CONTENTS

CW00358268

Printed by Pureprint Group Ltd   Maps by Alan Palfreyman

Cover image Carolside, Ettrick & Lauderdale © Andrea Jones

WHO'S WHO IN SCOTLAND'S GARDENS

BANKERS
Adam & Company plc, 25 St Andrew Square, Edinburgh EH2 1AF

SOLICITORS
Turcan Connell, Princes Exchange, Earl Grey Street, Edinburgh EH3 9EE

AUDITORS
Douglas Home & Co, 47-49 The Square, Kelso TD5 7HW

ISSN   2054-3301
ISBN   978-0-901549-29-7

SCOTTISH
CHARITY NO
SC011337

As a result of the lovely summer of 2014, I'm sure that all the Scotland's Gardens owners have seen their visitors increase; what better way to spend a sunny day than discovering a wonderful new garden to wander in…!

I would like to congratulate the organisers of the major events that took place during the year which are so important for Scotland's Gardens. As ever the Snowdrop Festival in February and March attracted many visitors and provided an encouraging start to the year. The Fife Garden Festival, the East Lothian Garden Trail and the Orkney Garden Trail in June and July all gave people the opportunity of visiting some really remarkable gardens and raised substantial sums for charity.

My heartfelt thanks go to the ever-increasing number of garden owners who open their garden gates to the public in order to raise funds for their chosen charities and Scotland's Gardens' beneficiary charities. I would also like to thank all the volunteers who cheerfully give their time and effort to enhance Scotland's Gardens.

As the President of Scotland's Gardens I wish you all good gardening and good weather for 2015!

Camilla

CHAIRMAN'S MESSAGE

I am writing this introduction to our Guide for 2015 in my office at home with the sun pouring through the window. Outside the leaves on the trees are marking the shorter days with a spectacular show of colour which contrasts vividly with the clear blue sky. Autumn has arrived and I am already looking forward to next spring and summer.

We have another exciting year in prospect with many familiar and some not so familiar gardens opening for us, as well as some lovely new ones. I always enjoy visiting new gardens to see how they have been designed and planted. Gardens take time to evolve and develop and very often they reflect their owners' own personalities, so it is always interesting to meet them and to hear their stories. Inspiration and new ideas are never far away.

In the last few years Garden Trails and Festivals have become a feature of the summer which our President refers to in her message. This year we have a trail encompassing Angus and Fife over an extended period in May and June and three Orkney trails. Village openings too have become popular and a regular feature over the summer. Village openings are always fun because of the range and diversity of gardens that participate and the sense of community that they generate.

It will not be long before the first snowdrops begin to show and remind us that spring is on its way. Early spring is an exciting time of year with longer days and a return of warmth to the sun. This year we have some glorious snowdrop gardens opening for us which will brighten up everyone's spirits whatever the weather.

I hope you enjoy browsing through the Guide and planning your visits to our listed gardens. Were it not for the generosity of our owners, openers and volunteers none of these gardens would be open, so on behalf of all our visitors, I would like to thank them for their loyal support. Finally, whether you are a visitor, volunteer or owner could I welcome you to our Guide for 2015 and wish you a contented season of growing and giving.

Mark Hedderwick
Chairman

SPONSORS

We would like to acknowledge and thank the following organisations that will be sponsoring Scotland's Gardens in 2015. Their support is invaluable and enables us to maximise the funds we give to our beneficiary charities.

Investec Wealth & Investment

Corney & Barrow

D C Thomson & Co

Lycetts

Rettie & Co

Savills (L&P) Ltd

The Edinburgh International Conference Centre

In addition we would like to say how grateful we are to the many private donors who give us their support.

Individuals \ International \ Financial Advisers \ Charities \ Court of Protection

Offices at: Bath Belfast Birmingham Bournemouth Cheltenham Edinburgh Exeter Glasgow Guildford Leeds Liverpool London Manchester Reigate Sheffield

Wealth & Investment. Home grown success

Visit us soon at our growing Edinburgh or Glasgow offices

Just like Scotland's Gardens, we are a national network with a local feel, and our offices in Glasgow and Edinburgh are well placed to tend to your investments, pensions or other financial matters.

Our specialist teams manage over £24 billion* on behalf of our clients, seeking the best and most tax-efficient returns on their capital. To see how we could best be of service to you please visit our website.

Please bear in mind that the value of investments and the income derived from them can go down as well as up and that you may not get back the amount that you have put in.

For more information on how we have supported Scotland's Gardens please visit **investecwin.co.uk/sponsorships**

Edinburgh – please contact Murray Mackay on **0131 226 5000**
Glasgow – please contact Stuart Light on **0141 333 9323**

Royal Caledonian Horticultural Society (The Caley)

Scotland's National Horticultural and Gardening Society

Encouraging the science, art and practice of all kinds of horticulture and gardening in Scotland for everyone.

he Caley has been recognising the skill of dividual gardeners since 1809. Scotland's ardens showcases many different gardens in cotland and some have received RCHS awards recognition of their work.

Membership of the Society includes professionals, generalists, amateurs and those who love and those who appreciate gardens.

Find out more by at www.rchs.co.uk
Or join us - only £26 for individuals
or £32 for family membership

Think property, think Savills.

RHS IN SCOTLAND

Cambo Gardens, Fife – RHS Partner Garden

SUPPORTING MEMBERS

Great days out to over 150 UK gardens, including 21 Partner Gardens in Scotland

Priority booking for the world-renowned RHS Flower Shows

Personalised gardening advice and The Garden Magazine

SUPPORTING COMMUNITIES

Supporting over 1200 schools in Scotland to learn and grow

Helping communities to transform their open spaces

Promoting horticultural education, training and volunteering

Royal Horticultural Society

Sharing the best in Gardening

For further information please contact: scotland@rhs.org.uk

rhs.org.uk

RHS Registered Charity No: 222879/SC038262

35 inspirational
gardens. Right on
your doorstep.

Crathes Castle, Garden & Estate, Aberdeenshire

**Discover one of the National Trust for Scotland's 35 magnificent gardens.
Located throughout Scotland, each one is a feast for the senses and
the imagination. A magical world awaits.**

Step into a world of wonder.
Visit *www.nts.org.uk/visitgardens*

the National Trust
for Scotland

a place for everyone

The National Trust for Scotland for Places of Historic Interest or Natural Beauty is a charity registered in Scotland, Charity Number SC 007410

Visit four Botanic Gardens to see one of the richest plant collections on Earth.

Royal Botanic Garden Edinburgh

Arboretum Place and Inverleith Row, Edinburgh EH3 5LR

Tel 0131 248 2909 | www.rbge.org.uk

Open every day from 10 am
(except 1 January and 25 December)
Garden is free
Entry charges apply to Glasshouses

Royal Botanic Garden Edinburgh at

Benmore

Dunoon,
Argyll PA23 8QU

Tel 01369 706261
www.rbge.org.uk/benmore

Open daily 1 March to 31 October
Admission charge applies

Royal Botanic Garden Edinburgh at

Logan

Port Logan, Stranraer,
Dumfries and Galloway DG9 9ND

Tel 01776 860231
www.rbge.org.uk/logan

Open daily 15 March to 31 October
Admission charge applies

Royal Botanic Garden Edinburgh at

Dawyck

Stobo, Scottish Borders
EH45 9JU

Tel 01721 760254
www.rbge.org.uk/dawyck

Open daily 1 February – 30 November
Admission charge applies

The Royal Botanic Garden Edinburgh is a Charity registered in Scotland (number SC007983) and is supported by the Scottish Government, Rural and Environment Science and Analytical Services (RESAS).

WHAT HAPPENS TO THE MONEY RAISED?

All garden owners who participate in the Scotland's Gardens programme are able to nominate a charity of their choice to receive 40% of the funds raised at their openings. 220 different charities will be supported in this manner in 2015 and these vary from small local ones to several large and well known organisations. Examples include:

- 1st Crail Brownies
- ABF Soldiers' Charity
- Ardgowan Hospice
- Bethany Christian Trust
- Caithness Samaritans
- Cystic Fibrosis Trust
- Dalhousie Day Care
- Erskine Hospital
- Forget Me Not
- Gardening Leave
- Laggan Church
- Margaret Kerr Unit, Borders General Hospital

- Motor Neurone Disease Scotland
- Newburgh Scout Group
- Poppy Scotland
- Riding for the Disabled
- Sandpiper Trust
- Scottish Charity Air Ambulance
- St Mary's Episcopal Church
- Save the Children
- The Breadmaker
- The Little Haven
- The Prince's Trust
- Westerkirk Parish Trust

60%, net of expenses, of the funds raised at each garden is given to Scotland's Gardens beneficiary charities which are:

- Maggie's Cancer Caring Centres
- The Queen's Nursing Institute Scotland
- The Gardens Fund of the National Trust for Scotland
- Perennial

Information on these organisations is provided on the following pages.

Several garden owners who open their garden on a regular basis and generously support Scotland's Gardens give a donation and the net sum is split between Scotland's Gardens beneficiaries.

In this book details of the charities nominated by the Garden Owners are provided and those gardens giving a donation are also indicated.

BENEFICIARY MESSAGES

maggie's

It is always heartening to see that, competing with the outstanding natural beauty that is the Scottish landscape, and an often challenging climate, gardeners in Scotland still manage to create some of the most captivating, fascinating gardens that Britain has to offer.

At Maggie's we recognise that being in a natural environment can have a positive effect on wellbeing, improving mindfulness and reducing stress levels. Run by experienced gardeners, our therapeutic gardening groups are open to anyone with cancer, their family and friends, and offer the chance to enjoy the gardens at Maggie's and take part in a creative activity with other people who are going through a similar experience.

I would like to take this opportunity to thank you all for your most welcome support of Maggie's in Scotland again this year. All of our Centres benefit from Scotland's Gardens donations.

And as we continue to grow in Scotland, with a brand new Centre in Lanarkshire in 2014 and plans for our Centre in Forth Valley well under way, we look forward to a wonderful year ahead – a year of growth, and enjoying the many green spaces and delightful gardens that Scotland's Gardens has made accessible to everyone.

With warmest wishes,

Laura Lee
Chief Executive
Maggie's

Please call 0300 123 1801 or visit **www.maggiescentres.org** for more information.

The latest Maggie's Centre opened in September 2014 in the grounds of Monklands Hospital, Lanarkshire.

THE QUEEN'S NURSING INSTITUTE SCOTLAND

125 years 1889-2014

Scotland's Gardens came into being in 1931 to raise money to fund Queen's Nurses, now known as District Nurses, so that the neediest in Scotland's communities had access to health care before the days of the NHS. In the early years, the donations received from garden openings were used to support the Queen's Nurses in their work and into their retirement.

Now care is provided by the NHS, some may wonder why we still need your support. Over 90% of all health care is provided outside of hospital. Today nurses in the community have many and varied roles including:

- Health visitors, who work with the under 5s,
- School nurses who promote the health of children,
- Community psychiatric nurses who promote mental health,
- Practice nurses who work in local surgeries alongside GPs,
- District nurses, who coordinate complex care,
- Nurses who work with the homeless,
- Nurses who work out of hours,
- Nurses who specialise in support for end of life care.

There is an urgent need to recruit and train more nurses to work in the community and QNIS is lobbying hard to ensure that the skills and expertise required are in place. We are working to set standards to promote excellence in education and practice so that patients receive the best possible care.

This is Margaret - she is a Community Nurse Consultant and with the help of QNIS, her role was developed to include the supervision of other advanced nurse practitioners who can support people who are acutely unwell by providing a 'hospital at home' service. With GP support the nurses visit several times a day delivering highly skilled acute care to allow people who prefer to remain at home, to do so safely.

This year, we have helped 22 nurses further their education by funding professional development opportunities. To promote innovation and excellence, we funded four projects to support the effective integration of health and social care. We also recognise and reward the dedication of our community nurses in Scotland – this year we are presenting over 110 Long Service Awards to individuals who had devoted over 21 years to nursing within the community.

In addition, we continue to support over 400 of the original Queen's Nurses across Scotland, who are now retired, by providing them with welfare, companionship and fellowship.

All of this work has been enabled by the financial support we have received from Scotland's Gardens and we would like to take this opportunity to thank you.

Clare Cable
Chief Executive and Nurse Director

the National Trust
for Scotland
a place for everyone

On behalf of the National Trust for Scotland's Gardens Community I would like to thank all of Scotland's Gardens owners for their ongoing support to the National Trust for Scotland in general and its gardens portfolio in particular. We really appreciate the financial (and other) support you provide that enables so much of the work that goes on in our gardens. Our gardens and designed landscapes continue to flourish and grow, prove popular with our visitors, providing perfect places for sanctuary and reflection away from the pressures of modern daily life. We are grateful to those people who support our work and the work of Scottish gardens by continuing to visit and enjoy the places in our care.

In 2014 twenty-eight of our gardens supported Scotland's Gardens, with over 50 successful events and activities held, including the serving of homemade scones on Branklyn Garden's patio; daffodil pot sales at Brodie Castle; artist and craft stalls at Kellie Castle; live music at Broughton House; and behind the scenes guided walks at Crarae Garden.

In 2015 we plan to build on last year's success by putting on the following events: a guided walk around Greenbank, tea/coffee and cake at Culross Palace, a herbaceous border workshop with Crathes Castle's expert gardeners and a harvest and produce plant sale in the unique setting of the Pineapple – and much, much more.

Through the School of Heritage Gardening, in part supported by Scotland's Gardens, the Trust continues to play an important part in growing future gardeners. There is a high quality framework to support gardener training in our gardens across the country, with student placements at Branklyn Garden, Craigievar Castle, Crathes Castle, Drum Castle, Kellie Castle and Threave Garden.

Arduaine Garden, Oban

Thanks to your generous financial donation, visitors can continue to enjoy our gardens across the seasons and enjoy the expertise and labours of our dedicated gardens staff, who help to create, develop and conserve these beautiful places.

Kate Mavor
Chief Executive

Perennial, the only charity that cares for all horticulturists

We celebrated our 175th birthday in 2014 and are looking forward to our next milestone. The Gardeners' Benevolent Institution was established in January 1839 to provide pensions for retired gardeners, often a key, long-serving member of household staff, who could face the workhouse after their service when their tied accommodation came to an end.

Perennial's founders financed a plan to support their staff and families into old-age. In 1840 the first pension of £75 was shared among three beneficiaries.

175 years later

175 years on we are living in very different times, yet Perennial continues to support those in the industry who are in need. We are now helping more than 1,000 individuals and their families cope and move on from a range of issues every year. It is not just the long-term unemployed, single parent families, or retired horticulturists who need our help. The vast majority of new cases are from those who are in work.

Low income working families are now struggling to keep their homes warm and to put sufficient food on the table, and they need our help in ever growing numbers too. To safeguard these vital services we need your support.

Perhaps you could make a commitment to raise send us a donation, remember us in your will, attend one of our Special Events at gardens throughout the summer or join us at the flower shows across the country?

If you would like to help us and feel you could spare time this year to encourage friends and colleagues to raise money and awareness of Perennial, please visit **www.perennial.org.uk** or contact us on 01372 373962.

Escape to Auchlochan Village to see our beautifully landscaped grounds, mature woodlands, spectacular gardens and expansive lochs.

Auchlochan Gardens

Escape to Auchlochan Garden Village to see our beautifully landscaped grounds, mature woodlands, spectacular gardens and lochs.

The gardens at Auchlochan are its undoubted glory, offering a wide range of attractions to visitors, walkers and residents alike.

Laid out over a 50 acre estate, the gardens feature not only the lochs that gave the village its name, but stunning herbaceous borders, terrace gardens, rhododendron beds and heather gardens. Along the River Nethan valley, the gardens merge with mature woodland which feature our prominent Sequoiadendron giganteum - giant Redwoods - which are native to California.

At Auchlochan's heart is the delightful 1.5 acre walled garden. Built around 1900, the garden was originally designed as a source of fruit and vegetables for the estate. Under the care of the current gardening team it has been transformed into a show garden.

The Auchlochan grounds attract many visitors - there is a 4 Star B&B and self catering accommodation available all year round - and enjoy a relaxing cup of tea or coffee or even lunch in our bistro, at the same time.

nd Grounds

Auchlochan
Garden Village

01555 893592
www.auchlochan.com

Auchlochan Garden Village, New Trows Road,
Lesmahagow, South Lanarkshire ML11 0GS

NEW HOPETOUN GARDENS

...so much more than just a garden centre

The perfect place for a relaxed visit at any time of year. Set in six acres of woodland with 20 small themed gardens to explore and probably the biggest range of garden plants for sale in Scotland.

The Orangery tearoom will revive you and the gift shop will tempt you with the most exciting range of presents for everyone.

art in the garden runs during July and August and features original works of art by artists working in Scotland installed in the gardens.

(Entry is always free to our gardens.)

OPEN EVERY DAY 10.00AM – 5.30PM
New Hopetoun Gardens, by Winchburgh
West Lothian EH52 6QZ   01506 834433
www.newhopetoungardens.co.uk

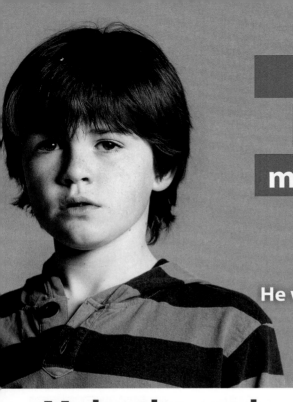

Meet Connor.

At the age of 10

he became the

man of the house.

Connor's dad died of a stroke at age 42.

He was the picture of health.

It was the last thing anyone expected.

Make the end
a new beginning.

A gift in your Will can mean life to those suffering from chest, heart and stroke illness in Scotland.

The funding that gifts in Wills provide is crucial to our work.

We are Scotland's Health Charity

Research • Advice • Support • Action

Chest Heart & Stroke Scotland

FRSB
FundRaising
Standards Board

0300 1212 555 | gifts@chss.org.uk | www.chss.org.uk

Guiding our clients every step of the way

The Turcan Connell Group is the country's leading firm of legal, wealth management and tax advisers with an interdisciplinary team of lawyers, tax planners, investment managers and financial planners working together out of offices in Edinburgh, Glasgow, London and Guernsey. We provide our clients with all the services and expertise they need under one roof:

- Wealth Management*
- Charity Law and Philanthropy
- Charity Office
- Divorce and Family Law
- Employment Law
- Family Businesses
- Financial Planning*
- Pensions*

- Land and Property
- Litigation and Dispute Resolution
- Tax Compliance
- Wills, Estate Planning and Succession
- Turcan Connell Family Office*
- Investment Management*
- Renewables

TURCAN CONNEL

LEGAL · WEALTH MANAGEMENT ·

Edinburgh   Glasgow   Lor

Princes Exchange, 1 Earl Grey Street, Edinburgh EH3 9EE Tel: 0131 228
Sutherland House, 149 St Vincent Street, Glasgow G2 5NW Tel: 0141 441

Follow us on Twitter 🐦 @TurcanCc
enquiries@turcanconnell.com www.turcanconnel

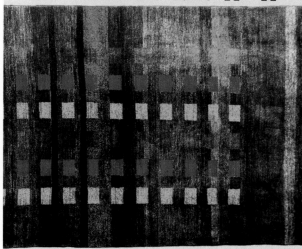

NEW GARDENS FOR 2015

Angus & Dundee

Glamis Castle
Hospitalfield Gardens
Kilry Village Gardens

Argyll

Barguillean House
Eas Mhor
Fasnacloich
Lorn Organic Growers

Ayrshire

Girvan Community Garden
Grougarbank House
High Fulwood

Caithness, Sutherland, Orkney & Shetland

14a Victoria Street (Orkney Trail Two)
Duncan Street Gardens
Fiddlers Green (The Herston Garden Trail)
Frakkafield
Gyre Cottage (Orkney Trail Two)
Lindaal
Millbank Gardens
Mucklejocks (The Herston Garden Trail)
New House (The Herston Garden Trail)
Quoylanks (Orkney Trail One)
Quoys of Herston (The Herston Garden Trail)
Schoolquoy (Orkney Trail Two)
South Banks (The Herston Garden Trail)
The Bu (Orkney Trail Two)
The Marengo Garden (The Herston Garden Trail)

Symmar's Cottage, East Lothian

The Steading at Blairgowrie, Perth & Kinross

Fiddler's Green, Orkney

7 Duncan Street, Thurso, Caithness & Sutherland

Dumfriesshire

Capenoch
Craig
Leap Cottage
Westwater Farm

Dunbartonshire

Brandon Grove
Milton Cottage
Rowanan

East Lothian

Hopefield
Lammerlaw House (Humbie Garden Circle)
Old Windymains Cottage (Humbie Garden Circle)
Symmar's Cottage (Humbie Garden Circle)

Edinburgh & West Lothian

20 Blackford Road
41 Hermitage Gardens
Gilmour Road Gardens

Fife

Kenly Green House (The Angus & Fife Garden Trail)
Millfield House (The Angus & Fife Garden Trail)
St Mary's Farm (The Angus & Fife Garden Trail)

Glasgow & District

53 Dalziel Drive
Ardlinnhe
Kamares

Isle of Arran

The Glades

Kirkcudbrightshire

Glenlivet

Midlothian

Greenfield Lodge

Moray & Nairn

Haugh Garden

Kamares, Glasgow & District

Fasnacloich, Argyll

41 Hermitage Gardens, Edinburgh

Haugh Garden, Moray & Nairn

Peeblesshire

Srongarbh
The Potting Shed

Perth & Kinross

Machany House
Mill of Forneth
The Steading

Renfrewshire

Gardening Leave

Ross, Cromarty, Skye & Inverness

2 Durnamuck
Old Allangrange

Stirlingshire

Fintry Village Gardens
Woodstone House

Wigtownshire

Burbainie
The Homestead
Whitehills House

Burbainie, Wigtownshire

Lindaal, Shetland

Kenly Green House, Fife

2 Durnamuck, Ross, Cromarty, Skye & Inverness

SCOTLAND'S GARDENS AUTUMN GATHERING
1 OCTOBER 2015

IN CONJUNCTION WITH THE ROYAL HORTICULTURAL SOCIETY

Join us at the Albert Halls, Stirling
from 10:30am - 4:00pm
for our biennial public lectures.

- Three first-class speakers
- Morning coffee
- Sandwich lunch with wine
- Stalls

£45.00 per ticket

*See www.scotlandsgardens.org
for reservations and more details.*

Royal
Horticultural
Society

Sharing the best in Gardening

SNOWDROP OPENINGS

Snowdrop openings during February and March provide some fabulous spectacles of white carpets and collections of unusual snowdrop species.

VisitScotland will be supporting our openings with their heavily marketed Snowdrop Festival which is an important part of their successful annual marketing programme.

The following properties will be opening and most will be participating in the Snowdrop Festival:

Aberdeenshire

Bruckhills Croft

Angus

Dunninald
Gagie House
Pitmuies Gardens

Ayrshire

Caprington Castle

Dumfriesshire

Craig

East Lothian

Shepherd House

Fife

Lindores House

Kincardine & Deeside

Ecclesgreig Castle

Kirkcudbrightshire

Brooklands
Danevale

Lanarkshire

Cleghorn

Midlothian

Greenfield Lodge
Kevock Garden

Brooklands, Kirkcudbrightshire
Snowdrops

Kailzie Gardens, Peeblesshire
© Ray Cox

Moray & Nairn

10 Pilmuir Road West

Peeblesshire

Dawyck Botanic Garden
Kailzie Gardens

Perth & Kinross

Braco Castle
Cluny House
Fingask Castle
Kilgraston School

Renfrewshire

Ardgowan

Ross, Cromarty, Skye & Inverness

Abriachan Garden Nursery

Stirlingshire

Duntreath Castle
Gargunnock House
The Linns
West Plean House

Wigtownshire

Castle Kennedy & Gardens
Craichlaw
Dunskey Garden and Maze
Logan Botanic Garden

Bruckhills Croft, Aberdeenshire
Galanthus 'Hippolyta'

We always like to hear about new snowdrop gardens. Please get in touch if you have a great display and would consider opening in 2016.

ANGUS & FIFE GARDEN TRAIL MAY - JUNE 2015

We are introducing an exciting new venture into our 2015 programme - The Angus & Fife Garden Trail. Following the fantastic success of the Fife Garden Trail in 2013, you will now be able to follow this Trail across the silvery Tay to include some beautiful gardens from Angus.

Running over May and June, this year's Angus & Fife Trail provides an opportunity to see 12 privately owned gardens, all different and several of which have rarely admitted visitors before. It also offers a very flexible way to visit the gardens whether you wish to visit the area and see all gardens in short succession (26-28 May and 2-4 June) or take the two months to see them all. The gardens can also be visited at different times of the day, with some open all day, some in the afternoon only and others in the afternoon and evening. Some include plants for sale, others the option of teas.

Follow this Trail *sans frontières* around four amazing Angus gardens and to Fife to eight more fabulous gardens! The gardens represent a diverse range of character and design from the beauty and scent of a bluebell wood in late spring to a garden designed around the ancient art of herbal medicine. Some gardens are symmetrical and formal while others are flowing and irregular. Others again are designed as a combination of formal structure with naturalist romantic perennial plantings within. There are gardens designed to entice and draw the garden visitor from one space to the next providing a sense of travel and discovery or to invite the curious to enjoy many unusual plants at close quarters. So please plan to join us for what we hope to be a memorable garden trail experience.

Please do note that all this is offered to raise money for charity, with two very worthwhile cancer charities in Angus and Fife earmarked along with Scotland's Gardens' traditional beneficiaries. So please help us to help our community while sharing some of our best gardens with you.

A ticket for The Garden Trail makes a perfect gift and do treat yourself as well!

See also pages 101 and 188 of this book.

Herbalist's Garden at Logie, Angus

Logie House, Fife

Opening times

Various dates and times:
Tuesdays, Wednesdays, Thursdays, 5 May to 25 June
Please see website for further details.

Admission

£25 (plus £1 P&P) for entrance to all gardens.
Early Bird Price: £20 (plus £1 P&P) available until
28 February 2014
Accompanied children free.

Tickets (limited in number) may be purchased by
credit card at **www.angusfifetrail.org.uk** or by cheque
payable to Scotland's Gardens from S. Lorimore,
Willowhill, Forgan, Newport on Tay, Fife DD6 8RA.

Beneficiary Charities

60% net of the proceeds from the Angus & Fife Trail
is shared between Scotland's Garden's beneficiary
charities:

- Maggie's Cancer Caring Centres
- Queen's Nursing Institute Scotland
- Gardens Fund of the National Trust for Scotland
- Perennial

The remaining 40% to be divided equally between the
charities Worldwide Cancer Research, St Andrews,
Fife and Macmillan Cancer Care, Brechin, Angus.

in aid of

Kirklands, Fife

Kirklands, Fife

Kirkside of Lochty, Angus

Kenlygreen House, Fife

Glassmount, Fife

Kirkton House, Angus

St Mary's Farm, Fife

Wormistoune, Fife

Kenly Green Farm, Fife

Millfield House, Falkland, Fife

The Garden Cottage, Dunnichen, Angus

HUMBIE GARDEN CIRCLE
MAY - JUNE 2015

Five beautiful gardens in the village of Humbie, East Lothian, are opening during May and June to show off their summer splendour.

Opening times

Wednesdays 20 May, 3 June, 17 June
2:00pm - 6:00pm
See p161 for further details.

See p161 for further details.

Admission

£15.00 for unlimited access to all five gardens over the three days. Tickets available at the gate.

£5.00 per garden for day tickets to Stobshiel House or Humbie Dean.

£5.00 for a day ticket to the combined three gardens at Symmar's Cottage, Old Windymains Cottage and Lammerlaw House.

Beneficiary Charities

60% net of the proceeds from the Humbie Garden Circle is shared between Scotland's Garden's beneficiary charities:

- Maggie's Cancer Caring Centres
- Queen's Nursing Institute Scotland
- Gardens Fund of the National Trust for Scotland
- Perennial

The remaining 40% will go to Circle.

Stobshiel

Old Windymains Cottage

Humbie Dean

Lammerlaw House

Symmar's Cottage

ORKNEY GARDEN TRAILS JUNE & JULY 2015

Visitors to Orkney this summer are in for a treat.
Keep your Sunday afternoons free for three garden trails,
showcasing 17 amazing gardens, most pictured here.

For further details please see pages 134-136.

Opening dates and times

The Herston Garden Trail
Sundays 28 June and 5 July
11:00am to 6:00pm

Orkney Garden Trail One
Sundays 7 and 14 June
11:00am to 5:00pm

Orkney Garden Trail Two
Sundays 12 and 19 July
11:00am to 5:00pm

Fiddlers Green, The Herston Garden Trail

Quoys of Herston,
The Herston Garden Trail

New House, The Herston Garden Trail

Gyre Cottage, Orkney Garden Trail Two

33 Hillside, Orkney Garden Trail One

The Quoy of Houton,
Orkney Garden Trail Two

Community Garden,
Orkney Garden Trail One

South Banks, The Herston Garden Trail

Marengo Community Garden,
The Herston Garden Trail

Mucklejocks Garden,
The Herston Garden Trail

Giles Garden,
Orkney Garden Trail One

Dalkeith Polytunnel, Orkney Garden Trail One

Kierfold,
Orkney Garden Trail Two

Stenwood, Orkney Garden Trail One

Schoolquoy Garden,
Orkney Garden Trail Two

SINCE 1931
SCOTLAND'S
GARDENS
GROWING AND GIVING

Two wonderful Private Garden Tours for 2015

Gardens of Galloway and Northern Ireland

Galloway's mild, moist climate allows for a wide range of rare and exotic plants to flourish in its gardens, as demonstrated to great effect at places such as Glenwhan, Logan Botanic Gardens and Castle Kennedy, all of which are filled with stunning plants and provide endless fascination and discovery. We then sail across the North Channel to the lush green hills of Co Antrim and Co Down, where a similar climate prevails, and at the dazzling Mount Stewart and selected private gardens there are further horticultural delights to be found.

Departs **June 6, 2015**
Five nights' half board from **£675pp**
Single room supplement **£125**

What's included
Visits to the gardens of Cosmic Speculation, Corsock House, Glenwhan, Logan Botanics, Castle Kennedy, Ballyrobert, Glenarm Castle, Benvarden, Mount Stewart, Rosemont House and two private gardens; Giant's Causeway, the Dark Hedges and Stormont.

Orkney's Garden Trail

Last year for the first time the determined gardeners of Orkney pooled their resources to create 'Orkney's Garden Trail'. It was a pleasant surprise to see how good they were at 'gardening on the edge' and such a success that we felt we had to arrange a holiday to enjoy their gardens, as well as some of the other gardens not easily visited in the far north. HRH The Queen Mother put gardening on the map in Caithness when she regularly opened the walled garden at her summer home The Castle of Mey, and we visit this along with other fine private gardens.

Departs **July 13, 2015**
Five nights' half board from **£795pp**
Single room supplement **£100**

What's included
Visits to the gardens of Old Allangrange, Langwell and the Castle of Mey; two private gardens in Thurso and some of the gardens of 'Orkney's Garden Trails'; guided tours of Orkney, including the Ring of Brodgar, Standing Stones of Stenness, the Italian Chapel and the archaeological sites at Skara Brae and Maeshowe.

For full details on both tours contact:
01334 657155

brightwater
holidays

Brightwater Holidays Ltd
Eden Park House,
Cupar, Fife KY15 4HS
info@brightwaterholidays.com
www.brightwaterholidays.com

PITMUIES GARDENS

I have often been asked how best to describe Pitmuies. To me it is simply a garden within a garden within a garden. It also has a unique feature in that the gardens surround the house. The garden walls date back to 1780 and create a micro climate of peace and tranquillity. Pitmuies has been in the hands of a number of owners over the centuries all whom have contributed in their own way to make the garden what it is today. My husband Ruaraidh's grandparents bought the house in 1945. Before then it was owned by a Major Crombie who had much to do with the redesigning of the garden and introduced the delphiniums for which the garden is now well known. Ruaraidh's grandparents continued to improve the gardens, planting many shrubs and trees. Pitmuies was inherited by my parents-in-law in 1966 and in the capable hands of my mother-in-law Marguerite the garden began its transformation. A conservatory was added that links the garden to the house.

There are in fact two walled gardens. Most visitors start their tour in the kitchen garden. It's a mixture of flowers, shrubs, fruit trees and vegetables. The centre comprises a formal potager in which vegetables are grown and we rotate them annually with the simple wooden beds making weeding much easier. Since we moved in, in 2013 we have planted five beds of asparagus which hopefully will be ready in May. There is a fruit cage, and in between that and the raspberries is a holding bed for indoor rhododendrons. Marguerite planted many beautiful magnolias and one of my favourite beds in this part of the garden has grape hyacinths planted under magnolia stellata. We also have very old apple trees which are underplanted with hellebores, and by cutting the leaves away in February they then flower and flower until late spring.

The second walled garden is the more formal garden, which is entered through white wrought iron gates which along with the main entrance gates were commissioned

Main border

to celebrate my parents-in-law's silver wedding anniversary although tragically my father-in-law died before they were installed. An archway of clipped pear frames the central herbaceous borders which are flanked by red hedges of cherry plum. To the right, below the house is a series of three rose terraces linked by stone steps and in the centre there is a pond and fountain. The children and I, together with Paul who helps in the garden, cleaned it out last year and restocked it with goldfish and we seem to have a continuous stream of babies which we hope the heron will not discover. The long delphinium borders lie alongside stretching the length of the terraces. On the far side a green trellis with climbing roses divides the rose garden from the blue and yellow herbaceous borders and the massive yew hedge that protects this part of the garden from the prevailing south-west wind.

At the foot of the rose garden is a line of eight shiny-barked cherry trees leading towards the old grass tennis court and backed by a white trellised walk where clematis mingle with climbing roses and Himalayan poppies flourish among ferns, hostas and iris. The huge lillies (lilium cardiocrinum) were grown from seed collected in Japan in 1992 and we allow them to self seed around the garden and in the kitchen garden. The former tennis court now has paved corners, in which scented dianthus and violas are planted and a central roundel sprouts stately spikes of acanthus mollis planted around a golden elm. The whole area is backed by low walls, shrubs and small trees. Beyond lies a shrub border.

At the bottom of the garden you go through another white gate leading down onto a small grass meadow which in the spring is a mass of purple and white crocuses planted by my mother-in-law when they

moved to Pitmuies. Over the years they have naturalised and spread. The meadow was a drying green for the house in the past and on the left is a beautiful Gothic washhouse, built over 200 years ago and often mistaken for a chapel. The walk along the riverside is lined by stately beech and lime trees which may date back to the 1770s. In the summer their shading branches are a welcome relief from the heat of the sun. Along the walk you pass a beautiful and unusual turreted doo'cot. On this building, a very worn carved stone bears the Ogilvy and Guthrie arms, and the date 1643. One of the turrets served as a feed-store for the pigeons which once occupied the hundreds of nest boxes which line the inside of the building and where we hope to reintroduce white doves. At the bottom of the walk the ground opens up to the Vinny Garden. In this secluded part of the grounds there is a small Cupid struggling with his bow and arrow, probably dating from Victorian times. The area now includes some huge variegated hollies and a monkey puzzle and a fine North American tulip tree. The paperbark maple (acer griseum) greets you as you enter the garden – a tree now believed to be extinct in its native Manchuria. A bridge takes you back across the Turbie Burn, and a path climbs up the bank, to a walk leading back towards the house, part of which is planted with native hornbeam trees. In the spring this whole area is a mass of daffodils and narcissi. To your left is a ha-ha or sunken wall which gives uninterrupted views from the house across the adjacent Policy Field. Fine copper beeches and a pair of venerable Spanish chestnut trees stand on the lawn in front of the house.

The drive beyond the house leads down to the Black Loch, where a broad grass walk leads round among the trees,

Delphiniums and roses

Doo'cot

rhododendrons and azaleas. Between the loch and the Policy Field are planted a variety of exotic rowans and maples noted for their autumn colours, many of them raised from wild seed collected in Oregon and Japan.

Pitmuies is a magical garden because every day there is something new to see. In early spring there are the masses of spring bulbs. By May the main gardens starts to take form with its subtle colours suggesting what is to come. It is perhaps my favourite time in the garden. In July the borders and rose garden are at their zenith. As autumn approaches the surrounding trees have splendid colour. We as a family are just the caretakers and hopefully in years to come the same pleasures will be enjoyed by future generations.

The gardens are open daily from 1 April to 31 October between 10:00am and 5:00pm.

Organised groups are asked to book in advance.

Jeanette Ogilvie

Loch

Border

Lily pond

ROYAL HORTICULTURAL SOCIETY, SCOTLAND

I am delighted to be asked to write an article for the 2015 Guidebook since it illustrates (to me at least) that Scottish gardeners and horticulturalists are prepared to trust and accept some of the initiatives which we have introduced in Scotland over the last two or three years.

In 2012, we established the small but dedicated team that is now Liz Stewart and Angela Smith who are based in Edinburgh and Glasgow. We cannot hope, or wish to take on existing institutions, started by others where we cannot add value. The essence therefore is that we work consensually with those in the industry, firming partnerships and helping where all parties feel that the RHS will add value. I am acutely aware that stepping on toes is a complete no-no!

Since I have been President of the RHS, I have always felt that Scottish gardeners have to an extent been undervalued by us. There are only a few RHS Partner Gardens, for example, but this is an area which we hope to rectify over the next few years. The RHS Scotland team that I chair represents a great cross section of the gardening community, and they would be the first to put

us back on the straight and narrow should we venture too far into the wrong areas!

I do hope that this group strengthens and together we can initiate some exciting projects. People on the ground are vital if we are able to make a difference. The Scottish team seem to achieve great things.

RHS Britain in Bloom groups and RHS It's Your Neighbourhood have increased 20% since last year and RHS Campaign for School Gardening is now reaching 1200 schools, 800 more since the Scotland team was established. 70 schools have signed up since September 2014 alone and much of that was owing to our attendance at Education Scotland events.

RHS Britain in Bloom would be significantly poorer without the Scottish Finalists. At the Awards in Bristol, we always expect the national dress, accompanied by the usual banter. It is good to see Aberdeen City still in the Finals having been associated with Bloom since 1964. As with many things in life, people make the difference and when a successful team changes, sometimes the enthusiasm

Cathedral Walk at Seaton Park - Horticultural excellence

and energy is not so compelling and the eye for detail is temporarily lost. But this has not happened in that case.

So often, a visit to a school is met with wild enthusiasm by the children, but we need to make sure that after we leave, the teachers can carry on the good work. The teachers, pulled hither and thither by regulators and requirements, don't necessarily have the expertise or confidence to teach practical horticulture to children. Part of our job is to teach them the rudiments of growing plants or vegetables so that they can then pass on that excitement to their classes. So far this year Liz and Angela have trained 190 teachers who will be able to pass on their knowledge to thousands of pupils for years to come.

In communities around Scotland, the RHS' £100,000 investment is now in its second year and is helping new community horticultural projects grow at grassroots level.

Last year, £30,000 was awarded to 17 wide-ranging projects which include the Toryglen Community Base in Glasgow who received more than £5,000 to help develop growing spaces on a substantial amount of vacant brown space.

We are also supporting the BBC's The Beechgrove Garden, helping to fund a number of wonderful projects. In 2013, we worked with four communities including Ninewells Hospital in Dundee where we helped build a medical garden for patients. More recently, we have been working alongside the BBC team and volunteers in projects around Scotland, to help revitalise a community park for local residents and visitors.

I hope that what I have said confirms that we want to add something of value in partnership with others, but not to interfere. That said, I am thrilled to say that we are certainly in Scotland to stay.

Sir Nicholas Bacon
RHS Scotland

Easthaven Bloom volunteers (RHS/Beechgrove project)

Glenrothes in Bloom 2014 display

Volunteers work on the Polmadie Plots Community Allotments and Market Garden Prospecthill Circus, Glasgow (received RHS funding)

SCOTLAND'S EXCITING GARDEN CLUB

The buzz address on the internet for the world's gardening pubic is **srgc.net.** This is the online home of Scotland's largest and most vibrant gardening society, The Scottish Rock Garden Club. Now in its 82nd year and known as simply the SRGC or 'The Rock Garden Club', it is a the epicentre through and from which, knowledge, pictures and ideas about rock garden plants and gardens is shared by enthusiasts everywhere. All the information on the SRGC web site is free for everyone, even access to 80 years of its fabulous journal. What's more the excellent new 'International Rock Gardener' magazine is also free to everyone, members and non-members. It is on-line every month. With contributions and pictures sent in continuously from all over the world it is always up to date and at the cutting edge of horticulture. Communicating with the world via the internet allows the SRGC to live up to its charitable function, 'to share information on and promote the cultivation of rock garden plants'. No matter how small or large any garden is there are bound to be rock plants in it, as the term includes small shrubs, herbaceous perennials and bulbs along with traditional mountain and alpine plants.

The Scottish Rock Garden Club provides gardening interest all year round. Two thirds of its membership is based in the UK, half of these in Scotland. The other third is scattered in 40 countries throughout the world. It is easy to see why Scottish gardeners join: there are 9 flower shows, 3 floral displays and a Discussion Weekend every year. As well as these, local groups of enthusiasts in most areas hold monthly lectures during the winter months and garden visits during summer. The quality of these presentations is unrivalled.

Flower shows

The SRGC holds nine excellent flower shows each year throughout the year in Scotland and Northern England. There are classes for experts and for beginners. Here you will see the wide diversity and quality of plants grown by members.

The rock garden

Every January and July 'The Rock Garden', the club's full-colour journal is published. This unique publication has recorded the fashions in rock gardening and plants

Rock plants in pots

since 1935. It has built up into a unique encyclopaedia of Scottish rock gardening and plants in cultivation in Scotland. Today's journals are, as you would expect from a world ranking gardening society, vibrantly illustrated with superb pictures of plants and habitats. Many of its articles are written by members, some of whom are professional horticulturists and others amateurs. Older journals contained mostly words but as the years passed and technology improved, first black and white and then colour pictures were introduced. Nowadays every page is printed in colour! As a result, now that there are close up pictures of plants in flower, fewer words are needed to describe it further.

Saxifraga oppositifolia in trough Scottish native

In this case less is more! There are hints on growing and propagation beside articles on members' gardens. Much of the information is timeless and is as relevant today as it was in the club's earliest days. Right from issue 1, a practical thread has run through 'The Rock Garden'. This first issue contained an article on troughs and suitable plants to grow in them. In it you discover an incredible range of plants, whether for a traditional rock garden, a raised bed or a woodland area. Inspiration wafts from every page. 'The Rock Garden' is without doubt the finest publication of its kind. At the back of each issue a dozen pages are devoted to adverts for nurseries, seed sellers, holidays and other sister societies.

Tulipa sprengeri

Electronic membership

Through our web site **srgc.net** you can take out an Electronic Membership of the SRGC. For £10 per year you get all the benefits of membership except no paperwork is sent out. With electronic membership you get each issue of the journal, 'The Rock Garden', as soon as paper copies are posted. The seed list is posted on the website in December and all members can make their choices.

srgc.net is also home to the SRGC Forum. Here gardeners from all over the world post pictures and discuss gardening. Its threads cover many aspects of gardening and related pursuits. It is overseen by Maggi Young in Aberdeen and with her guidance is now the pre-eminent site for amateur gardeners worldwide. You don't have to be a member to visit the site. In this modern era many people prefer paperless communication. Reports of every flower show on the website combine to provide a running record of the winning plants and exhibitors. New and unusual plants feature strongly in the reports. For those who can't get to the shows they tell who won what with which plant.

World class seed list

Each December members the SRGC is sent to members, who can choose from over 4000 different varieties. The seed is collected by gardeners from all over the world and offers an unrivalled selection. Many of these are unavailable commercially. This sharing of seed from cultivated plants reduces the pressure on rare plants in the wild. SRGC members recognise the need to maintain a wide variety of plants in cultivation in our gardens where they are a real resource for horticulture. Once a species is introduced to cultivation we have a duty to maintain it and pass it on to future generations of gardeners. One of the advantages in growing plants from seed is that there will be some variation in the seedlings and some will be better suited than others to grow in your garden. This is a kind of self self-selection. Sometimes hybrids occur and your seedling might very well be unique. This excitement is a far cry from the uniformity of F1 hybrids offered commercially. Surplus seed is sold at SRGC events.

Specialist nurseries

Today's gardeners often spend a lot of money in big garden centres. This is usually because of convenience and perceived savings in cost. They certainly have an unrivalled choice of sundries. Their tea rooms are well worth visiting for excellent sandwiches and mouth-watering cakes. While they may stock thousands of plants the choice offered is often surprisingly limited. The trouble with the uniform, mass produced plants offered commercially is that they may have been grown far away, perhaps overseas and they are at a stage of growth not particularly suited for transplanting.

Celmisia viscosum

Much better is to buy rock plants from the people who produce them in specialist nurseries. They offer a huge range of plants that big garden centres cannot match. Locally raised and propagated, perhaps in small numbers, their selection of plants, already acclimatised and habituated to their environment is unsurpassed. It is only to be expected that these specialist nurseries are spread throughout the country. This way each has a different local clientele. When you are close to one, it is great to visit and part with a few pounds for some new treasures for your garden. A good way to source new plants for rock gardens is on the nursery web sites. Since its inception it has had a symbiotic relationship with the nurseries. They recognised that the rock gardeners needed the suppliers and vice versa. It is surprising how each specialises in different plants. By visiting SRGC shows you can select many alpines in flower from the specialists. This way you know exactly what you are buying. As postal charges continue to rise mail order is increasingly expensive. Most of the nurseries will deliver orders to flower the shows which they attend.

Plants for small gardens and busy people

Working people these days are said to have very little free time for gardening. Others think that rock gardening is difficult and that you require special skill to grow rock plants. The truth is that many are very easy to cultivate in normal gardens and that the plants live for a long time. Many are basically smaller versions of 'run of the mill' herbaceous plants. Of course there are others which need a bit more care when they are planted. Usually they need better drainage, which is easily arranged by increasing the amount of grit in the soil or by planting in a raised bed. Troughs are excellent homes for alpines and rock plants. The SRGC has pioneered the use of polystyrene fish boxes as troughs. To find out how, consult the SRGC website.

Unlike your local garden club the SRGC is national and worldwide. It is not in competition with local clubs. It is here to help. Membership of the SRGC enhances your membership of local garden clubs and societies. You can share your seedlings and plants with local gardeners. Your horizons will expand and before long you too may be travelling to places you had never thought of visiting to see mountain plants. Back at home you can share your adventures with friends and probably show your pictures of wild places and plants at your local garden club.

The SRGC extends its invitation to everyone to attend any show or local group event. The SRGC is truly Scotland's gift to the world of gardening. We offer free membership to horticultural students and our Diana Aitchison Fund provides grants to young people who wish to pursue a career in horticulture.

Single Membership of the SRGC costs £18, Family membership £21, Junior £3.

Find out more at srgc.net or from the SRGC Subscription Secretary, 10 Quarry Avenue, Acklington, Morpeth, Northumberland, NE65 9BZ

HAMILTON

FINANCIAL

Investment Managers & Financial Planners

*Know your perennials
from your hardy annuals.*

www.hamilton-financial.co.uk

enquiries@hamilton-financial.co.uk   Tel:0131 315 4888

Hamilton Financial registered by the FCA no. 485546

NB GIN

Botanical infusions are just the tonic

Reassuringly classic but contemporary in character, NB Gin is handmade in North Berwick by husband-and-wife team Steve and Viv Muir, from pure British grain spirit and eight meticulously selected botanicals.

It's delicious, distinct and smooth, with subtle notes of citrus and an assertive hit of juniper. It's also uncompromising on quality, with every part of this award-winning spirit having an attention to detail which makes it stand out from the rest. It works either on its own with a block or two of ice, traditionally mixed with a quality tonic, or is equally at home in a classic cocktail.

It has been described as 'everything gin fans are looking for, and a bit more besides'.*

We're not going to argue with that.

This is NB Gin. Unique in its own perfection.

Classic NB&T

Fill a highball glass with ice cubes

Pour a shot or two of NB Gin over the ice and top up with Fever Tree Naturally Light Tonic Water

Drop in a slice of orange

Sláinte!

www.nbgin.com

NB Gin, The Distillery, North Berwick
T: 0845 4674547 E: info@nbgin.co.uk

mmer Fruit Cup review, January 2014

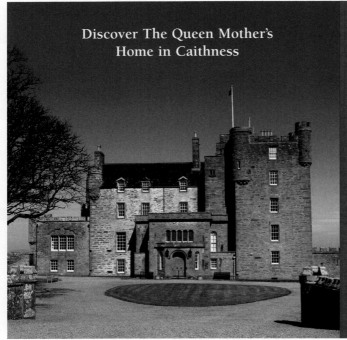

Every one of our retirement homes comes with a 40 acre garden.
And a gardening team.

Remember Flower Power? It's alive and well in the gardens at Inchmarlo.

You can enjoy the handiwork of our green-fingered workers everywhere (they do the spadework so you don't have to).

Then, slightly off the well-manicured path, our woods are home for red squirrels, deer and all kinds of birds.

And while woodland and gardens surround the village, the whole estate is surrounded by the regal grandeur of Royal Deeside.

Homes at Inchmarlo range from one-bedroom apartments to four bedroom houses, all well proportioned and all carefully designed for retirement living.

An added comfort is Inchmarlo House. This magnificent Georgian mansion is now a care home, so as your needs change, help and support is right on your doorstep.

Here too is a private lounge for Home Owners' events and a bar/restaurant serving dishes inspired by Michelin starred chefs.

To find out more call +44 (1330) 824981 or email info@inchmarlo-retirement.co.uk

Then come and see why Inchmarlo is the ideal spot to put down some roots.

INCHMARLO
RETIREMENT VILLAGE

Where Gracious Living Comes Naturally

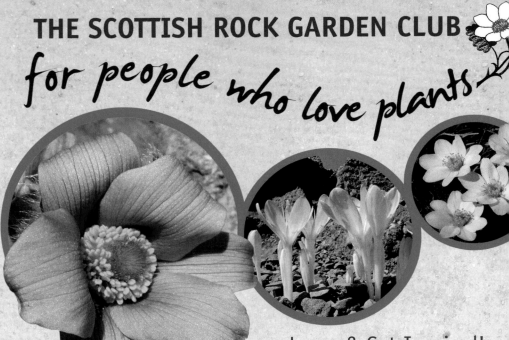

VISIT OUR WEBSITE
for last minute offers

the National Trust
for Scotland
a place for everyone

SCOTTISH BREAKS

Enjoy a relaxing break surrounded by breathtaking Scottish scenery in our extensive range of self-catering accommodation

Find out more and book online at **www.nts.org.uk**
or call **0131 458 0305** to request a brochure

GARDENS OPEN ON A SPECIFIC DATE

February

Date to be advised

Kirkcudbrightshire   Danevale Park, Crossmichael
Ross, Cromarty, Skye & Inverness   Cardon, Balnafoich

Sunday 1 February

Wigtownshire   Logan Botanic Garden, Port Logan

Sunday 8 February

Perth & Kinross   Fingask Castle, Rait
Renfrewshire   Ardgowan, Inverkip
Wigtownshire   Logan Botanic Garden, Port Logan

Saturday 14 February

Wigtownshire   Dunskey Gardens and Maze, Portpatrick

Sunday 15 February

Ayrshire   Caprington Castle, Kilmarnock
Dumfriesshire   Craig, Langholm
Wigtownshire   Dunskey Gardens and Maze, Portpatrick
Wigtownshire   Logan Botanic Garden, Port Logan

Saturday 21 February

East Lothian   Shepherd House, Inveresk
Kincardine & Deeside   Crathes Castle Garden, Banchory
Wigtownshire   Dunskey Gardens and Maze, Portpatrick

Sunday 22 February

East Lothian   Shepherd House, Inveresk
Kirkcudbrightshire   Brooklands, Crocketford
Lanarkshire   Cleghorn, by Lanark
Stirlingshire   West Plean House, by Stirling
Wigtownshire   Dunskey Gardens and Maze, Portpatrick
Wigtownshire   Logan Botanic Garden, Port Logan

Saturday 28 February

Perth & Kinross   Kilgraston School, Bridge of Earn
Angus & Dundee   Dunninald, Montrose

March

Sunday 1 March

Fife   Lindores House, by Newburgh

Kincardine & Deeside	Ecclesgreig Castle, St Cyrus
Midlothian	Kevock Road Gardens, Lasswade
Angus & Dundee	Dunninald, Montrose

Tuesday 3 March
Argyll	Torosay Castle Gardens, Isle of Mull

Saturday 7 March
Aberdeenshire	Hatton Castle Garden Workshop, Turriff
Angus & Dundee	Dunninald, Montrose

Sunday 8 March
Angus & Dundee	Dunninald, Montrose

April

Friday 3 April
Roxburghshire	Floors Castle, Kelso

Saturday 4 April
Glasgow & District	Holmwood, Cathcart
Roxburghshire	Floors Castle, Kelso

Sunday 5 April
Edinburgh & West Lothian	61 Fountainhall Road, Edinburgh
Fife	Balcarres, Colinsburgh
Glasgow & District	Holmwood, Cathcart
Roxburghshire	Floors Castle, Kelso

Monday 6 April
Roxburghshire	Floors Castle, Kelso

Saturday 11 April
Moray & Nairn	Brodie Castle, Forres

Sunday 12 April
Aberdeenshire	Auchmacoy, Ellon
Edinburgh & West Lothian	61 Fountainhall Road, Edinburgh
Moray & Nairn	Brodie Castle, Forres
Perth & Kinross	Megginch Castle, Errol

Thursday 16 April
Ross, Cromarty, Skye & Inverness	Dundonnell House, Little Loch Broom

Saturday 18 April
Kincardine & Deeside	Crathes Castle Garden, Banchory
Renfrewshire	Kilmacolm Plant Sale, Kilmacolm

Sunday 19 April
Aberdeenshire	Westhall Castle, Inverurie
East Lothian	Winton House, Pencaitland

Edinburgh & West Lothian	Redcroft, Edinburgh
Fife	Cambo House Spring Plant and Craft Fair, Kingsbarns
Stirlingshire	West Plean House, by Stirling

Saturday 25 April

East Lothian	Shepherd House, Inveresk

Sunday 26 April

Argyll	Benmore Botanic Garden, Dunoon
Dunbartonshire	Kilarden, Rosneath
East Lothian	Shepherd House, Inveresk
Edinburgh & West Lothian	Gilmour Road Gardens, Edinburgh
Ettrick & Lauderdale	Bemersyde, Melrose
Stirlingshire	The Pass House, Callander

Wednesday 29 April

Ayrshire	Grougarbank House, Kilmarnock

May

Saturday 2 May

Aberdeenshire	Castle Fraser Garden, Inverurie
Edinburgh & West Lothian	41 Hermitage Gardens, Edinburgh
Lanarkshire	The Scots Mining Company House, Leadhills
Lochaber	Canna House Walled Garden, Isle of Canna
Ross, Cromarty, Skye & Inverness	Old Allangrange, Munlochy

Sunday 3 May

Aberdeenshire	Castle Fraser Garden, Inverurie
Angus & Dundee	Brechin Castle, Brechin
Dumfriesshire	Portrack House, Holywood
Edinburgh & West Lothian	41 Hermitage Gardens, Edinburgh
Fife	Earlshall Castle, Leuchars
Lanarkshire	The Scots Mining Company House, Leadhills
Perth & Kinross	Branklyn Garden, Perth
Perth & Kinross	Fingask Castle, Rait
Stirlingshire	Broich, Kippen

Friday 8 May

Dumfriesshire	Peilton, Moniaive

Saturday 9 May

Angus & Dundee	3 Balfour Cottages, Menmuir
Argyll	Knock Cottage, Lochgair
Lochaber	Arisaig House, Arisaig

Sunday 10 May

Angus & Dundee	Dalfruin, Kirriemuir
Argyll	Arduaine Garden, Oban

Argyll	Knock Cottage, Lochgair
Ayrshire	Kilmaurs Village Gardens, Kilmaurs
Dumfriesshire	Capenoch, Thornhill
East Lothian	Tyninghame House and The Walled Garden, Dunbar
Edinburgh & West Lothian	Dean Gardens, Edinburgh
Kirkcudbrightshire	Netherhall, Glenlochar
Kirkcudbrightshire	Threave Garden, Castle Douglas
Stirlingshire	Bridge of Allan Gardens, Bridge of Allan

Thursday 14 May

Isle of Arran	Brodick Castle & Country Park

Friday 15 May

Dumfriesshire	Peilton, Moniaive

Saturday 16 May

Argyll	Drim na Vullin, Lochgilphead
Argyll	Knock Cottage, Lochgair
East Lothian	Broadwoodside, Gifford
Ettrick & Lauderdale / Peeblesshire	Borders Plant and Produce Sale, Melrose

Sunday 17 May

Angus & Dundee	Dunninald, Montrose
Argyll	Drim na Vullin, Lochgilphead
Argyll	Knock Cottage, Lochgair
Dumfriesshire	Dalswinton House, Dalswinton
Dunbartonshire	Ross Priory, Gartocharn
Edinburgh & West Lothian	101 Greenbank Crescent, Edinburgh
Edinburgh & West Lothian	61 Fountainhall Road, Edinburgh
Edinburgh & West Lothian	Redcroft, Edinburgh
Fife	Northwood Cottage, Newport-on-Tay
Fife	Tayfield, Forgan
Fife	Willowhill, Forgan
Perth & Kinross	Machany House, Auchterarder
Stirlingshire	Dunblane Community Gardens, Dunblane
Stirlingshire	Gargunnock House Plant Sale, Gargunnock
Wigtownshire	Logan House Gardens, Port Logan

Monday 18 May

Caithness, Sutherland, Orkney & Shetland	Frakkafield, Gott

Tuesday 19 May

Caithness, Sutherland, Orkney & Shetland	Frakkafield, Gott

Wednesday 20 May

Caithness, Sutherland, Orkney & Shetland	Frakkafield, Gott
East Lothian	Humbie Garden Circle, Humbie
Ross, Cromarty, Skye & Inverness	Inverewe Garden and Estate, Poolewe

Thursday 21 May
Caithness, Sutherland, Orkney & Shetland   Frakkafield, Gott

Friday 22 May
Caithness, Sutherland, Orkney & Shetland   Frakkafield, Gott

Saturday 23 May
Angus & Dundee   Gallery, Montrose
Argyll   Colintraive Gardens, Colintraive
Argyll   Strachur House Flower & Woodland Gardens
Caithness, Sutherland, Orkney & Shetland   Frakkafield, Gott
Edinburgh & West Lothian   Dr Neil's Garden, Edinburgh
Perth & Kinross   Wester House of Ross, Comrie
Ross, Cromarty, Skye & Inverness   Oldtown of Leys Garden, Inverness

Sunday 24 May
Argyll   Colintraive Gardens, Colintraive
Argyll   Crarae Garden, Inveraray
Argyll   Fasnacloich, Appin
Argyll   Strachur House Flower & Woodland Gardens
Ayrshire   Borlandhills, Dunlop
Berwickshire   Anton's Hill, Leitholm
Caithness, Sutherland, Orkney & Shetland   Frakkafield, Gott
Dumfriesshire   Dabton, Thornhill
East Lothian   Belhaven Hill School, Dunbar
East Lothian   Belhaven House, Dunbar
Edinburgh & West Lothian   20 Blackford Road, Edinburgh
Edinburgh & West Lothian   61 Fountainhall Road, Edinburgh
Edinburgh & West Lothian   Dr Neil's Garden, Edinburgh
Fife   Kirklands, Saline
Kincardine & Deeside   Inchmarlo House Garden, Banchory
Kirkcudbrightshire   Corsock House, Castle Douglas
Lanarkshire   Nemphlar Village Garden Trail, Lanark
Lochaber   Aberarder with Ardverikie, Kinlochlaggan
Lochaber   Ardverikie with Aberarder, Kinlochlaggan
Moray & Nairn   Newbold House, Forres
Perth & Kinross   Dowhill, Cleish
Perth & Kinross   Wester House of Ross, Comrie
Ross, Cromarty, Skye & Inverness   Aultgowrie Mill, Muir of Ord
Stirlingshire   Dun Dubh, Aberfoyle
Stirlingshire   Touch, Stirling
Wigtownshire   Logan Botanic Garden, Port Logan

Monday 25 May
Caithness, Sutherland, Orkney & Shetland   Frakkafield, Gott

Tuesday 26 May
Caithness, Sutherland, Orkney & Shetland   Frakkafield, Gott

Wednesday 27 May

Caithness, Sutherland, Orkney & Shetland	Frakkafield, Gott
Ross, Cromarty, Skye & Inverness	House of Gruinard, by Achnasheen

Thursday 28 May

Aberdeenshire	Leith Hall Garden, Huntly
Caithness, Sutherland, Orkney & Shetland	Frakkafield, Gott
Ross, Cromarty, Skye & Inverness	Dundonnell House, Little Loch Broom

Friday 29 May

Caithness, Sutherland, Orkney & Shetland	Frakkafield, Gott

Saturday 30 May

Caithness, Sutherland, Orkney & Shetland	Frakkafield, Gott
Moray & Nairn	Carestown Steading, Deskford
Ross, Cromarty, Skye & Inverness	Duirinish Lodge, Kyle of Lochalsh

Sunday 31 May

Angus & Dundee	Glamis Castle, Glamis
Ayrshire	1 Burnside Cottages, Coylton
Caithness, Sutherland, Orkney & Shetland	Frakkafield, Gott
Dumfriesshire	Leap Cottage, Dumfries
Dunbartonshire	Brandon Grove, Helensburgh
Dunbartonshire	Milton Cottage, Helensburgh
Ettrick & Lauderdale	Laidlawstiel House, Galashiels
Glasgow & District	Ardlinnhe, Glasgow
Kincardine & Deeside	Woodend House, Banchory
Kirkcudbrightshire	Cally Gardens, Gatehouse of Fleet
Peeblesshire	Srongarbh, West Linton
Renfrewshire	Carruth, Bridge of Weir
Ross, Cromarty, Skye & Inverness	Duirinish Lodge, Kyle of Lochalsh
Stirlingshire	Fintry Village Gardens, by Glasgow
Wigtownshire	Burbainie, Stranraer
Wigtownshire	Claymoddie Garden, Whithorn

June

Monday 1 June

Caithness, Sutherland, Orkney & Shetland	Frakkafield, Gott
East Lothian	St Mary's Pleasance, Haddington
Ross, Cromarty, Skye & Inverness	Duirinish Lodge, Kyle of Lqchalsh

Tuesday 2 June

Caithness, Sutherland, Orkney & Shetland	Frakkafield, Gott
East Lothian	St Mary's Pleasance, Haddington
Ross, Cromarty, Skye & Inverness	Duirinish Lodge, Kyle of Lochalsh

Wednesday 3 June

Caithness, Sutherland, Orkney & Shetland	Frakkafield, Gott

East Lothian	Humbie Garden Circle, Humbie
East Lothian	St Mary's Pleasance, Haddington
Ross, Cromarty, Skye & Inverness	Duirinish Lodge, Kyle of Lochalsh
Ross, Cromarty, Skye & Inverness	Inverewe Garden and Estate, Poolewe

Thursday 4 June

Caithness, Sutherland, Orkney & Shetland	Frakkafield, Gott
East Lothian	St Mary's Pleasance, Haddington
Perth & Kinross	Bradystone House, Murthly
Ross, Cromarty, Skye & Inverness	Duirinish Lodge, Kyle of Lochalsh

Friday 5 June

Caithness, Sutherland, Orkney & Shetland	Frakkafield, Gott
East Lothian	St Mary's Pleasance, Haddington
Ross, Cromarty, Skye & Inverness	Duirinish Lodge, Kyle of Lochalsh

Saturday 6 June

Ayrshire	Holmes Farm, by Irvine
Caithness, Sutherland, Orkney & Shetland	Amat, Ardgay
Caithness, Sutherland, Orkney & Shetland	Frakkafield, Gott
Ross, Cromarty, Skye & Inverness	Duirinish Lodge, Kyle of Lochalsh
Ross, Cromarty, Skye & Inverness	The New House, Dingwall
Wigtownshire	Whitehills House, Newton Stewart

Sunday 7 June

Aberdeenshire	Birken Cottage, Inverurie
Aberdeenshire	Kildrummy Castle Gardens, Alford
Aberdeenshire	Tillypronie, Tarland
Ayrshire	Holmes Farm, Drybridge
Caithness, Sutherland, Orkney & Shetland	Amat, Ardgay
Caithness, Sutherland, Orkney & Shetland	Orkney Garden Trail One
Dumfriesshire	Newtonairds Lodge, Newtonairds
Dumfriesshire	Westerhall, Langholm
Dunbartonshire	Geilston Garden, Cardross
East Lothian	Hopefield, Gladsmuir
Edinburgh & West Lothian	The Glasshouses at the Royal Botanic Garden Edinburgh
Fife	Earlshall Castle, Leuchars
Glasgow & District	Aeolia with Blackmill, Kilsyth
Glasgow & District	Blackmill with Aeolia, Kilsyth
Isle of Arran	The Glades, Whiting Bay
Kirkcudbrightshire	Brooklands, Crocketford
Midlothian	Temple Village Gardens, Temple
Moray & Nairn	Gordonstoun, Duffus
Peeblesshire	Stobo Japanese Water Garden, Stobo
Perth & Kinross	Delvine, Murthly
Perth & Kinross	Explorers Garden, Pitlochry
Renfrewshire	Quarriers Village Gardens, Bridge of Weir
Ross, Cromarty, Skye & Inverness	Field House, Belladrum

Stirlingshire	Thornhill Village, near Stirling

Monday 8 June

East Lothian	St Mary's Pleasance, Haddington

Tuesday 9 June

East Lothian	St Mary's Pleasance, Haddington

Wednesday 10 June

East Lothian	St Mary's Pleasance, Haddington
Peeblesshire	The Potting Shed, Broughton
Ross, Cromarty, Skye & Inverness	Gorthleck, Stratherrick

Thursday 11 June

East Lothian	St Mary's Pleasance, Haddington
Kirkcudbrightshire	Broughton House Garden, Kirkcudbright
Perth & Kinross	Bradystone House, Murthly

Friday 12 June

East Lothian	St Mary's Pleasance, Haddington
Kirkcudbrightshire	Stockarton, Kirkcudbright

Saturday 13 June

Edinburgh & West Lothian	Rocheid Garden, Edinburgh
Glasgow & District	53 Dalziel Drive, Glasgow
Kirkcudbrightshire	Stockarton, Kirkcudbright
Midlothian	Kevock Road Gardens, Lasswade
Moray & Nairn	Glenrinnes Lodge, Dufftown
Perth & Kinross	Blair Castle Gardens, Blair Atholl

Sunday 14 June

Angus & Dundee	Letham Village, Letham
Caithness, Sutherland, Orkney & Shetland	Duncan Street Gardens, Thurso
Caithness, Sutherland, Orkney & Shetland	Orkney Garden Trail One
Dumfriesshire	Dunesslin, Dunscore
Fife	Greenhead Farmhouse, Greenhead of Arnot
Kincardine & Deeside	Kincardine, Kincardine O'Neil
Kirkcudbrightshire	Stockarton, Kirkcudbright
Kirkcudbrightshire	The Waterhouse Gardens at Stockarton, Kirkcudbright
Lanarkshire	Dippoolbank Cottage, Carnwath
Midlothian	Kevock Road Gardens, Lasswade
Peeblesshire	Halmyre Mains Plant Sale, West Linton
Perth & Kinross	Bonhard House, Perth
Perth & Kinross	Mill of Forneth, Blairgowrie
Renfrewshire	Duchal, Kilmacolm
Stirlingshire	Lanrick, Doune
Wigtownshire	Castle Kennedy and Gardens, Stranraer

Wednesday 17 June

East Lothian	Humbie Garden Circle, Humbie

Peeblesshire   The Potting Shed, Broughton
Ross, Cromarty, Skye & Inverness   Brackla Wood, Culbokie

Thursday 18 June
Aberdeenshire   Leith Hall Garden, Huntly
Isle of Arran   Brodick Castle & Country Park
Perth & Kinross   Bradystone House, Murthly

Saturday 20 June
Argyll   Dal an Eas and Dalnaneun, Oban
Ayrshire   Gardens of West Kilbride and Seamill

Sunday 21 June
Angus & Dundee   Edzell Village & Castle, Edzell
Argyll   Dal an Eas and Dalnaneun, Oban
Dumfriesshire   Cowhill Tower, Holywood
Caithness, Sutherland, Orkney & Shetland   The Quoy of Houton, Orphir
East Lothian   Amisfield Walled Garden, Haddington
Edinburgh & West Lothian   61 Fountainhall Road, Edinburgh
Edinburgh & West Lothian   Merchiston Cottage, Edinburgh
Ettrick & Lauderdale   Harmony Garden, Melrose
Ettrick & Lauderdale   Priorwood Gardens, Melrose
Fife   Culross Palace Garden, Culross
Fife   Kinghorn Village Gardens,
Fife   Pittenweem: Gardens in the Burgh
Kincardine & Deeside   Ecclesgreig Castle, St Cyrus
Kirkcudbrightshire   Seabank, Rockcliffe
Stirlingshire   Doune Village Gardens,
Wigtownshire   Damnaglaur House, Stranraer
Wigtownshire   The Homestead, Stranraer
Wigtownshire   Woodfall Gardens, Glasserton

Wednesday 24 June
Peeblesshire   The Potting Shed, Broughton

Thursday 25 June
Moray & Nairn   Bruntlands Bungalow, Elgin
Perth & Kinross   Bradystone House, Murthly

Saturday 27 June
Angus & Dundee   Kilry Village Gardens, Glen Isla
Argyll   Ascog Hall, Isle of Bute
Argyll   Seafield, Dunoon
Fife   Gilston House, Leven
Moray & Nairn   Haugh Garden, College of Roseisle
Perth & Kinross   The Bield at Blackruthven, Tibbermore

Sunday 28 June
Angus & Dundee   Newtonmill House, by Brechin

Argyll	Seafield, Dunoon
Ayrshire	10 Grange Terrace and The Allotments of Annanhill Park, Kilmarnock
Caithness, Sutherland, Orkney & Shetland	Pentland Firth Gardens, Dunnet
Caithness, Sutherland, Orkney & Shetland	The Herston Garden Trail
East Lothian	Tyninghame House and The Walled Garden, Dunbar
Fife	Strathmiglo Village Gardens
Kirkcudbrightshire	Glenlivet with The Limes, Kirkcudbright
Kirkcudbrightshire	The Limes with Glenlivet, Kirkcudbright
Ross, Cromarty, Skye & Inverness	House of Aigas and Field Centre, by Beauly
Stirlingshire	Thorntree with Woodstone House, Arnprior
Stirlingshire	Woodstone House with Thorntree, Kippen

July

Wednesday 1 July

Caithness, Sutherland, Orkney & Shetland	The Castle & Gardens of Mey
Isle of Arran	Dougarie
Kincardine & Deeside	Drum Castle Garden, by Banchory
Peeblesshire	Portmore, Eddleston
Peeblesshire	The Potting Shed, Broughton

Thursday 2 July

Perth & Kinross	Bradystone House, Murthly

Friday 3 July

Ettrick & Lauderdale	Carolside, Earlston

Saturday 4 July

Ettrick & Lauderdale	Carolside, Earlston

Sunday 5 July

Aberdeenshire	Bruckhills Croft, Inverurie
Angus & Dundee	Montrose and Hillside Gardens, Montrose
Argyll	Torosay Castle Gardens, Isle of Mull
Ayrshire	Gardening Leave, SAC Auchincruive
Berwickshire	Lennel Bank, Coldstream
Berwickshire	Netherbyres, Eyemouth
Caithness, Sutherland, Orkney & Shetland	Bighouse Lodge, by Melvich
Caithness, Sutherland, Orkney & Shetland	The Herston Garden Trail
Glasgow	Kamares, Newton Mearns
Kincardine & Deeside	Findrack, Torphins
Kirkcudbrightshire	Crofts, Castle Douglas
Kirkcudbrightshire	Southwick House, Southwick
Moray & Nairn	10 Pilmuir Road West , Forres

Wednesday 8 July

Peeblesshire	Portmore, Eddleston
Peeblesshire	The Potting Shed, Broughton

Thursday 9 July

Perth & Kinross	Bradystone House, Murthly

Friday 10 July

Ettrick & Lauderdale	Carolside, Earlston

Saturday 11 July

Aberdeenshire	Middle Cairncake, Turriff
Angus & Dundee	Gallery, Montrose
Ettrick & Lauderdale	Carolside, Earlston
Ross, Cromarty, Skye & Inverness	The New House, Dingwall

Sunday 12 July

Aberdeenshire	Middle Cairncake, Turriff
Ayrshire	Carnell, by Hurlford
Caithness, Sutherland, Orkney & Shetland	Holmlea, Mid Yell
Caithness, Sutherland, Orkney & Shetland	Lea Gardens, Tresta
Caithness, Sutherland, Orkney & Shetland	Orkney Garden Trail Two
Lanarkshire	Lindsaylands, Biggar
Perth & Kinross	Hollytree Lodge, Dollar
Ross, Cromarty, Skye & Inverness	Aultgowrie Mill, Muir of Ord
Roxburghshire	Yetholm Village Gardens, Town Yetholm
Stirlingshire	Moon Cottage, Dunblane
Wigtownshire	Woodfall Gardens, Glasserton

Tuesday 14 July

Ayrshire	Culzean, Maybole

Wednesday 15 July

Aberdeenshire	Haddo House, Ellon
Caithness, Sutherland, Orkney & Shetland	The Castle & Gardens of Mey
Kincardine & Deeside	Drum Castle Garden, by Banchory
Peeblesshire	Portmore, Eddleston
Peeblesshire	The Potting Shed, Broughton

Thursday 16 July

Caithness, Sutherland, Orkney & Shetland	15 Linkshouse, Mid Yell
Isle of Arran	Brodick Castle & Country Park
Perth & Kinross	Bradystone House, Murthly

Friday 17 July

Ettrick & Lauderdale	Carolside, Earlston

Saturday 18 July

Angus & Dundee	Hospitalfield Gardens, Arbroath
Ettrick & Lauderdale	Carolside, Earlston
Fife	Crail: Small Gardens in the Burgh
Moray & Nairn	Bruntlands Bungalow, Elgin
Moray & Nairn	Haugh Garden, College of Roseisle

Sunday 19 July

Aberdeenshire	Glenkindie House, Alford
Ayrshire	Cairnhall House, Ochiltree
Berwickshire	Anton's Hill with The Walled Garden, Leitholm
Berwickshire	The Walled Garden with Anton's Hill, Leitholm
Caithness, Sutherland, Orkney & Shetland	Holmlea, Mid Yell
Caithness, Sutherland, Orkney & Shetland	Orkney Garden Trail Two
Dumfriesshire	Westwater Farm, Langholm
Edinburgh & West Lothian	Hunter's Tryst, Edinburgh
Fife	Crail: Small Gardens in the Burgh
Lanarkshire	Dippoolbank Cottage, Carnwath
Moray & Nairn	Bruntlands Bungalow, Elgin
Peeblesshire	8 Halmyre Mains, West Linton
Roxburghshire	West Leas, Bonchester Bridge
Stirlingshire	The Tors, Falkirk

Wednesday 22 July

Kincardine & Deeside	Drum Castle Garden, by Banchory
Peeblesshire	Portmore, Eddleston
Ross, Cromarty, Skye & Inverness	House of Gruinard, by Achnasheen

Thursday 23 July

Caithness, Sutherland, Orkney & Shetland	15 Linkshouse, Mid Yell
Perth & Kinross	Bradystone House, Murthly

Saturday 25 July

Aberdeenshire	Knockmuir, Auchry, Turriff
Caithness, Sutherland, Orkney & Shetland	House of Tongue, Lairg
Edinburgh & West Lothian	45 Northfield Crescent, Bathgate

Sunday 26 July

Aberdeenshire	Knockmuir, Turriff
Angus & Dundee	The Herbalist's Garden at Logie, Kirriemuir
Argyll	Ardchattan Priory, North Connel
Argyll	Crarae Garden, Inveraray
Caithness, Sutherland, Orkney & Shetland	Holmlea, Mid Yell
Caithness, Sutherland, Orkney & Shetland	Langwell, Berriedale
Edinburgh & West Lothian	45 Northfield Crescent, Bathgate
Fife	Balcaskie with Kellie Castle, Pittenweem
Fife	Falkland Palace, Cupar
Fife	Kellie Castle with Balcaskie, Pittenweem
Kirkcudbrightshire	Glensone Walled Garden, Southwick
Lanarkshire	Wellbutts, Elsrickle
Moray & Nairn	Newbold House, Forres
Ross, Cromarty, Skye & Inverness	House of Aigas and Field Centre, by Beauly
Wigtownshire	Balker Farmhouse, Stranraer

Tuesday 28 July

Stirlingshire	Gean House, Alloa

Wednesday 29 July

Kincardine & Deeside	Drum Castle Garden, by Banchory
Peeblesshire	Portmore, Eddleston

Thursday 30 July

Aberdeenshire	Leith Hall Garden, Huntly
Caithness, Sutherland, Orkney & Shetland	15 Linkshouse, Mid Yell

August

Saturday 1 August

Argyll	Eas Mhor, Oban

Sunday 2 August

Argyll	Eas Mhor, Oban
Caithness, Sutherland, Orkney & Shetland	Holmlea, Mid Yell
Dunbartonshire	Glebeside House with Rowanan, Rhu
Dunbartonshire	Rowanan with Glebeside House, Rhu
Kincardine & Deeside	Glenbervie House, Stonehaven
Kirkcudbrightshire	Cally Gardens, Gatehouse of Fleet
Peeblesshire	West Linton Village Gardens
Perth & Kinross	Drummond Castle Gardens, Crieff

Wednesday 5 August

Peeblesshire	Portmore, Eddleston

Thursday 6 August

Caithness, Sutherland, Orkney & Shetland	15 Linkshouse, Mid Yell

Friday 7 August

Ross, Cromarty, Skye & Inverness	2 Durnamuck, Little Loch Broom

Saturday 8 August

Argyll	Barguillean House, Taynuilt
Argyll	Barguillean's "Angus Garden", Taynuilt
Argyll	Lorn Organic Growers, Taynuilt
Ayrshire	Girvan Community Garden, Girvan
Ross, Cromarty, Skye & Inverness	2 Durnamuck, Little Loch Broom,
Ross, Cromarty, Skye & Inverness	Hugh Miller's Birthplace Cottage & Museum, Cromarty

Sunday 9 August

Aberdeenshire	Pitmedden Garden, Ellon
Ayrshire	Girvan Community Garden, Girvan
Caithness, Sutherland, Orkney & Shetland	Holmlea, Mid Yell
Kincardine & Deeside	Fasque House, Laurencekirk
Kirkcudbrightshire	Threave Garden, Castle Douglas
Lochaber	Roshven House, Lochailort
Ross, Cromarty, Skye & Inverness	2 Durnamuck, Little Loch Broom

Wednesday 12 August

Lochaber	Canna House Walled Garden, Isle of Canna
Peeblesshire	Portmore, Eddleston

Thursday 13 August

Caithness, Sutherland, Orkney & Shetland	15 Linkshouse, Mid Yell
Ross, Cromarty, Skye & Inverness	Dundonnell House, Little Loch Broom,

Saturday 15 August

Caithness, Sutherland, Orkney & Shetland	The Castle & Gardens of Mey
Moray & Nairn	Haugh Garden, College of Roseisle

Sunday 16 August

Caithness, Sutherland, Orkney & Shetland	Holmlea, Mid Yell
Caithness, Sutherland, Orkney & Shetland	Millbank Gardens, Thurso
Lanarkshire	Culter Allers, Culter
Midlothian	Kirkhill Gardens, Penicuik
Stirlingshire	The Steading, by Dollar
Wigtownshire	Lochnaw Castle, Stranraer

Wednesday 19 August

Peeblesshire	Portmore, Eddleston

Thursday 20 August

Caithness, Sutherland, Orkney & Shetland	15 Linkshouse, Mid Yell

Saturday 22 August

Ross, Cromarty, Skye & Inverness	Rubha Phoil Forest Gardens, Isle of Skye

Sunday 23 August

Argyll	Duart Castle, Isle of Mull
Renfrewshire	Gardening Leave, Bishopton

Wednesday 26 August

Aberdeenshire	Haddo House, Methlick, Ellon
Peeblesshire	Portmore, Eddleston

Thursday 27 August

Aberdeenshire	Leith Hall Garden, Huntly

Sunday 30 August

Aberdeenshire	Tillypronie, Tarland
Ross, Cromarty, Skye & Inverness	Highland Liliums, Kiltarlity
Stirlingshire	The Pineapple, Falkirk

September

Wednesday 2 September

Aberdeenshire	Cruickshank Botanic Gardens, Aberdeen

Sunday 6 September

Argyll	Torosay Castle Gardens, Isle of Mull

Dunbartonshire   Hill House Plant Sale, Helensburgh
Edinburgh & West Lothian   61 Fountainhall Road, Edinburgh

Saturday 12 September
Renfrewshire   Kilmacolm Plant Sale, Kilmacolm
Ross, Cromarty, Skye & Inverness   Old Allangrange, Munlochy

Sunday 13 September
Edinburgh & West Lothian   61 Fountainhall Road, Edinburgh

Thursday 17 September
Ross, Cromarty, Skye & Inverness   Dundonnell House, Little Loch Broom

Saturday 19 September
Glasgow & District   Greenbank Garden, Clarkston
Perth & Kinross   Wester House of Ross, Comrie

Sunday 20 September
Glasgow & District   Greenbank Garden, Clarkston
Perth & Kinross   Wester House of Ross, Comrie

Sunday 27 September
Aberdeenshire   Kildrummy Castle Gardens, Alford

October

Sunday 4 October
Fife   Hill of Tarvit
Peeblesshire   Dawyck Botanic Garden, Stobo
Stirlingshire   Little Broich, Kippen

GARDENS OPEN BY ARRANGEMENT

Aberdeenshire

Birken Cottage, Burnhervie	1 May - 31 August
Bruckhills Croft, Inverurie	1 February - 15 March
Grandhome, Aberdeen	1 April - 31 October
Greenridge, Cults	1 July - 31 August
Hatton Castle, Turriff	On request
Laundry Cottage, Huntly	On request
Westfield Lodge, Milltimber	1 July - 17 July

Angus & Dundee

Dunninald, Montrose	On request
Gallery, Montrose	1 May - 30 September
Kirkside of Lochty, Menmuir, by Brechin	1 March - 31 October
Kirkton House, Kirkton of Craig, Montrose	1 May - 30 September
The Garden Cottage, Dunnichen	31 May - 28 June

Argyll

Kinlochlaich House Gardens, Appin	12 October - 31 December
Knock Cottage, Lochgair	15 April - 15 June

Ayrshire

Burnside, Littlemill Road, Drongan	1 April - 30 September
High Fulwood, Stewarton	20 April - 6 September

Berwickshire

Anton's Hill, Leitholm	On request
Lennel Bank, Coldstream	On request
Netherbyres, Eyemouth	1 May - 31 August

Caithness, Sutherland, Orkney & Shetland

Cruisdale, Sandness	1 March - 31 October
Keldaberg, Cunningsburgh	1 June - 31 October
Lindaal, Tingwall	1 May - 30 September
Nonavaar, Levenwick	1 March - 12 September

Dunbartonshire

8 Laggary Park, Rhu, Helensburgh	1 August - 30 September
Glenarn, Rhu	21 March - 21 September

Edinburgh & West Lothian

101 Greenbank Crescent, Edinburgh	1 March - 31 October
Hunter's Tryst, Edinburgh	On request
Redcroft, Edinburgh	8 September - 30 September
Rocheid Garden, Edinburgh	On request

Fife

Barham, Bow of Fife	1 April - 31 July
Earlshall Castle, Leuchars	On request
Glassmount House, By Kirkcaldy	1 April - 30 September
Logie House, Crossford	1 April - 31 October
South Flisk, Blebo Craigs	15 April - 31 May
Strathairly House, Upper Largo	1 April - 31 August
The Tower, Wormit	1 April - 30 September
Willowhill, Forgan	1 May - 29 August
Wormistoune House, Crail	1 April - 30 September

Glasgow & District

Aeolia with Blackmill, Kilsyth	1 April - 30 September
Blackmill with Aeolia, Kilsyth	1 April - 30 September

Kincardine & Deeside

14 Arbeadie Avenue, Banchory	1 May - 31 July

Kirkcudbrightshire

Anwoth Old Schoolhouse, Anwoth	15 February - 15 November
Barholm Castle, Gatehouse of Fleet	1 February - 4 October
Corsock House, Corsock	1 April - 30 June
The Mill House at Gelston, Gelston	12 July - 13 September

Lanarkshire

20 Smithycroft, Hamilton	1 April - 30 September
Carmichael Mill, Lanark	On request
The Scots Mining Company House, Leadhills	1 April - 30 September

Lochaber

Ard-Daraich, Ardgour	On request

Midlothian

Newhall, Carlops	1 June - 31 July
The Old Sun Inn, Newbattle	1 June - 31 July

Moray & Nairn

Bruntlands Bungalow, Alves	1 June - 31 August
Castleview, Dufftown	1 June - 31 August
10 Pilmuir Road West, Forres	1 February - 15 March

Peeblesshire

Portmore, Eddleston	1 June - 16 September
Stobo Japanese Water Garden, Stobo	1 May - 31 October

Perth & Kinross

Bradystone House, Murthly	5 June - 22 July
Carig Dhubh, Bonskeid	1 May - 30 September
Croftcat Lodge, Grandtully	15 May - 15 October
Delvine, Murthly	15 April - 15 October
Easter Meikle Fardle, Meikleour	31 March - 1 September
Hollytree Lodge, Muckhart	1 April - 30 October
Little Tombuie, Killiechassie	15 May - 15 June
Little Tombuie, Killiechassie	15 September - 15 October
Mill of Forneth, Forneth	30 April - 30 September
Parkhead House, Perth	1 June - 31 August
The Steading, Newmill of Kinloch	25 April - 17 May
The Steading, Newmill of Kinloch	6 June - 21 June

Ross, Cromarty, Skye & Inverness

Brackla Wood, Culbokie	6 April - 27 September
Cardon, Balnafoich	1 March - 30 September
Dundonnell House, Little Loch Broom	1 April - 30 November
Glenkyllachy Lodge, Tomatin	1 May - 31 July
Glenkyllachy Lodge, Tomatin	1 September - 31 October
House of Aigas and Field Centre, By Beauly	1 March - 25 October
Leathad Ard, Isle of Lewis	1 May - 31 May
Leathad Ard, Isle of Lewis	1 September - 30 September
The Lookout, Kilmuir	On request

Roxburghshire

Lanton Tower, Jedburgh	On request
West Leas, Bonchester Bridge	On request

Stirlingshire

Arndean, by Dollar	15 May - 15 June
Duntreath Castle, Blanefield	1 February - 30 November
Milseybank, Bridge of Allan	1 April - 31 May
Rowberrow, Dollar	1 February - 31 December
The Linns, Sheriffmuir	15 February - 30 September

The Steading, Yetts O'Muckhart	1 April - 15 October
The Tors, Falkirk	1 May - 30 September
Thorntree, Arnprior	1 April - 15 October

Wigtownshire

Balker Farmhouse, Stranraer	1 May - 30 September
Castle Kennedy and Gardens, Stranraer	2 November - 31 December
Claymoddie Garden, Whithorn	1 April - 30 September
Craichlaw, Kirkcowan	On request
Woodfall Gardens, Glasserton	On request

GARDENS OPEN ON A REGULAR BASIS

Aberdeenshire

Fyvie Castle, Turriff	1 July - 31 October

Angus & Dundee

Dunninald, Montrose	4 July - 2 August not Mondays
Gagie House, by Dundee	21 February - 25 May
Glamis Castle, Glamis	3 April - 1 November
Hospitalfield Gardens, Arbroath	11 April - 26 September Saturdays
Pitmuies Gardens, by Forfar	1 February - 15 March
Pitmuies Gardens, by Forfar	1 April - 31 October
The Angus and Fife Garden Trail	5 May - 25 June
The Herbalist's Garden at Logie, Kirriemuir	1 June - 31 August Tuesdays & Saturdays

Argyll

Achnacloich, Connel	28 March - 31 October Saturdays
An Cala, Isle of Seil	1 April - 31 October
Ardchattan Priory, North Connel	1 April - 31 October
Ardkinglas Woodland Garden, Cairndow	1 January - 31 December
Ardmaddy Castle, by Oban	1 January - 31 December
Barguillean's "Angus Garden", Taynuilt	1 January - 31 December
Benmore Botanic Garden, Benmore	1 March - 31 October
Crinan Hotel Garden, Crinan	1 May - 31 August
Druimneil House, Port Appin	2 April - 31 October
Fairwinds, Dunoon	1 April - 31 October
Inveraray Castle Gardens, Inveraray	1 April - 31 October
Kinlochlaich House Gardens, Appin	1 Jan - 28 Feb & 12 Oct - 31 Dec Saturdays
Kinlochlaich House Gardens, Appin	1 Mar - 11 Oct
Oakbank, Ardrishaig	1 May - 31 August

Berwickshire

Bughtrig, by Leitholm	1 June - 1 September

Caithness, Sutherland, Orkney & Shetland

Highlands, Scalloway	1 May - 30 September
Lea Gardens, Tresta	1 April - 31 October closed Thursdays
Nonavaar, Levenwick	1 March - 12 September Thursdays and Fridays
Norby, Sandness	1 January - 31 December

The Castle & Gardens of Mey | 13 May - 26 July
The Castle & Gardens of Mey | 11 August - 30 September

Dumfriesshire

Newtonairds Lodge, Newtonairds | 7 May - 13 August

Dunbartonshire

Glenarn, Rhu | 21 March - 21 September

East Lothian

Inwood, Carberry, Musselburgh | 1 May - 30 September Tuesdays and Thursdays
Shepherd House, Inveresk | 10 February - 26 February Tuesdays and Thursdays
Shepherd House, Inveresk | 14 April - 9 July Tuesdays and Thursdays

Edinburgh & West Lothian

Newliston, Kirkliston | 1 May - 4 June except Mondays and Tuesdays
The Glasshouses at the Royal Botanic Garden Edinburgh | 2 January - 31 December

Fife

The Angus and Fife Garden Trail | 5 May - 25 June
Glassmount House, By Kirkcaldy | 1 April - 30 September Monday to Friday
Willowhill, Forgan | 11 June - 29 August Thursdays, Fridays and Saturdays

Kincardine & Deeside

Drum Castle Garden, by Banchory | 1 April - 31 October

Lochaber

Ardtornish, by Lochaline | 1 January - 31 December

Peeblesshire

Dawyck Botanic Garden, Stobo | 1 February - 30 November
Kailzie Gardens, Peebles | 1 January - 31 December

Perth & Kinross

Ardvorlich, Lochearnhead | 1 May - 1 June
Blair Castle Gardens, Blair Atholl | 1 April - 31 October
Bolfracks, Aberfeldy | 1 January - 31 December
Braco Castle, Braco | 1 February - 31 October
Cluny House, Aberfeldy | 1 January - 31 December
Dowhill, Cleish | 18 May - 31 May
Drummond Castle Gardens, Crieff | 1 May - 31 October
Glendoick, by Perth | 1 April - 31 May
Glenericht House, Blairgowrie | 1 January - 31 December

Ross, Cromarty, Skye & Inverness

Abriachan Garden Nursery, Loch Ness Side	1 February - 30 November
Applecross Walled Garden, Strathcarron	15 March - 31 October
Attadale, Strathcarron	1 April - 31 October closed Sundays
Balmeanach House, Isle of Skye	5 May - 31 October Mondays and Thursdays
Clan Donald Skye, Isle of Skye	1 January - 31 March
Clan Donald Skye, Isle of Skye	1 April - 31 October
Clan Donald Skye, Isle of Skye	1 November - 31 December
Coiltie Garden, Divach, Drumnadrochit	22 June - 12 July
Dunvegan Castle and Gardens, Isle of Skye	1 April - 15 October
Highland Liliums, Kiltarlity	1 January - 31 December
Leathad Ard, Isle of Lewis	1 June - 31 August except Fridays & Sundays and Wednesday 5 August
Oldtown of Leys Garden, Inverness	1 January - 31 December
The Lookout, Kilmuir, North Kessock	1 May - 31 August Saturdays and Sundays

Roxburghshire

Floors Castle, Kelso	1 May - 25 October
Monteviot, Jedburgh	1 April - 31 October

Stirlingshire

Duntreath Castle, Blanefield	1 March - 8 March
Gargunnock House, Gargunnock	1 February - 16 March
Gargunnock House, Gargunnock	13 April - 30 September weekdays only

Wigtownshire

Ardwell House Gardens, Ardwell	1 April - 30 September
Castle Kennedy and Gardens, Stranraer	1 February - 29 March weekends only
Castle Kennedy and Gardens, Stranraer	30 March - 1 November
Claymoddie Garden, Whithorn	1 April - 30 September Fridays, Saturdays and Sundays
Glenwhan Gardens, Dunragit	1 April - 31 October
Logan Botanic Garden, Port Logan	15 March - 31 October
Logan House Gardens, Port Logan	1 March - 30 September

PLANT SALES

Renfrewshire

Kilmacolm Plant Sale, Kilmacolm	Saturday 18 April	10:00am - 12:00pm

Ettrick & Lauderdale

Borders Plant and Produce Sale, Melrose	Saturday 16 May	10:30am - 4:00pm

Peeblesshire

Borders Plant and Produce Sale, Melrose	Saturday 16 May	10:30am - 4:00pm

Stirlingshire

Gargunnock House Plant Sale, Gargunnock	Sunday 17 May	2:00pm - 5:00pm

Peeblesshire

Halmyre Mains Plant Sale, West Linton	Sunday 14 June	10:00am - 12:00pm

Dunbartonshire

Hill House Plant Sale, Helensburgh	Sunday 6 September	11:00am - 4:00pm

Renfrewshire

Kilmacolm Plant Sale, Kilmacolm	Saturday 12 September	10:00am - 12:00pm

Fife

Hill of Tarvit Plant Sale and Autumn Fair, Cupar	Sunday 4 October	10:30am - 4:00pm

GENERAL INFORMATION

MAPS
A map of each district is provided at the start of each section. These show the location of gardens as per the postal codes provided. Directions can be found in the garden descriptions.

HOUSES
Houses are not open unless specifically stated; where the house or part of the house is open, an additional charge is usually made.

TOILETS
Private gardens do not normally have outside toilets. For security reasons owners have been advised not to admit visitors into their houses.

PHOTOGRAPHY
No photographs taken in a garden may be used for sale or reproduction without the prior permission of the garden owner.

CHILDREN
Children are always welcome but must be accompanied by an adult. Children's activities are often available at openings.

CANCELLATIONS
All cancellations will be posted on our website www.scotlandsgardens.org

KEY TO SYMBOLS

	New in 2015		Homemade teas		Accommodation
	Teas		Dogs on a lead allowed		Plant stall
	Cream teas		Wheelchair access		Scottish Snowdrop Festival

MAP OF DISTRICTS

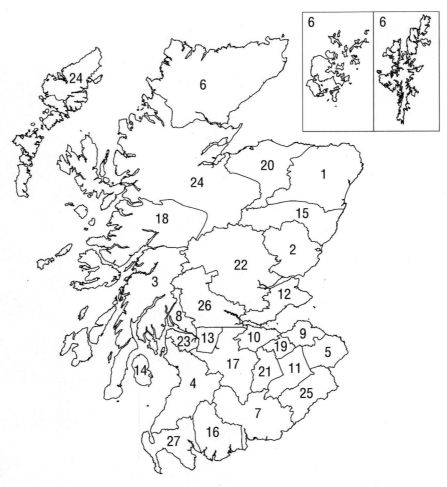

1. Aberdeenshire
2. Angus & Dundee
3. Argyll
4. Ayrshire
5. Berwickshire
6. Caithness, Sutherland, Orkney & Shetland
7. Dumfriesshire
8. Dunbartonshire
9. East Lothian
10. Edinburgh & West Lothian
11. Ettrick & Lauderdale
12. Fife
13. Glasgow & District
14. Isle of Arran
15. Kincardine & Deeside
16. Kirkcudbrightshire
17. Lanarkshire
18. Lochaber
19. Midlothian
20. Moray & Nairn
21. Peeblesshire
22. Perth & Kinross
23. Renfrewshire
24. Ross, Cromarty, Skye & Inverness
25. Roxburghshire
26. Stirlingshire
27. Wigtownshire

ABERDEENSHIRE

Scotland's Gardens 2015 Guidebook is sponsored by **INVESTEC WEALTH & INVESTMENT**

District Organiser

Mrs V Walters	Tillychetly, Alford AB33 8HQ

Area Organisers

Mrs H Gibson	6 The Chanonry, Old Aberdeen AB24 1RP
Mrs F G Lawson	Asloun, Alford AB33 8NR
Mrs Jan Oag	Old Balgove, Oldmeldrum, Inverurie AB51 0AX
Mrs Penny Orpwood	Middle Cairncake, Cuminestown, Turriff AB53 5YS
Mrs A Robertson	Drumblade House, Huntly AB54 6ER
Mrs H Rushton	Bruckhills Croft, Rothienorman, Inverurie AB51 8YB
Mrs F M K Tuck	Stable Cottage, Allargue, Gorgarff AB36 8YP

Treasurer

Mr A H J Coleman	Templeton House, Arbroath DD11 4QP

Gardens open on a specific date

Hatton Castle Garden Workshop, Turriff	Saturday 7 March	2:00pm		
Auchmacoy, Ellon	Sunday 12 April	1:15pm	-	4:00pm
Westhall Castle, Inverurie	Sunday 19 April	1:00pm	-	4:00pm
Castle Fraser Garden, Inverurie	Saturday 2 May	11:00am	-	4:00pm
Castle Fraser Garden, Inverurie	Sunday 3 May	11:00am	-	4:00pm
Leith Hall Garden, Huntly	Thursday 28 May	7:00pm		
Birken Cottage, Inverurie	Sunday 7 June	2:00pm	-	5:00pm
Kildrummy Castle Gardens, Alford	Sunday 7 June	10:00am	-	5:00pm
Tillypronie, Tarland	Sunday 7 June	2:00pm	-	5:00pm
Leith Hall Garden, Huntly	Thursday 18 June	7:00pm		
Bruckhills Croft, Inverurie	Sunday 5 July	12:00pm	-	5:00pm
Middle Cairncake, Turriff	Saturday 11 July	1:00pm	-	5:00pm
Middle Cairncake, Turriff	Sunday 12 July	1:00pm	-	5:00pm
Haddo House, Ellon	Wednesday 15 July	11:00am	-	5:00pm
Glenkindie House, Alford	Sunday 19 July	1:00pm	-	4:00pm
Knockmuir, Turriff	Saturday 25 July	1:00pm	-	5:00pm
Knockmuir, Turriff	Sunday 26 July	1:00pm	-	5:00pm
Leith Hall Garden, Huntly	Thursday 30 July	7:00pm		
Pitmedden Garden, Ellon	Sunday 9 August	1:30pm		
Haddo House, Ellon	Wednesday 26 August	11:00am	-	5:00pm
Leith Hall Garden, Huntly	Thursday 27 August	7:00pm		

ABERDEENSHIRE

Tillypronie, Tarland	Sunday 30 August	2:00pm - 5:00pm
Cruickshank Botanic Gardens, Aberdeen	Wednesday 2 September	6:15pm - 8:30pm
Kildrummy Castle Gardens, Alford	Sunday 27 September	10:00am - 5:00pm

Gardens open regularly

| Fyvie Castle, Turriff | 1 July - 31 October | 9:00am - Dusk |

Gardens open by arrangement

Birken Cottage, Inverurie	1 May - 31 August	01467 623013
Bruckhills Croft, Inverurie	1 February - 15 March	01651 821596
Grandhome, Aberdeen	1 April - 31 October	01224 722202
Greenridge, Craigton Road, Cults	1 July - 31 August	01224 860200 F: 01224 860210
Hatton Castle, Turriff	On request	01888 562279
Laundry Cottage, Huntly	On request	01466 720768
Westfield Lodge, Milltimber	1 July - 17 July	07435 969628

Birken Cottage, Aberdeenshire

Key to symbols

	New in 2015		Homemade teas		Accommodation
	Teas		Dogs on a lead allowed		Plant stall
	Cream teas		Wheelchair access		Scottish Snowdrop Festival

Garden locations

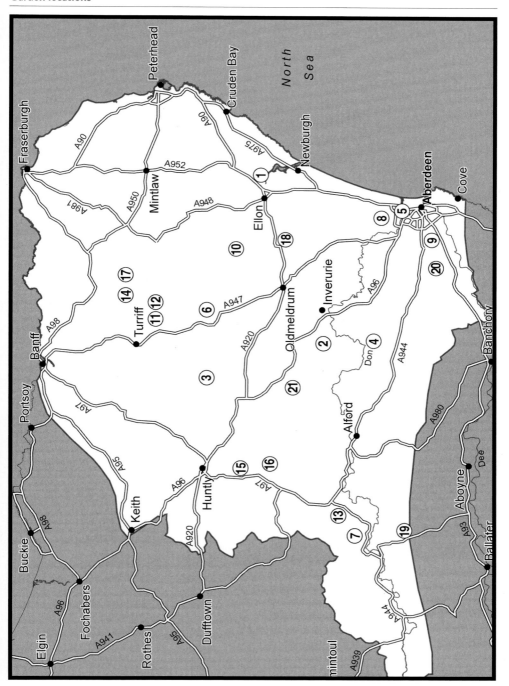

AUCHMACOY
Ellon AB41 8RB
Mr and Mrs Charles Buchan

Auchmacoy House's attractive policies feature spectacular displays of thousands of daffodils.

Directions: A90 from Aberdeen. Turn right to Auchmacoy/Collieston.

Disabled Access:
Partial

Opening Times:
Sunday 12 April
1:15pm - 4:00pm

Admission:
£4.00, children free

Charities:
Royal National Mission to Deep Sea Fishermen receives 40%, the net remaining to SG Beneficiaries

---

BIRKEN COTTAGE
Burnhervie, Inverurie AB51 5JR
Clare and Ian Alexander T: 01467 623013
E: i.alexander@abdn.ac.uk

This steeply sloping garden of just under one acre is packed with plants. It rises from a wet streamside gully and woodland, past sunny terraces and a small parterre, to dry flowery banks.

Directions: Burnhervie is about three miles west of Inverurie. Leave Inverurie by the B9170 (Blackhall Road) or B993 (St James' Place).

Disabled Access:
None

Opening Times:
Sunday 7 June
2:00pm - 5:00pm
Also by arrangement
1 May - 31 August

Admission:
£4.00

Charities:
Friends of Anchor receives 40%, the net remaining to SG Beneficiaries

---

BRUCKHILLS CROFT
Rothienorman, Inverurie AB51 8YB
Paul and Helen Rushton T: 01651 821596
E: helenrushton1@aol.com

A slate built croft-house surrounded by an informal country cottage garden with numerous flower borders, an orchard and a productive fruit and vegetable patch with polytunnel. Flowers range from the tiny Primula scotica to the giant Himalayan Lily, and include 280 named snowdrops. Below the main garden is a wildflower meadow and pond which attracts a great deal of wildlife. You can relax on the decking overlooking the fledgling River Ythan or try out the labyrinth.

Other Details: Snowdrop openings are by appointment only, due to the unpredictability of the weather at that time of year, and because of limited parking. Please let the owner know if you would like teas provided.

Directions: At Rothienorman take the B9001 north, just after Badenscoth Nursing Home turn left, after one mile you will be directed where to park depending if it is the winter or summer opening.

Disabled Access:
Partial

Opening Times:
Sunday 5 July
12:00pm - 5:00pm
By arrangement
1 February - 15 March for the Snowdrop Festival.

Admission:
£4.00, children free

Charities:
Advocacy Service Aberdeen receives 20%, Befriend A Child, Aberdeen receives 20%, the net remaining to SG Beneficiaries

CASTLE FRASER GARDEN
Sauchen, Inverurie AB51 7LD
The National Trust for Scotland T: 0844 493 2164
E: castlefraser@nts.org.uk   www.nts.org.uk

Castle Fraser's designed landscape and parkland is the work of Thomas White dating from 1794. Castle Fraser, one of the most spectacular of the Castles of Mar, has a traditional walled garden of trees, shrubs and herbaceous plantings, a medicinal and culinary border and organically grown fruit and vegetables. You can stroll through the woodland garden with its azaleas and rhododendrons or take the young at heart to the Woodland Secrets adventure playground and trails.

Other Details: A sale of herbaceous plants lifted straight from the garden and a raffle to win the Castle Fraser Gardeners for a day's work in your garden.

Directions: Near Kemnay, off A944.

Disabled Access:
Partial

Opening Times:
Saturday 2 May
11:00am - 4:00pm
Sunday 3 May
11:00am - 4:00pm

Admission:
All donations welcome

Charities:
Donation to SG Beneficiaries

CRUICKSHANK BOTANIC GARDENS
23 St Machar Drive, Aberdeen AB24 3UU
Cruickshank Botanic Garden Trust, Aberdeen University
www.abdn.ac.uk/botanic-garden/

An evening tour with the Curator, Mark Paterson and Head Gardener, Richard Walker. The garden comprises a sunken garden with alpine lawn, a rock garden built in the 1960s complete with waterfalls and pond system, a long unbroken herbaceous border, a formal rose garden with drystone walling, and an arboretum. It has a large collection of flowering bulbs and rhododendrons, and many unusual shrubs and trees including two mature Camperdown Elms. It is sometimes known as The Secret Garden of Old Aberdeen.

Directions: Come down St Machar Drive over the mini roundabout, just before the first set of traffic lights turn left into the Cruickshank Garden car park. The pedestrian Garden entrance is off The Chanonry.

Disabled Access:
Partial

Opening Times:
Wednesday 2 September
6:15pm - 8:30pm

Admission:
£5.00 per person, includes tea/coffee and biscuits

Charities:
Cruickshank Botanic Gardens Trust receives 40%, the net remaining to SG Beneficiaries

FYVIE CASTLE
Fyvie, Turriff AB53 8JS
The National Trust for Scotland T: 01651 891363 / 891266
E: gthomson@nts.org.uk   www.nts.org.uk

An 18th century walled garden developed as a garden of Scottish fruits and vegetables. There is also the American garden, Rhymer's Haugh woodland garden, a loch and parkland to visit. Expert staff are always on hand to answer any questions. Learn about the collection of Scottish fruits and their cultivation, and exciting projects for the future. From 1 July to 31 October 2015 we will be selling produce from our garden shop (known as the 'Fruit Store').

Other Details: Large fresh produce stall selling a wide selection of organic fruit and vegetables. Proceeds to be donated to Scotland's Gardens.

Directions: Off A947 8 miles SE of Turriff and 25 miles NW of Aberdeen.

Disabled Access:
Full

Opening Times:
1 July - 31 October
9:00am - Dusk

Admission:
Fyvie Castle: £12.50, concession £9.00, family £29.50, one parent £23.00. Garden and grounds: free. N.B. Prices correct at time of going to print.

Charities:
Donation to SG Beneficiaries

7 GLENKINDIE HOUSE
Glenkindie, Alford AB33 8SU
Mr and Mrs JP White

Glenkindie House gardens are laid out around the house in an Arts and Crafts style. The lawns are resplendent with unusual topiary figures: look out for teddy bears, soldiers and Alice in Wonderland characters. There are ancient rubble walls, rose beds planted with R.'Braveheart', herbaceous borders and a large pond.

Directions: On the A97 Alford/Strathdon road, 12 miles west of Alford.

Disabled Access:
Full

Opening Times:
Sunday 19 July
1:00pm - 4:00pm

Admission:
£4.00, concessions £3.00, children free

Charities:
Willow Foundation receives 40%, the net remaining to SG Beneficiaries

8 GRANDHOME
Danestone, Aberdeen AB22 8AR
Mr and Mrs D R Paton T: 01224 722202
E: davidpaton@btconnect.com

18th century walled garden, incorporating rose garden (replanted 2010); policies with daffodils, tulips, rhododendrons, azaleas, mature trees and shrubs.

Directions: From north end of North Anderson Drive, continue on A90 over Persley Bridge, turning left at Tesco roundabout. 1¾ miles on left, through the pillars on a left hand bend.

Disabled Access:
Partial

Opening Times:
By arrangement
1 April - 31 October

Admission:
£4.00, concessions £3.00

Charities:
Children 1st receives 40%, the net remaining to SG Beneficiaries

9 GREENRIDGE
Craigton Road, Cults AB15 9PS
BP Exploration T: 01224 860200 or Fax 01224 860210
E: greenrid@bp.com

Large secluded garden surrounding 1840 Archibald Simpson house. For many years winner of Britain in Bloom 'Best Hidden Garden'. The garden has mature specimen trees and shrubs, a kitchen garden and sloping, walled rose garden and terraces.

Directions: Will be advised when booking.

Disabled Access:
Partial

Opening Times:
By arrangement
1 July - 31 August

Admission:
£3.50

Charities:
Cancer Research Scotland receives 40%, the net remaining to SG Beneficiaries

HADDO HOUSE
Methlick, Ellon AB41 7EQ
The National Trust for Scotland T: 0844 493 2179
E: haddo@nts.org.uk www.nts.org.uk

The Haddo Terrace Garden's geometric flower beds and fountain are being transformed through a lavish restoration. Meet the gardeners and learn about this exciting project. Visitors will also enjoy the secluded glades and knolls. A magnificent avenue of lime trees leads to adjacent Haddo Country Park with its lakes, monuments, walks and wildlife.

Other Details: The guided tours will set off at 2:00pm and 4:00pm. There will be plant sales and other activities.

Directions: Off B999 near Tarves, at Raxton crossroads, 19 miles north of Aberdeen, four miles north of Pitmedden and ten miles NW of Ellon. Cycle: one mile from NCN 1. Bus: Stagecoach Bluebird from Aberdeen bus station 01224 212666, c. four miles walk.

Disabled Access:
Partial

Opening Times:
Wednesday 15 July
11:00am - 5:00pm
Wednesday 26 August
11:00am - 5:00pm

Admission:
Guided tours £4.00

Charities:
Donation to SG Beneficiaries

HATTON CASTLE
Turriff AB53 8ED
Mr and Mrs D James Duff T: 01888 562279
E: jjdgardens@btinternet.com

Hatton Castle has a two acre walled garden featuring mixed borders and shrub roses with yew and box hedges and alleys of pleached hornbeam. Also, a kitchen garden, fan trained fruit trees, a lake and woodland walks.

Directions: On A947, two miles south of Turriff.

Disabled Access:
Full

Opening Times:
By arrangement on request

Admission:
£5.00, children free

Charities:
Juvenile Diabetes Research
Foundation receives 40%,
the net remaining to
SG Beneficiaries

HATTON CASTLE GARDEN WORKSHOP
Turriff AB53 8ED
Mr and Mrs D James Duff T: 01888 562279
E: jjdgardens@btinternet.com

Join garden designer Jayne James Duff on Saturday 7 March for a fascinating afternoon learning some great tips and guidelines about how to breathe new life into garden borders. Jayne will be giving demonstrations in the garden to illustrate her talk.

Other Details: A gardener's working afternoon tea may be in the garden, weather permitting. Tickets will be sold on a first come first served basis as space is limited. To order a ticket email or send a letter to Hatton Castle.

Directions: On A947, two miles south of Turriff.

Disabled Access:
Full

Opening Times:
Saturday 7 March 2:00pm
"Rethink your Garden
Borders"

Admission:
£25.00. Tickets must be
purchased in advance. See
other details for information
on how to order tickets.

Charities:
Juvenile Diabetes Research
Foundation receives 40%,
the net remaining to
SG Beneficiaries

13 KILDRUMMY CASTLE GARDENS

Alford AB33 8RA
Kildrummy Garden Trust T: 01975 571203
www.kildrummy-castle-gardens.co.uk

April shows the gold of the lysichitons in the water garden and the small bulbs naturalised beside the copy of the 14th century Brig o' Balgownie. Rhododendrons and azaleas feature from April (frost permitting). September/October brings colchicums and brilliant colour with acers, fothergillas and viburnums.

Directions: On A97, ten miles from Alford, seventeen miles from Huntly. Car park free inside hotel main entrance. Coaches park up at hotel delivery entrance.

Disabled Access:
Partial

Opening Times:
Sunday 7 June
10:00am - 5:00pm
Sunday 27 September
10:00am - 5:00pm

Admission:
£4.50, concessions £4.00, children free

Charities:
Aberdeen Branch Multiple Sclerosis Society receives 40%, the net remaining to SG Beneficiaries

14 KNOCKMUIR

Auchry, Turriff AB53 5UR
Mr and Mrs Ian Hamilton

Set in half an acre, our garden can be found in a countryside setting surrounded by farmland. When we purchased the property it had a well structured garden with many mature plants. During the last few years it has evolved with the addition of a polytunnel and a vegetable garden producing a large range of crops. We have colourful herbaceous beds, vibrant annual bedding, there are also shrubs, trees, a rockery, a wildlife pond and a wild flower area beside a small burn. These all produce a riot of colour throughout spring and summer.

Directions: Situated near Turriff on the B9170 between the A947 and Cuminestown.

Disabled Access:
Partial

Opening Times:
Saturday 25 July
1:00pm - 5:00pm
Sunday 26 July
1:00pm - 5:00pm

Admission:
£3.00, children free

Charities:
All proceeds to
SG Beneficiaries

15 LAUNDRY COTTAGE

Culdrain, Gartly, Huntly AB54 4PY
Simon and Judith McPhun T: 01466 720768
E: simon.mcphun@btinternet.com

An informal, cottage-style garden of about one and a half acres. Upper garden around the house of mixed borders, vegetables and fruit. Steep grass banks to the south and east are planted with native and non-native flowers, specimen trees and shrubs. Narrow grass paths, not suitable for wheelchairs, lead down to the River Bogie.

Directions: Four miles south of Huntly on A97.

Disabled Access:
Partial

Opening Times:
By arrangement on request

Admission:
£3.00, children free

Charities:
Amnesty International receives 40%, the net remaining to SG Beneficiaries

LEITH HALL GARDEN
Huntly AB54 4NQ
The National Trust for Scotland T: 01464 831148
E: leithhall@nts.org.uk www.nts.org.uk

A series of evening guided tours with the Head Gardener. The west garden was made by Charles and Henrietta Leith-Hay around the beginning of the 20th century. In summer the magnificent zigzag herbaceous and serpentine catmint borders provide a dazzling display. A lot of project work is ongoing in the garden including a rose catenary along with large borders being redeveloped in a Gertrude Jekyll style and a Laburnum archway with spring interest borders.

Other Details: The guided tours with the Head Gardener start at 7:00pm and include refreshments. Booking is essential.

Directions: On B9002 one mile west of Kennethmont.

Disabled Access:
Partial

Opening Times:
Thursday 28 May 7:00pm
Thursday 18 June 7:00pm
Thursday 30 July 7:00pm
Thursday 27 August 7:00pm

Admission:
£5.00 for the guided tour

Charities:
Donation to SG Beneficiaries

MIDDLE CAIRNCAKE
Cuminestown, Turriff AB53 5YS
Mr and Mrs N Orpwood T: 01888 544432

Our garden has evolved from grass circling the house and steading to a series of small garden areas with places to sit and enjoy the surroundings. Our aim has been to create a pleasing environment to delight the senses through different garden themes and planting. It includes cottage gardens, a pond, formal rose garden, heathers and a productive kitchen garden for self-sufficiency. We have many trees and the lower woodland walk completes the garden.

Directions: Middle Cairncake is on the A9170 between New Deer and Cuminestown. It is clearly signposted.

Disabled Access:
Partial

Opening Times:
Saturday 11 July
1:00pm - 5:00pm
Sunday 12 July
1:00pm - 5:00pm

Admission:
£3.50, children free

Charities:
Parkinson's UK receives
40%, the net remaining to
SG Beneficiaries

PITMEDDEN GARDEN
Ellon AB41 7PD
The National Trust for Scotland T: 01651 842 352
E: sburgess@nts.org.uk www.nts.org.uk

Join Property Manager/Head Gardener Susan Burgess on one of a series of mini guided walks conducted throughout the afternoon in the tranquil setting of Pitmedden's historic walled garden. Enjoy the sights and scents of the newly stocked rose border and fine herbaceous borders, and marvel at the immaculate boxwood parterres brimming with summer annuals. Hear about the planning and preparation which goes into creating and presenting this highly acclaimed formal garden.

Other Details: Self-catering accommodation available. Tearoom and gift shop.

Directions: On A920, one mile west of Pitmedden village and fourteen miles north of Aberdeen.

Disabled Access:
Partial

Opening Times:
Sunday 9 August
1:30pm onwards
Tours: 1:30pm, 2:30pm
and 3.30pm

Admission:
Usual admission charges
apply. Donations for guided
walk.

Charities:
Donation to SG Beneficiaries

TILLYPRONIE
Tarland AB34 4XX
The Hon Philip Astor

Late Victorian house for which Queen Victoria laid the foundation stone, with superb views over the Dee Valley. Herbaceous borders, heather beds, water garden and rockery with alpines. Golden Jubilee garden containing trees, shrubs and plants of a golden hue. Fine collection of trees, including recently planted acers and a well-established pinetum with rare specimens. There is also a fruit garden and greenhouses. In June there is a wonderful show of azaleas, rhododendrons and spring heathers.

Directions: Off A97 between Ballater and Strathdon.

Disabled Access:
Partial

Opening Times:
Sunday 7 June
2:00pm - 5:00pm
Sunday 30 August
2:00pm - 5:00pm

Admission:
£5.00, children £2.00

Charities:
All proceeds to
SG Beneficiaries

WESTFIELD LODGE
Contlaw Road, Milltimber, Aberdeen AB13 0EX
Mr and Mrs L. Kinch T: 07435 969628
E: fraserdesigner@aol.com

The gardens at Westfield are unique in that they are completely 'new' gardens, first laid out formally in the 1990s and gradually improved and reworked since that date. The commitment and investment of the Kinch family has allowed this peaceful and beautiful site to be transformed into the horticultural oasis you see today. The current Head Gardener, James Fraser, is responsible for the design and execution of many of the stunning features, such as the Reflection Pond, Boathouse and Tropical House. James have brought a flair and passion which has elevated the garden to a higher level. The team at Westfield work extremely hard year-round to ensure that the gardens and grounds are kept in immaculate condition.

Directions: On A93 at Milltimber turn into Contlaw Road. Continue for one mile; turn right into single track road signposted Westfield. From A944 turn at Mason Lodge on to B979, straight over Carnie Crossroads, turn second left signposted Contlaw, take first left and follow road for one mile. Westfield turning is on the left.

Disabled Access:
Partial

Opening Times:
By arrangement 1 July - 17 July Wednesday to Friday only, for pre-arranged groups

Admission:
£8.00 including refreshments

Charities:
CLAN Aberdeen receives 40%, the net remaining to SG Beneficiaries

WESTHALL CASTLE
Oyne, Inverurie AB52 6RW
Mr Gavin Farquhar and Mrs Pam Burney T: 01224 214301
E: enquiries@ecclesgreig.com

Set in an ancient landscape in the foothills of the impressive foreboding hill of Bennachie. A circular walk through glorious daffodils with outstanding views. Interesting garden in early stages of restoration, with large groupings of rhododendrons and specimen trees. Westhall Castle is a 16th century tower house, incorporating a 13th century building of the bishops of Aberdeen. There were additions in the 17th, 18th and 19th centuries. The castle is semi-derelict, but stabilised from total dereliction. A fascinating house encompassing 600 years of alteration and additions.

Directions: Marked from the A96 at Old Rayne and from Oyne Village.

Disabled Access:
Partial

Opening Times:
Sunday 19 April
1:00pm - 4:00pm

Admission:
£4.00, children free

Charities:
Bennachie Guides receives 40%, the net remaining to SG Beneficiaries

ANGUS & DUNDEE

Scotland's Gardens 2015 Guidebook is sponsored by **INVESTEC WEALTH & INVESTMENT**

District Organiser

Mrs Terrill Dobson	Logie House, Kirriemuir DD8 5PN

Area Organisers

Mrs Helen Brunton	Cuthlie Farm, Arbroath DD11 2NT
Mrs Moira Coleman	Templeton House, Arbroath DD11 4QP
Mrs Katie Dessain	Lawton House, Inverkeilor, by Arbroath DD11 4RU
Mrs Jeanette Ogilvie	House of Pitmuies, Guthrie DD8 2SN
Mrs Rosanne Porter	West Scryne Farm, Carnoustie DD7 6LL
Mrs Sue Smith	Balintore House, Balintore, by Kirriemuir DD8 5JS
Mrs Gladys Stewart	Ugie-Bank, Ramsay Street, Edzell DD9 7TT
Mrs Claire Tinsley	Ethie Mains, Ethie DD11 5SN
Mrs Tracey Williams	Alma Lodge, 51 Duncan Road, Letham DD8 2PN

Treasurer

Mrs Mary Stansfeld	Dunninald, By Montrose DD10 9TD

Gardens open on a specific date

Dunninald, Montrose	Saturday 28 February	12:00pm	- 5:00pm
Dunninald, Montrose	Sunday 1 March	12:00pm	- 5:00pm
Dunninald, Montrose	Saturday 7 March	12:00pm	- 5:00pm
Dunninald, Montrose	Sunday 8 March	12:00pm	- 5:00pm
Brechin Castle, Brechin	Sunday 3 May	2:00pm	- 5:00pm
3 Balfour Cottages, Menmuir	Saturday 9 May	1:00pm	- 5:00pm
Dalfruin, Kirriemuir	Sunday 10 May	2:00pm	- 5:00pm
Dunninald, Montrose	Sunday 17 May	2:00pm	- 5:00pm
Gallery, Montrose	Saturday 23 May	2:00pm	- 5:00pm
Glamis Castle, Glamis	Sunday 31 May	10:00am	- 4:30pm
Letham Village, Letham	Sunday 14 June	12:00pm	- 5:00pm
Edzell Village & Castle, Edzell	Sunday 21 June	1:00pm	- 5:00pm
Kilry Village Gardens, Glen Isla	Saturday 27 June	12:00pm	- 5:00pm
Newtonmill House, By Brechin	Sunday 28 June	2:00pm	- 5:00pm
Montrose and Hillside Gardens	Sunday 5 July	1:00pm	- 6:00pm
Gallery, Montrose	Saturday 11 July	2:00pm	- 5:00pm
Hospitalfield Gardens, Arbroath	Saturday 18 July	2:00pm	- 5:00pm
The Herbalist's Garden at Logie, Kirriemuir	Sunday 26 July	2:00pm	- 5:00pm

ANGUS & DUNDEE

Gardens open regularly

Gagie House, by Dundee	21 February - 25 May	10:00am - 5:00pm
Glamis Castle, Glamis	3 April - 1 November	10:00am - 4:30pm
Hospitalfield Gardens, Arbroath	11 April - 26 Sept (Sats only)	2:00pm - 5:00pm
Pitmuies Gardens, By Forfar	1 February - 15 March and 1 April - 31 October	10:00am - 5:00pm
The Angus and Fife Garden Trail	5 May - 25 June	Times vary
The Herbalist's Garden at Logie, Kirriemuir	1 June - 31 Aug (Tues & Sats)	1:00pm - 5:00pm
Dunninald, Montrose	4 July - 2 Aug (Closed Mons)	12:00pm - 5:00pm

Gardens open by arrangement

Dunninald, Montrose	On request for groups	01674 672031
Gallery, Montrose	1 May - 30 September	01674 840550
Kirkside of Lochty, Menmuir	1 March - 31 October	01356 660431
Kirkton House, Montrose	1 May - 30 September	01674 673604
The Garden Cottage, Dunnichen	31 May - 28 June	01307 818392

Dalfruin

Key to symbols

	New in 2015		Homemade teas		Accommodation
	Teas		Dogs on a lead allowed		Plant stall
	Cream teas		Wheelchair access		Scottish Snowdrop Festival

Garden locations

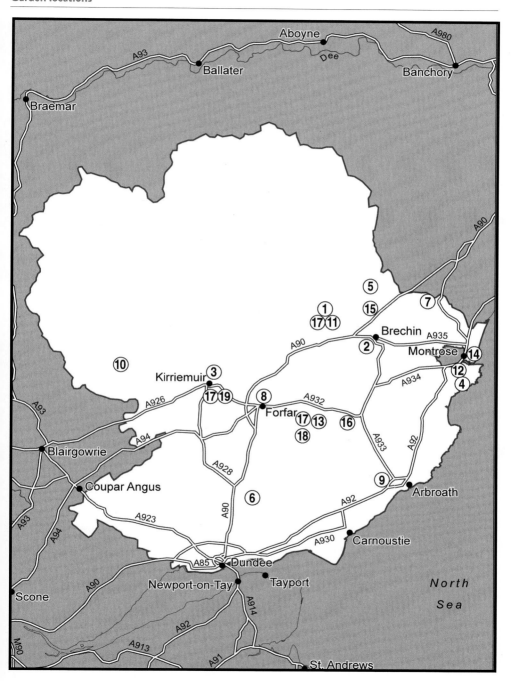

3 BALFOUR COTTAGES
Menmuir DD9 7RN
Dr Alison Goldie and Mark A Hutson T: 01356 660280
E: alisongoldie@btinternet.com www.angusplants.co.uk

Small cottage garden packed with rare and unusual plants. It comprises various 'rooms', containing myriad plants from potted herbs, spring bulbs and alpines in a raised bed, to a 'jungle' with a range of bamboos. Many other interesting plants include primula, hosta, meconopsis, fritillaria, trillium, allium, a large display of bonsai and auriculas.

Other Details: National Plant Collection®: Primula auricula (alpine).

Directions: Leave the A90 two miles south of Brechin and take the road to Menmuir (3½ miles). At the T-junction turn right and it is in the first group of cottages on your left (175 yards).

Disabled Access:
None

Opening Times:
Saturday 9 May
1:00pm - 5:00pm

Admission:
£3.00, accompanied children free

Charities:
Plant Heritage receives 40%, the net remaining to SG Beneficiaries

BRECHIN CASTLE
Brechin DD9 6SG
The Earl and Countess of Dalhousie T: 01356 624566
E: mandyferries@dalhousieestates.co.uk www.dalhousieestates.co.uk

The uniquely curving walls of the garden at Brechin Castle are just the first of many delightful surprises in store. The luxurious blend of ancient and modern plantings is the second. Find charm and splendour in the wide gravelled walks, secluded small paths and corners. May sees the rhododendrons and azaleas hit the peak of their flowering to wonderful effect; and with complementary under-planting and a framework of great and beautiful trees to set the collection in the landscape. This is a lovely garden at any time of year and a knockout in the spring.

Other Details: Dogs on leads please.

Directions: A90 southernmost exit to Brechin, one mile past Brechin Castle Centre, Castle gates on right.

Disabled Access:
Partial

Opening Times:
Sunday 3 May
2:00pm - 5:00pm

Admission:
£5.00, OAPs £4.00, accompanied children free

Charities:
Dalhousie Day Care receives 20%, Unicorn Preservation Society receives 20%, the net remaining to SG Beneficiaries

DALFRUIN
Kirktonhill Road, Kirriemuir DD8 4HU
Mr and Mrs James A Welsh

A well-stocked connoisseur's garden of about ⅓ acre situated at the end of a short cul-de-sac. There are many less common plants like varieties of Trilliums, Meconopsis (blue poppies), tree peonies (descendants of ones collected by George Sherriff and grown at Ascreavie), Dactylorhiza and Codonopsis. There is a scree and collection of ferns. Vigorous climbing roses, Kiftsgate and Paul's Himalayan Musk grow over pergolas. Interconnected ponds encourage wildlife.

Other Details: Good plant stall which may include Trilliums, Meconopsis and tree peonies. Teas served at St Mary's Episcopal Church.

Directions: From centre of Kirriemuir turn left up Roods. Kirktonhill Road is on left near top of hill. Please park on Roods or at St Mary's Episcopal Church. Disabled parking only in Kirktonhill Road.

Disabled Access:
Partial

Opening Times:
Sunday 10 May
2:00pm - 5:00pm

Admission:
£3.00, accompanied children free

Charities:
St Mary's Episcopal Church receives 40%, the net remaining to SG Beneficiaries

DUNNINALD
Montrose DD10 9TD
The Stansfeld Family T: 01674 672031
E: visitorinformation@dunninald.com www.dunninald.com

Dunninald is a family home built in 1824, set in policies developed during the 17th and 18th centuries. It offers many attractive features to the visitor including a beech avenue planted around 1670. Snowdrops in spring and bluebells in May carpet the woods and wild garden. At its best in July, the highlight of Dunninald is the walled garden with traditional mixed borders, vegetables, soft fruits, fruit trees and a greenhouse.

Other Details: Open for the Snowdrop Festival February and March. Sunday 17 May open for bluebells. Teas and plant stall on Sunday 17 May only.

Directions: Two miles south of Montrose, signposted off A92 Arbroath/Montrose road (turning marked Usan).

Disabled Access:
Partial

Opening Times:
Sat/Sun 28 Feb & 1 Mar and
Sat/Sun 7 & 8 March
12:00pm - 5:00pm
Sunday 17 May
2:00pm - 5:00pm
4 July - 2 August 12:00pm -
5:00pm (closed Mondays)
Also open by arrangement
for groups

Admission:
£4.00, accomp. children free

Charities:
Donation to SG Beneficiaries

EDZELL VILLAGE & CASTLE
Edzell DD9 7TT
The Gardeners of Edzell & Historic Scotland

Walk round several fabulous and different gardens in Edzell village including those of Edzell Castle.

Directions: On B966.

Disabled Access:
Partial

Opening Times:
Sunday 21 June
1:00pm - 5:00pm

Admission:
£4.00, accompanied children
free

Charities:
Stracathro Cancer Care Fund
UK receives 40%, the net
remaining to SG Beneficiaries

GAGIE HOUSE
Duntrune, by Dundee DD4 0PR
France and Clare Smoor T: 01382 380207
E: smoor@gagie.com www.gagie.com

A one mile springtime woodland walk in a delightful secluded dell along the Sweet Burn and its artesian ponds. Also a semi-wild pond garden in the policies of early 17th century Gagie House. Naturalised and more recent plantations of snowdrops followed by daffodils, bluebells, hellebores, erythroniums, primroses and candelabra primulas. Snowdrops are at their best from late February to mid-March.

Other Details: Rustic do-it-yourself tea facilities in farm building.

Directions: From A90 about two miles north of Dundee take turning to east signposted Murroes. Continue for two miles, wood on left, sharp right bend ahead; turn left along far side of wood, signpost Gagie; follow this road through stone gateposts at end (marked Private Road). Car park immediately to right.

Disabled Access:
None

Opening Times:
21 February - 25 May
10:00am - 5:00pm
for the Snowdrop Festival 21
February - 15 March and for
snowdrops till 22 March

Admission:
£4.00, accompanied children
free

Charities:
Donation to SG Beneficiaries

GALLERY
Montrose DD10 9LA
Mr John Simson T: 01674 840550
E: galleryhf@googlemail.com

The redesign and replanting of this historic garden have preserved and extended its traditional framework of holly, privet and box. A grassed central alley, embellished with circles, links themed gardens, including a fine collection of old roses, yellow and blue floral borders of the entrance garden and the fountain and pond in the formal white garden. A walk through the woodland garden, home to rare breed sheep, with its extensive border of mixed heathers, leads to the river North Esk. From there rough paths lead both ways along the bank.

Directions: From A90 south of Northwater Bridge take exit to Hillside and next left to Gallery and Marykirk. From A937 west of rail underpass follow signs to Gallery and Northwater Bridge.

Disabled Access:
Partial

Opening Times:
Saturday 23 May
2:00pm - 5:00pm
Saturday 11 July
2:00pm - 5:00pm
Also by arrangement
1 May - 30 September

Admission:
£4.00, accompanied children free

Charities:
Practical Action receives 40%, the net remaining to SG Beneficiaries

---

GLAMIS CASTLE
Glamis DD8 1RJ
The Earl and Countess of Strathmore & Kinghorne
E: enquiries@glamis-castle.co.uk   www.glamis-castle.co.uk

Glamis Castle has been the family home of the Earls of Strathmore & Kinghorne since 1372. The mile long drive, through the park landscaped in the style of Capability Brown, offers breathtaking views of the Castle. The Walled Garden, formally the kitchen garden, has recently undergone major development with new flower beds being planted and the installation of a spectacular fountain. The beautiful Italian Garden, to the east of the castle, laid out by Countess Cecilia, c.1910 and bounded by yew hedges, offers quiet seclusion with wonderful views of the castle. Walking eastward you enter The Pinetum. This area, planted by the 13th Earl in 1864, has a variety of exotic trees, many of which are conifers native to North America. Following difficulties in managing the Pinetum for some years, the 18th Earl commenced a programme of replanting and restoration.

Directions: Glamis one mile A94.

Disabled Access:
Full

Opening Times:
Sunday 31 May
10:00am - 4:30pm
3 April - 1 November
10:00am - 4:30pm

Admission:
Grounds & gardens incl. Pinetum: **£7**, OAPs £6, accomp. children free, **Castle, grounds & gardens: £11**, OAPs £10, children £8

Charities:
Proceeds to SG Beneficiaries on 31 May. Other days donation

HOSPITALFIELD GARDENS
Hospitalfield House, Westway, Arbroath DD11 2NH
Hospitalfield Arts
E: info@hospitalfield.org.uk   www.hospitalfield.org.uk

Hospitalfield Arts is the historic home of Patrick Allan-Fraser (1813–1890), left in trust to support contemporary artists and education in the arts. The delightful walled garden and surrounding landscapes are a work in progress and feature an enchanting Victoria fernery, currently under restoration. Gardens are maintained by an enthusiastic team of talented volunteers.

Other Details: Activities for children, teas and cake are available each Saturday. The house is accessible during open weekends in June and Sept. See website.

Directions: Car- A92 from Dundee. After the 'Welcome to Arbroath' sign turn left at the roundabout onto the Westway. Hospitalfield is 200 yds up the hill. From Aberdeen take the A90, then A92. Or take the slightly longer route but very scenic along the east coast take the A93 and the B974.
Train- Hospitalfield House is a 20 minute walk from Arbroath Station.
Bus- There are regular buses from Dundee and Aberdeen.

Disabled Access:
Partial

Opening Times:
Saturday 18 July
2:00pm - 5:00pm
11 April - 26 September
2:00pm - 5:00pm Sats only

Admission:
£3.50, accompanied children free

Charities:
The Patrick Allan Fraser of Hospitalfield Trust receives 40%, the net remaining to SG Beneficiaries

KILRY VILLAGE GARDENS
Kilry, Glen Isla PH11 8HS
Kilry Garden Club

A varied selection of delightful and interesting gardens in a beautiful glen setting, featuring meconopsis, primulas and rhododendrons and vegetables. One garden also has some unusual trees and shrubs.

Other Details: Soup, teas and plants with tickets, toilet and maps from the central point of Kilry Village Hall (PH11 8HS).

Directions: From Perth take A94 to Coupar Angus and just before Meigle take B964 and follow signs to Glen Isla and then to Kilry with sign on left.
From Dundee take B954 to Coupar Angus and follow as from Perth.

Disabled Access:
Partial

Opening Times:
Saturday 27 June
12:00pm - 5:00pm

Admission:
£4.00, accompanied children free

Charities:
Scotland's Charity Air Ambulance receives 40%, the net remaining to SG Beneficiaries

---

 KIRKSIDE OF LOCHTY
Menmuir, by Brechin DD9 6RY
James & Irene Mackie T: 01356 660431

The garden contains a large collection of plants, several rare and unusual, also many different varieties of ferns. It is approached by a strip of woodland and expands into various compartments in an overall area of two acres, part of which is cultivated as a flowering meadow.

Other Details: Groups welcome. No dogs allowed. Also part of The Angus & Fife Garden Trail, see page 101.

Directions: Leave the A90 two miles south of Brechin and take the road to Menmuir. After a further two miles, pass a wood on the left and a long beech hedge in front of the house.

Disabled Access:
None

Opening Times:
By arrangement
1 March - 31 October
Also part of the Angus & Fife Garden Trail, see page 101.

Admission:
£4.00, accompanied children free

Charities:
All proceeds to SG Beneficiaries

 KIRKTON HOUSE
Kirkton of Craig, Montrose DD10 9TB
Campbell Watterson T: 01674 673604
E: campbellkirktonhouse@btinternet.com

A regency manse set in over two acres of garden. The walled garden includes herbaceous borders, a sunken garden, lime allee, statuary and formal rose garden. The wild garden includes a pond and water lilies. There is also a large flock of Jacobs sheep in the adjoining glebe.

Other Details: Also part of The Angus & Fife Garden Trail, see page 101.

Directions: One mile south of Montrose, off A92 at the Balgove turn-off.

Disabled Access:
Partial

Opening Times:
By arrangement
1 May - 30 September
Also part of the Angus & Fife Garden Trail, see page 101.

Admission:
£3.50, accompanied children free

Charities:
All proceeds to SG Beneficiaries

LETHAM VILLAGE
Letham DD8 2PD
Letham Gardening Club

Be inspired by the diverse range of gardens from cottage style to shady gardens to small gardens and those newly developed by keen gardeners. Several new gardens added this year.

Other Details: Tickets and maps available in village Scout Hut, Auldbar Road DD8 2PD. Teas and plant stall at Letham Church Hall in the village centre.

Directions: From north take A90 exiting for Forfar town centre, then take A932 towards Arbroath and pickup signs to Letham. From south via Dundee take B978 Kellas/Wellbank Road, pick up signs.

Disabled Access:
Partial

Opening Times:
Sunday 14 June
12:00pm - 5:00pm

Admission:
£4.00, accompanied children free

Charities:
1st Letham and Dunnichen Scout Group receives 40%, the net remaining to SG Beneficiaries

MONTROSE AND HILLSIDE GARDENS
Montrose DD10 8AL & Hillside DD10 9HZ
Montrose & Hillside Gardeners

An eclectic mix of fascinating and sometimes hidden gardens in Montrose and neighbouring Hillside. These range from older established gardens to newly designed and planted. Tickets and maps available at The Croft, Main Street, Hillside DD10 9HZ and Straton House, 10 Castle Place, Montrose DD10 8AL

Other Details: No dogs allowed. Refreshments available at certain gardens. Plants for sale in certain gardens. Parking around the town.

Directions: Approach Montrose on A92 or A90 via Brechin.

Disabled Access:
Partial

Opening Times:
Sunday 5 July
1:00pm - 6:00pm

Admission:
£4.00, accompanied children free

Charities:
Friends of Stracathro Hospital receives 40%, the net remaining to SG Beneficiaries

NEWTONMILL HOUSE
By Brechin DD9 7PZ
Mr and Mrs S Rickman
E: rrickman@srickman.co.uk   www.newtonmillhouse.co.uk

Newtonmill House looks over and into the semi-formal walled garden. The entrance to the garden is through a wrought iron gate that reflects the mill wheel from which Newtonmill derives its name. The central pathway is flagged by herbaceous borders, sheltered by a fine prunus pissardi hedge. The garden is divided into four squares of vegetables, fruit, spring garden and croquet lawn with summer house. The construction of an autumn garden in this area will involve work in progress. Through the rose arch at the south end of the garden are peony and shrub rose beds, a small pond area and doocot. Adjacent to the house is a rose-garlanded terrace and raised beds.

Directions: From A90, exit B966 Brechin/Edzell towards Edzell.

Disabled Access:
Full

Opening Times:
Sunday 28 June
2:00pm - 5:00pm

Admission:
£4.00, accompanied children free

Charities:
RNLI (Montrose Ladies Branch) receives 40%, the net remaining to SG Beneficiaries

PITMUIES GARDENS
House of Pitmuies, Guthrie, By Forfar DD8 2SN
Jeanette & Ruaraidh Ogilvie

Two semi-formal walled gardens adjoin the 18th century house and shelter long borders of herbaceous perennials, superb delphiniums, old fashioned roses and pavings with violas and dianthus. Spacious lawns, river and lochside walks beneath fine trees. A wide variety of shrubs with good autumn colour. Interesting picturesque turreted doocot and 'Gothick' washhouse. Myriad spring bulbs include carpets of crocus following the massed snowdrops.

Other Details: Dogs on leads, please.

Directions: A932. Friockheim 1½ miles.

Disabled Access:
Partial

Opening Times:
1 February - 15 March and
1 April - 31 October
10:00am - 5:00pm

Admission:
£5.00, accompanied children free

Charities:
Donation to SG Beneficiaries

 THE ANGUS AND FIFE GARDEN TRAIL
Various locations in Fife and Angus
The Gardeners of Fife and Angus
www.angusfifetrail.org.uk

ANGUS
1. The Herbalist's Garden at Logie
Tuesdays 26 May - 23 June   1:00pm - 6:00pm   Teas and plant sale.
2. Kirkside of Lochty
Tuesdays 19 May - 23 June   11:00am - 5:00pm
3. Kirkton House
Tuesdays 5 May - 23 June   11:00am - 5:00pm
4. The Garden Cottage
Tuesdays 5 May - 23 June   1:00pm - 7:00pm
SOUTH/CENTRAL FIFE
5. Glassmount House
Wednesdays 6 May - 24 June   12 noon - 4:00pm
6. Kirklands
Wednesdays 20 May - 10 June   11:00am - 4:00pm   Plant sale.
7. Logie House
Wednesdays 6 May - 24 June   11:00am - 3:00pm   Plant sale.
8. Millfield House
Wednesdays 20 May - 24 June   4:00pm - 8:00pm
EAST/CENTRAL FIFE
9. Kenlygreen House
Thursdays 14 May - 4 June   10:00am - 4:00pm
10. Kenly Green Farm
Thursdays 21 May - 25 June   3:00pm - 7:00pm
11. St Mary's Farm
Thursdays 21 May - 25 June   4:00pm - 8:00pm
12. Wormistoune
Thursdays 7 May - 25 June   11:00am - 4:00pm   Plant sale.

Disabled Access:
Partial

Opening Times:
5 May - 25 June 10:00am -
8:00pm times and dates vary
for all gardens.

Admission:
£25.00 (plus £1.00 p&p)
for entrance to all gardens.
Early Bird Price £20.00 (plus
£1.00 p&p) available until
28 February 2015.
Accompanied children free.

Charities:
Macmillan Cancer Support
receives 20%, Worldwide
Cancer Research receives
20%, the net remaining to
SG Beneficiaries

Other Details: A limited number of tickets are available and may be purchased by debit/credit card at www.angusfifetrail.org.uk or by cheque payable to Scotland's Gardens from S. Lorimore, Willowhill, Forgan, Newport on Tay, Fife DD6 8RA. See also pages 34 - 36 of this book.

Directions: Further information and directions for all gardens will be supplied with tickets and are available at www.angusfifetrail.org.uk.

THE GARDEN COTTAGE
Dunnichen DD8 2NX
Nora Craig T: 01307 818392

This half acre garden was an orchard at one time but by 1974 only two apple trees. remained together with four mature deciduous trees and a cottage. Mown grass covered rather less than a third of the area and this has been developed to surround large beds in which a few small trees, several shrubs, hardy herbaceous plants, grasses, ferns and bulbs intermingle. Narrow paths criss-cross the plantings inviting the curious to discover many unusual plants.

Other Details: Also part of The Angus & Fife Garden Trail, see page 101.

Directions: Four miles south-east of Forfar on the 9128. Bear left ¼ mile after Kingsmuir to Letham. On entering Dunnichen turn left immediately, the cottage is on the right and is signposted.

Disabled Access:
None

Opening Times:
By arrangement
31 May - 28 June
Also part of The Angus & Fife
Garden Trail, see page 101.

Admission:
£3.50, accompanied children
free

Charities:
Scotland's Charity Air
Ambulance receives 40%,
the net remaining to
SG Beneficiaries

THE HERBALIST'S GARDEN AT LOGIE
Logie House, Kirriemuir DD8 5PN
Terrill and Gavin Dobson
E: terrill@angusherbalists.co.uk www.angusherbalists.co.uk

This garden, featured on *The Beechgrove Garden*, is set amid an 18th century walled garden and large Victorian greenhouse within Logie's organic farm. Featuring more than 150 herbs, the physic garden is divided into eight rectangles including medicinal herbs for different body systems. All the herbs are labelled with a brief description of actions to help novices learn more about this ancient art. The garden also features a herbaceous border and productive fruit and vegetable garden.

Other Details: Groups welcome by arrangement. Homemade teas on 26 July. DIY teas on other days. No dogs please. Also part of The Angus & Fife Garden Trail, see page 101.

Directions: From the A926 leaving Kirriemuir, fork left at Beechwood Place onto the single track road, or if approaching Kirriemuir take sharp left after "Welcome to Kirriemuir sign". Take the first left and follow signs to The Walled Garden.

Disabled Access:
Partial

Opening Times:
Sunday 26 July
2:00pm - 5:00pm
1 June - 31 August
1:00pm - 5:00pm
Tuesdays & Saturdays
See also page 101.

Admission:
£4.00, accompanied children
free

Charities:
Charity to be advised
will receive 40%, the net
remaining to SG Beneficiaries

Montrose and Hillside Gardens: Union Street

ARGYLL

Scotland's Gardens 2015 Guidebook is sponsored by **INVESTEC WEALTH & INVESTMENT**

District Organiser

Minette Struthers	Ardmaddy Castle, Balvicar, By Oban PA34 4QY

Area Organisers

Mrs Grace Bergius	Craignish House, Ardfern, By Lochgilphead PA31 8QN
Mrs G Cadzow	Duachy, Kilninver, Oban PA34 4RH
Mrs Mary Lindsay	Dal an Eas, Kilmore, Oban PA34 4XU
Mrs Patricia McArthur	Bute Cottage, Newton, Strachlachan PA27 8DB

Treasurer

Minette Struthers	Ardmaddy Castle, Balvicar, By Oban PA34 4QY

Gardens open on a specific date

Torosay Castle Gardens, Isle of Mull	Tuesday 3 March	10:00am -	5:00pm
Benmore Botanic Garden, Dunoon	Sunday 26 April	10:00am -	6:00pm
Knock Cottage, Lochgair	Saturday 9 May	1:00pm -	5:30pm
Arduaine Garden, Oban	Sunday 10 May	9:30am -	5:00pm
Knock Cottage, Lochgair	Sunday 10 May	1:00pm -	5:30pm
Drim na Vullin, Lochgilphead	Saturday 16 May	2:00pm -	5:00pm
Knock Cottage, Lochgair	Saturday 16 May	1:00pm -	5:30pm
Drim na Vullin, Lochgilphead	Sunday 17 May	2:00pm -	5:00pm
Knock Cottage, Lochgair	Sunday 17 May	1:00pm -	5:30pm
Colintraive Gardens, Colintraive	Saturday 23 May	1:00pm -	5:00pm
Strachur House Flower & Woodland Gardens, Strachur	Saturday 23 May	1:00pm -	5:00pm
Colintraive Gardens, Colintraive	Sunday 24 May	1:00pm -	5:00pm
Crarae Garden, Inveraray	Sunday 24 May	10:00am -	5:00pm
Fasnacloich, Appin	Sunday 24 May	10:00am -	5:00pm
Strachur House Flower & Woodland Gardens, Strachur	Sunday 24 May	1:00pm -	5:00pm
Dal an Eas and Dalnaneun, Oban	Saturday 20 June	1:30pm -	6:00pm
Dal an Eas and Dalnaneun, Oban	Sunday 21 June	1:30pm -	6:00pm
Ascog Hall, Isle of Bute	Saturday 27 June	10:00am -	5:00pm
Seafield, Dunoon	Saturday 27 June	2:00pm -	5:00pm
Seafield, Dunoon	Sunday 28 June	2:00pm -	5:00pm
Torosay Castle Gardens, Isle of Mull	Sunday 5 July	10:00am -	5:00pm
Ardchattan Priory, North Connel	Sunday 26 July	12:00pm -	4:00pm
Crarae Garden, Inveraray	Sunday 26 July	10:00am -	5:00pm

ARGYLL

Eas Mhor, Oban	Saturday 1 August	2:00pm - 5:30pm
Eas Mhor, Oban	Sunday 2 August	2:00pm - 5:30pm
Barguillean House, Taynuilt	Saturday 8 August	10:00am - 4:00pm
Barguillean's "Angus Garden", Taynuilt	Saturday 8 August	10:00am - 4:00pm
Lorn Organic Growers, Taynuilt	Saturday 8 August	10:00am - 4:00pm
Duart Castle, Isle of Mull	Sunday 23 August	11:00am - 4:00pm
Torosay Castle Gardens, Isle of Mull	Sunday 6 September	10:00am - 5:00pm

Gardens open regularly

Achnacloich, Oban	28 Mar - 31 Oct (Sats)	10:00am - 4:00pm
An Cala, Isle of Seil	1 April - 31 October	10:00am - 6:00pm
Ardchattan Priory, North Connel	1 April - 31 October	9:30am - 5:30pm
Ardkinglas Woodland Garden, Cairndow	1 January - 31 December	Dawn - Dusk
Ardmaddy Castle, by Oban	1 January - 31 December	9:00am - Dusk
Barguillean's "Angus Garden", Taynuilt	1 January - 31 December	9:00am - Dusk
Benmore Botanic Garden, Dunoon	1 March - 31 October	10:00am - 6:00pm ex. Mar & Oct 5.00pm
Crinan Hotel Garden, Crinan	1 May - 31 August	Dawn - Dusk
Druimneil House, Port Appin	2 April - 31 October	Dawn - Dusk
Fairwinds, Dunoon	1 April - 31 October	9:00am - 6:00pm
Inveraray Castle Gardens, Inveraray	1 April - 31 October	10:00am - 5:45pm
Kinlochlaich House Gardens, Appin	1 Jan - 28 Feb (Sats) 1 March - 11 October 12 Oct - 31 Dec (Sats)	9:30am - 4:00pm 9:30am - 5:00pm 9:30am - 4:00pm
Oakbank, Ardrishaig	1 May - 31 August	10:30am - 6:00pm

Gardens open by arrangement

Kinlochlaich House Gardens, Appin	1 Jan - 28 Feb and 12 Oct - 31 Dec (Sun - Fri)	07881 525754
Knock Cottage, Lochgair	15 April - 15 June	01546 886331

Key to symbols

 New in 2015

 Teas

 Cream teas

 Homemade teas

 Dogs on a lead allowed

 Wheelchair access

 Accommodation

 Plant stall

 Scottish Snowdrop Festival

Garden locations

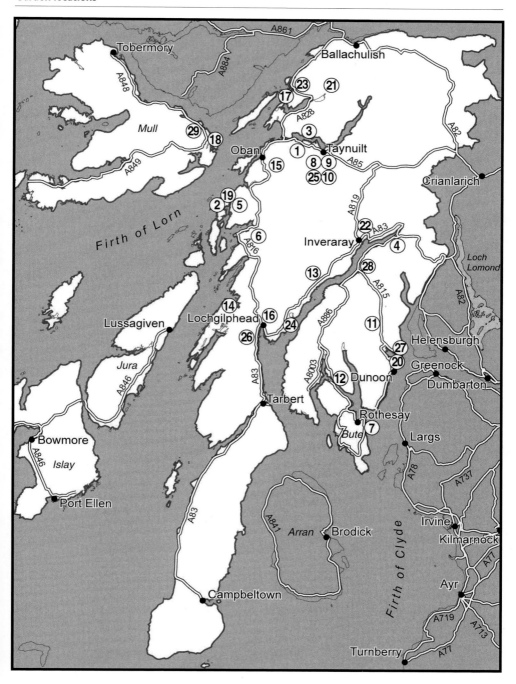

ACHNACLOICH
Connel, Oban PA37 1PR
Mr T E Nelson T: 01631 710796
E: charlie_milne@msn.com

Scottish baronial house by John Starforth of Glasgow. Succession of wonderful bulbs, flowering shrubs, rhododendrons, azaleas, magnolias and primulas. Woodland garden with ponds above Loch Etive. Good autumn colours.

Directions: On A85 three miles east of Connel. Parking on the right at the bottom of the drive.

Disabled Access:
Partial

Opening Times:
28 March - 31 October
10:00am - 4:00pm
Saturdays

Admission:
£4.00

Charities:
All proceeds to
SG Beneficiaries

AN CALA
Ellenabeich, Isle of Seil PA34 4RF
Mrs Thomas Downie T: 01852 300237
www.gardens-of-argyll.co.uk

A wonderful example of a 1930s designed garden, An Cala sits snugly in its horseshoe shelter of surrounding cliffs. A spectacular and very pretty garden with streams, waterfall, ponds, many herbaceous plants as well as azaleas, rhododendrons and cherry trees in spring. Archive material of Mawson's design found recently.

Directions: Proceed south from Oban on Campbeltown road for eight miles, turn right at Easdale sign, a further eight miles on B844; garden is between school and village.

Disabled Access:
Partial

Opening Times:
1 April - 31 October
10:00am - 6:00pm

Admission:
£4.00

Charities:
Cancer Research UK receives
40%, the net remaining to
SG Beneficiaries

ARDCHATTAN PRIORY
North Connel PA37 1RQ
Mrs Sarah Troughton T: 01796 481355
E: sh.troughton@virgin.net www.ardchattan.co.uk

Beautifully situated on the north side of Loch Etive. In front of the house there is a rockery, extensive herbaceous and rose borders, with excellent views over the loch. West of the house there are shrub borders and a wild garden, numerous roses and many different varieties of sorbus providing excellent autumn colour. The Priory, founded in 1230, is now a private house. The ruins of the chapel and graveyard are in the care of Historic Scotland and open with the garden.

Other Details: Garden Fete on Sunday 26 July, on this day only there will be soup lunches, homemade teas, stalls including plant stall and other attractions.

Directions: Oban ten miles. From north, turn left off A828 at Barcaldine onto B845 for six miles. From East/Oban on A85, cross Connel Bridge and turn first right, proceed east on Bonawe Road.

Disabled Access:
Partial

Opening Times:
Sunday 26 July
12:00pm - 4:00pm
for Garden Fete
1 April - 31 October
9:30am - 5:30pm

Admission:
£4.00, children up to 16 free

Charities:
Donation to SG Beneficiaries

ARDKINGLAS WOODLAND GARDEN
Cairndow PA26 8BG
Ardkinglas Estate T: 01499 600261
www.ardkinglas.com

In a peaceful setting overlooking Loch Fyne the garden contains one of the finest collections of rhododendrons and conifers in Britain. This includes the mightiest conifer in Europe, a silver fir, as well as many other champion trees. A gazebo with unique "Scriptorium" based around a collection of literary quotes. The garden has a woodland lochan, ancient mill ruins and many woodland walks. It is a Visit Scotland 3* garden.

Other Details: Champion Trees: includes the mightiest conifer in Europe and the tallest tree in Scotland. There are five Champion Trees in total. Nearby, the Tree Shop garden centre café offers fabulous food.

Directions: Entrance through Cairndow village off A83 Loch Lomond/Inveraray road.

Disabled Access:
Partial

Opening Times:
1 January - 31 December
Dawn - Dusk

Admission:
£4.50, children under 16 free

Charities:
Donation to SG Beneficiaries

ARDMADDY CASTLE
by Oban PA34 4QY
Mr and Mrs Charles Struthers T: 01852 300353
E: ardmaddycastle@btinternet.com www.gardens-of-argyll.co.uk

Ardmaddy Castle gardens, in a most spectacular setting, are shielded to the north by mature woodlands, carpeted with bluebells and daffodils and protected from the Atlantic winds by the elevated Castle. The Walled Garden is full of magnificent rhododendrons, some huge, an increasing collection of rare and unusual shrubs and plants, the 'Clock Garden' with its cutting flowers, fruit and vegetables grown with labour saving formality, all within dwarf box hedging. Beyond, a woodland walk, with its amazing hydrangea climbing to 60 feet, leads to the water gardens - in early summer a riot of candelabra primulas, irises, rodgersias and other damp loving plants and grasses. Lovely autumn colour. A garden for all seasons.

Other Details: Plant stalls and veg and summer fruit stalls in season. Toilet suitable for disabled. Six self catering cottages, details at www.ardmaddy.com.

Directions: Take A816 south of Oban for eight miles. Turn right B844 to Seil Island/Easdale. Four miles on, take Ardmaddy road for a further two miles.

Disabled Access:
Full

Opening Times:
1 January - 31 December
9:00am - Dusk

Admission:
£4.00, children free

Charities:
Donation to SG Beneficiaries

ARDUAINE GARDEN
Oban PA34 4XQ
The National Trust for Scotland T: 0844 493 2216
E: mwilkins@nts.org.uk www.nts.org.uk

Outstanding 20 acre coastal garden created over 100 years ago on the south facing slope of a promontory separating Asknish Bay from Loch Melfort. This remarkable hidden paradise, protected by tall shelterbelts and influenced favourably by the North Atlantic Drift, grows a wide variety of plants from all over the globe. Internationally known for the rhododendron species collection, the garden also features magnolias, camellias, azaleas and other wonderful trees and shrubs, many being tender and rarely seen. A broad selection of perennials, bulbs, ferns and water plants ensure year-long interest.

Other Details: Free walks with garden staff at 11:00am and 2:30pm. Teas available in local hotel.

Directions: Off A816 Oban-Lochgilphead, sharing an entrance with the Loch Melfort Hotel.

Disabled Access:
Partial

Opening Times:
Sunday 10 May
9:30am - 5:00pm

Admission:
£6.50 including NTS
members.
N.B. These prices are correct
at the time of going to print.

Charities:
Donation to SG Beneficiaries

ASCOG HALL
Ascog, Isle of Bute PA20 9EU
Karin Burke T: 01700 503 461
E: karin@ascogfernery.com   www.ascogfernery.com

The most outstanding feature of this three acre garden is the Victorian Fernery, a beautiful sunken structure fed by natural spring waters and housing many fern species, including a 1,000 year old King Fern - the only survivor from the original collection. Rare and exotic plants and trees also await the observant visitor wandering the paths of the original Victorian garden "rooms" while the stables and coach house ruin will feed the imagination of long lost times. Teas are available.

Other Details: Guest toilet facilities. Parking for restricted mobility citizens at top of drive (close to house). Personal assistance available for disabled access to Fernery. Guide dogs permitted. Tea and biscuits £2.00.

Directions: Either thirty minutes on ferry from Wemyss Bay, three miles south of Rothesay on A844, or five minutes on ferry from Colintraive and eleven miles south on A844. Close to the picturesque Ascog Bay.

Disabled Access:
Partial

Opening Times:
Saturday 27 June
10:00am - 5:00pm

Admission:
£4.00, including seal viewing.
There are no concessions.

Charities:
Scoliosis Association UK
receives 40%, the net
remaining to SG Beneficiaries

BARGUILLEAN HOUSE WITH BARGUILLEAN'S "ANGUS GARDEN" AND LORN ORGANIC GROWERS
Barguillean, Glen Lonan, Taynuilt PA35 1HY
Mr Robin Marshall T: 01866 822 333
E: info@barguillean.co.uk

One acre of well kept traditional garden with herbaceous perennials, espaliered fruit trees and a fruit and vegetable garden. The attractive farmhouse was designed by Robert Lorimer.

Other Details: Teas in the Farmhouse Barn. Toilet available. Plants and produce for sale.

Directions: Turn off at Taynuilt Hotel on A85 and follow garden signs for two miles up the Glen Lonan Road. Parking at nursery and Angus woodland garden. All three gardens within walking distance. Disabled parking at all sites.

Disabled Access:
Partial

Opening Times:
Saturday 8 August
10:00am - 4:00pm

Admission:
£5.00 for all three gardens

Charities:
Alzheimer Scotland (Oban)
receives 40%, the net
remaining to SG Beneficiaries

BARGUILLEAN'S "ANGUS GARDEN"
Taynuilt PA35 1HY
The Josephine Marshall Trust T: 01866 822333
E: info@barguillean.co.uk   www.barguillean.co.uk

Nine acre woodland garden around an eleven acre loch set in the Glen Lonan hills. Spring flowering shrubs and bulbs, extensive collection of rhododendron hybrids, deciduous azaleas, conifers and unusual trees. The garden contains a large collection of North American rhododendron hybrids from famous contemporary plant breeders. Some paths can be steep. Three marked walks from 30 minutes to 1½ hours.

Other Details: Self catering accommodation in comfortable wing of the main house. Coach Tours by appointment.

Directions: Three miles south off A85 Glasgow/Oban road at Taynuilt; road marked Glen Lonan; three miles up single track road; turn right at sign.

Disabled Access:
None

Opening Times:
1 January - 31 December
9:00am - Dusk

Admission:
£3.00, children under 14 free

Charities:
Donation to SG Beneficiaries

BARGUILLEAN'S "ANGUS GARDEN" WITH BARGUILLEAN HOUSE AND LORN ORGANIC GROWERS
Taynuilt PA35 1HY
The Josephine Marshall Trust T: 01866 822333
E: info@barguillean.co.uk www.barguillean.co.uk

Nine acre woodland garden around an 11 acre loch set in the Glen Lonan hills. Extensive collection of rhododendron hybrids, deciduous azaleas, conifers and unusual trees. The garden contains a large collection of North American rhododendron hybrids from famous contemporary plant breeders. Some steep paths. Three marked walks from 30 minutes to 1½ hours. Self catering accommodation in comfortable wing of the main house.

Other Details: Toilets are available at Barguillean Farmhouse barn. Teas available in Barguillean Farmhouse barn. Plants and produce for sale. Sturdy shoes advised for the Nursery and Angus woodland garden.

Directions: Three miles south off A85 Glasgow/Oban road at Taynuilt; road marked Glen Lonan; three miles up single track road; turn right at sign. Parking at Nursery site and Angus woodland garden. All three gardens within walking distance. Disabled parking at all sites.

Disabled Access:
None

Opening Times:
Saturday 8 August
10:00am - 4:00pm

Admission:
£5.00 for all three gardens

Charities:
Alzheimer Scotland (Oban) receives 40%, the net remaining to SG Beneficiaries

BENMORE BOTANIC GARDEN
Benmore, Dunoon PA23 8QU
A Regional Garden of the Royal Botanic Garden Edinburgh T: 01369 706261
E: benmore@rbge.org.uk www.rbge.org.uk

Benmore with its magnificent mountainside setting is a joy to behold. Its 49 hectares/120 acres boast a world famous collection of flowering trees and shrubs including over 300 species of rhododendron. Visitors are welcomed by an impressive avenue of giant redwoods, arguably one of the finest entrances to any botanic garden in the world. Established in 1863, these majestic giants now stand over 50 metres high.

Other Details: Seven miles of trails throughout the Garden lead to beautiful spots such as the restored Victorian Fernery and dramatic viewpoint at 450 feet (140 metres) overlooking the surrounding mountains and Holy Loch.

Directions: Seven miles north of Dunoon or 22 miles south from Glen Kinglass below Rest and Be Thankful pass. On A815.

Disabled Access:
Partial

Opening Times:
Sunday 26 April
10:00am - 6:00pm
1 March - 31 October
10:00am - 6:00pm (closes 5:00pm March and October)

Admission:
£6.00, conc. £5.00, under 16 free (includes donation to garden, for prices without donation check rbge.org.uk)

Charities:
Donation to SG Beneficiaries

COLINTRAIVE GARDENS
Colintraive PA22 3AR
The Gardeners of Colintraive

Three delightful and varied spring gardens in this very beautiful corner of Argyll - two within easy reach of each other on the old B866 shore road looking out over Loch Riddon and the Kyles of Bute. The gardens are Altavoil (Mrs Caroline Sinclair) and Caol Ruadh (Mr and Mrs C Scotland). Caol Ruadh has the additional attraction of a unique outdoor sculpture park featuring works from a variety of Scottish artists. The third, Milton Wood (Greg and Grace Morris), is straight through the village past the hotel and heritage centre to the first house on the right hand side.

Other Details: Tickets and maps can be obtained at all gardens. Teas and homebaking are available at Caol Ruadh.

Directions: A815 and A866 (Dunoon 20 miles via B836, Strachur 22 miles).

Disabled Access:
None

Opening Times:
Saturday 23 May
1:00pm - 5:00pm
Sunday 24 May
1:00pm - 5:00pm

Admission:
£4.00 (includes all three gardens), children free

Charities:
All proceeds to
SG Beneficiaries

13 CRARAE GARDEN
Inveraray PA32 8YA
The National Trust for Scotland T: 0844 4932210
E: CraraeGarden@nts.org.uk www.nts.org.uk

A spectacular 50 acre garden in a dramatic setting. Crarae has a wonderful collection of woody plants centred on the Crarae Burn, which is spanned by several bridges and tumbles through a rocky gorge in a series of cascades. A wide variety of shrubs and trees chosen for spring flowering and autumn colour grow in the shelter of towering conifers. The lush naturalistic planting and rushing water give the garden the feel of a valley in the Himalayas.

Other Details: National Plant Collection®: Nothofagus (Southern Beech). This collection is the most northerly of its type in the UK. Champion Trees: Abies, Acer and Chamaecyparis. Price includes behind the scenes guided walk by our expert staff. Sturdy footwear is recommended. Plant sales throughout the season.

Directions: On A83 ten miles south of Inveraray.

Disabled Access:
Partial

Opening Times:
Sunday 24 May
10:00am - 5:00pm
Sunday 26 July
10:00am - 5:00pm

Admission:
£6.50 (including NTS members). N.B. Prices correct at time of going to print

Charities:
Donation to SG Beneficiaries

---

14 CRINAN HOTEL GARDEN
Crinan PA31 8SR
Mr and Mrs N Ryan T: 01546 830261
E: nryan@crinanhotel.com www.crinanhotel.com

Small rock garden with azaleas and rhododendrons created into a steep hillside over a century ago with steps leading to a sheltered, secluded garden with sloping lawns, herbaceous beds and spectacular views of the canal and Crinan Loch.

Other Details: Raffle of painting by Frances Macdonald (Ryan). Tickets at coffee shop, art gallery and hotel. Homemade teas available in the coffee shop.

Directions: Lochgilphead A83, then A816 to Oban, then A841 Cairnbaan to Crinan.

Disabled Access:
None

Opening Times:
1 May - 31 August
Dawn - Dusk

Admission:
By donation

Charities:
Feedback Madagascar receives 40%, the net remaining to SG Beneficiaries

---

15 DAL AN EAS AND DALNANEUN
Kilmore, Oban PA34 4XU
Mary Lindsay and Ms C Boswell T: 01631 770 246 or 209
E: dalaneas@live.com

Recently created informal country garden with the aim of increasing the biodiversity of native plants and insects while adding interest and colour with introduced trees, shrubs and naturalised perennials. It has a structured garden with pond, a burn with pool, wildflower meadow with five different species of native orchid and a vegetable plot. Grass paths lead to waterfalls, views and ancient archaeological sites. The enclosed garden of Dalnaneun is accessed through the Dal an Eas garden and comprises lawns, flowerbeds, vegetables and herbs. A burn runs through the garden and local stone has been imaginatively used for various features.

Other Details: Sturdy footwear is recommended.

Directions: Take A816 to Kilmore turn (3½ miles south of Oban) on the road marked Barran and Musdale. Keep left at junction. Follow the Connel road. Dal an Eas is on the left over the cattle grid.

Disabled Access:
Partial

Opening Times:
Saturday 20 June
1:30pm - 6:00pm
Sunday 21 June
1:30pm - 6:00pm

Admission:
£4.00

Charities:
Mary's Meals receives 40%, the net remaining to SG Beneficiaries

DRIM NA VULLIN
Blarbuie Road, Lochgilphead PA31 8LE
Mr and Mrs Robin Campbell Byatt T: 01546 602615
E: byatt.drim@virgin.net

Drim na Vullin, originally a mill, and its woodland garden have been owned by the same family since 1829. Most of the development of the garden was landscaped and planted in the 1950s by Sybil Campbell OBE, Britain's first female professional magistrate, assisted by Percy Cane, the garden designer. It lies along a cleft formed by the Cuilarstitch Burn with a spectacular waterfall at the top. Mature species and hybrid rhododendrons, magnolias, azaleas and other shrubs are under a canopy of mostly native trees. The present owners' planting brings the developed area to about five acres.

Other Details: Waterproof shoes are recommended. Uphill walking.

Directions: A83 to Lochgilphead. At the top of main street in front of parish church, turn right up Manse Brae. The garden is ⅓ mile up the hill on the left. Beyond the houses on the left a high fence leads to Drim na Vullin's entrance. Please park on the road.

Disabled Access:
None

Opening Times:
Saturday 16 May
2:00pm - 5:00pm
Sunday 17 May
2:00pm - 5:00pm

Admission:
£4.00

Charities:
Wildfowl and Wetlands Trust,
Caerlaverock receives 20%,
Christchurch Episcopal
Church, Lochgilphead
receives 20%, the net
remaining to SG Beneficiaries

DRUIMNEIL HOUSE
Port Appin PA38 4DQ
Mrs J Glaisher (Gardener: Mr Andrew Ritchie) T: 01631 730228
E: druimneilhouse@btinternet.com

Large garden overlooking Loch Linnhe with many fine varieties of mature trees and rhododendrons and other woodland shrubs. Nearer the house, an impressive bank of deciduous azaleas is underplanted with a block of camassia and a range of other bulbs. A small Victorian walled garden is currently being restored.

Other Details: Teas normally available. Lunch by prior arrangement.

Directions: Turn in for Appin off A828 (Connel/Fort William Road). Two miles, sharp left at Airds Hotel, second house on right.

Disabled Access:
None

Opening Times:
2 April - 31 October
Dawn - Dusk

Admission:
By donation

Charities:
All proceeds to
SG Beneficiaries

DUART CASTLE
Isle of Mull PA64 6AP
Sir Lachlan & Lady Maclean
E: office@duartcastle.com

At Duart Castle we have recently created a new walled garden. Yew hedges have been planted within to afford greater protection from the wind. Raised beds and a polytunnel grow organic vegetables for use in the tearoom. There is a small ornamental rose garden with shrubs and herbaceous plants. There are climbing roses, honeysuckle, clematis and fruit trees being trained up the walls.

Other Details: Tearoom open for light lunches, teas and coffee and delicious home baking.

Directions: Two and a half miles on the A849 on the road to Iona from Craignure. Then follow the sign to Duart Castle.

Disabled Access:
Full

Opening Times:
Sunday 23 August
11:00am - 4:00pm

Admission:
By donation

Charities:
RNLI receives 40%, the net
remaining to SG Beneficiaries

19 **EAS MHOR**
Cnoc-a-challtuinn, Clachan Seil, Oban PA34 4TR
Mrs Kimbra Lesley Barrett T: 01852 300 469
E: flora99@maxvall.plus.com

All the usual joys of a west coast garden plus some delightful surprises! A small contemporary garden on a sloping site - the emphasis being on scent and exotic plant material. Unusual and rare blue Borinda bamboos (only recently discovered in China) and bananas. The garden is at its best in mid to late summer when shrub roses and sweet peas fill the air with scent. The delightful sunny deck overlooks stylish white walled ponds with cascading water blades.

Other Details: Cream tea in small artist studio off the deck - enjoy to the sound of gentle music.

Directions: At Kilninver turn off A816 from Oban onto B844 signed Easdale and Atlantic Bridge. Over Bridge onto Seil Island, pass Tigh an Truish pub and turn right after ¼ mile (at bus shelter) up Cnoc-a-Challtuin road. Public car park on left at bottom, please park there, walk up road. Eas Mhor with high deer gates is on right after second speed bump. Please do not block shared driveway.

Disabled Access:
None

Opening Times:
Saturday 1 August
2:00pm - 5:30pm
Sunday 2 August
2:00pm - 5:30pm

Admission:
Minimum £5.00 donation to include cream tea.

Charities:
MS Therapy Centre (Oban) receives 40%, the net remaining to SG Beneficiaries

20 **FAIRWINDS**
14 George Street, Hunter's Quay, Dunoon PA23 8JU
Mrs Carol Stewart T: 01369 702666
E: carol.argyll@talk21.com

This mature garden was created in the fifties from a small orchard. The present owner is constantly trying to add colour and interest for all seasons. Spring brings a flourish of spring flowers, rhododendrons and azaleas. Trees of all kinds display their constantly changing shades throughout the year and in autumn the acers and copper beech are at their very best. Around every corner there is yet another plant of interest, a goldfish pond or a swing.

Other Details: Please call if coming from a distance. Teas available on request.

Directions: On A815. Enter Dunoon on loch side road, right up Cammesreinach Brae just before the Royal Marine Hotel opp W Ferries terminal. The Brae becomes George Street, Fairwinds is on left.

Disabled Access:
Partial

Opening Times:
1 April - 31 October
9:00am - 6:00pm

Admission:
£2.50, children free

Charities:
The Cowal Hospice receives 40%, the net remaining to SG Beneficiaries

21 **FASNACLOICH**
Appin PA38 4BJ
Mr David Stewart

South-facing 15 acre woodland garden sloping down to Loch Baile Mhic Cailein in Glen Creran. Partly laid out in the mid-19th century with extensive structural water features added in the early 20th century. The garden mainly consists of hybrid and species rhododendrons, azaleas and magnolias with, over the last 25 years, a more recent addition of trees from Eastern Europe, Central Asia and the Northern United States (including a small Pinetum).

Other Details: Tea available in the Stables from 12:00pm to 5:00pm.

Directions: Fasnacloich is located off the roundabout on the north side of Creagan Bridge. Creagan Bridge is on the A828 between Benderloch and Appin. Follow the road signed Invercreran. At the end of Loch Creran take the single road straight ahead for approximately 1½ miles. The house gates are on the right side. GPS: 'Fasnacloich'.

Disabled Access:
Partial

Opening Times:
Sunday 24 May
10:00am - 5:00pm

Admission:
£5.00

Charities:
Mary's Meals receives 40%, the net remaining to SG Beneficiaries

INVERARAY CASTLE GARDENS
Inveraray PA32 8XF
The Duke and Duchess of Argyll T: 01499 302203
E: enquiries@inveraray-castle.com www.inveraray-castle.com

Rhododendrons and azaleas abound and flower from April to June. Very fine specimens of Cedrus deodars, Sequoiadendron wellingtonia, Cryptomeria japonica, Taxus baccata and others thrive in the damp climate. The 'Flag-Borders' on each side of the main drive with paths in the shape of Scotland's national flag, the St Andrew's Cross, are outstanding in spring with Prunus "Ukon" and "Subhirtella" and are underplanted with rhododendrons, Eucryphias, shrubs and herbaceous plants giving interest all year. Bluebell Festival during flowering period in May.

Other Details: Guide dogs allowed. Wheelchair users please note there are gravel paths.

Directions: Inveraray is 60 miles north of Glasgow on the banks of Loch Fyne on the A83 with a regular bus service from Glasgow and 15 miles from Dalmally on A819.

Disabled Access:
Partial

Opening Times:
1 April - 31 October
10:00am - 5:45pm

Admission:
£4.00

Charities:
Donation to SG Beneficiaries

KINLOCHLAICH HOUSE GARDENS
Appin PA38 4BD
Mr and Mrs D E Hutchison and Miss F M M Hutchison T: 07881 525754
E: gardens@kinlochlaich-house.co.uk www.kinlochlaichgardencentre.co.uk

Walled garden incorporating the Western Highlands' largest Nursery Garden Centre. Amazing variety of plants growing and for sale. Extensive grounds with woodland walk, spring garden, vegetable gardens and formal garden. Extensive display of rhododendrons, azaleas, trees, shrubs and herbaceous, including many unusuals - Embothrium, Davidia, Magnolia, Eucryphia and Tropaeolum.

Other Details: The gardens surround the historic Kinlochlaich House, which has cottages and apartments to let for self catering.

Directions: On the A828 in Appin between Oban, 18 miles to the south, and Fort William, 27 miles to the north. The entrance is next to the Police Station.

Disabled Access:
Partial

Opening Times:
1 Jan - 28 Feb (Sats) 9:30am
- 4:00pm or by arrangement
1 Mar - 11 Oct every day
9:30am - 5:00pm
12 Oct - 31 Dec (Sats)
9:30am - 4:00pm or by
arrangement

Admission:
£2.50

Charities:
Appin Village Hall receives
40%, the net remaining to
SG Beneficiaries

KNOCK COTTAGE
Lochgair PA31 8RZ
Mr David Sillar T: 01546 886331
E: birkhill@btinternet.com

A five acre woodland and water garden centred round a small loch and lily pond. Started in the 1960s most of the garden dates from the creation of the lochan in 1989 and the plantings of the 1990s. Development entered a new phase following the severe storms of 2011/12. Some 80 different rhododendron species and hybrids along with camellias, azaleas and other shrubs are scattered throughout the garden in a natural setting, sheltered by conifers, eucalyptus, birch, rowan, alder and beech.

Other Details: Please note there is very limited parking. Waterproof footwear is recommended.

Directions: On the A83, ½ mile south of Lochgair Hotel on the west side of the road between two sharp bends.

Disabled Access:
Partial

Opening Times:
Saturday & Sunday 9-10 May
1:00pm - 5:30pm
Saturday & Sunday 16-17 May
1:00pm - 5:30pm
Also by arrangement
15 April - 15 June

Admission:
£4.00

Charities:
Marie Curie Cancer Care
receives 40%, the net
remaining to SG Beneficiaries

25 LORN ORGANIC GROWERS WITH BARGUILLEAN'S "ANGUS GARDEN" AND BARGUILLEAN HOUSE

Barguillean Nursery, Glen Lonan, Taynuilt PA35 1HY
Lorn Organic Growers
E: lornorganicgrowers@gmail.com

Disabled Access:
Partial

Opening Times:
Saturday 8 August
10:00am - 4:00pm

Admission:
£5.00 for all three gardens

Charities:
Alzheimer Scotland (Oban)
receives 40%, the net
remaining to SG Beneficiaries

Adjacent to Barguilleans' Angus Garden is Barguillean Nursery Polytunnel project - an ex-commercial nursery first converted in 2013 to an organic community growing project. Expanding in 2015 to six very large tunnels, divided into allotments of varying sizes. All the participants are growing organic fruit and vegetables either to sell or for personal use. The rest of the site is still under development with plans for an orchard and a netted fruit tunnel.

Other Details: The nursery site has limited facilities (compost toilet only) but toilets are available at Barguillean Farmhouse barn. Teas available in Barguillean Farmhouse barn. Plants and produce for sale. Sturdy shoes advised for the Nursery and Angus woodland garden.

Directions: Turn off at Taynuilt Hotel on A85 and follow garden signs for two miles up the Glen Lonan road. Parking at Nursery site and Angus Garden. All three gardens are within walking distance. Disabled parking at all sites.

26 OAKBANK

Ardrishaig PA30 8EP
Helga Macfarlane T: 01546 603405
E: helgamacfarlane@onetel.com www.gardenatoakbank.blogspot.com

Disabled Access:
None

Opening Times:
1 May - 31 August
10:30am - 6:00pm

Admission:
£3.00, children free

Charities:
Diabetes UK receives
40%, the net remaining to
SG Beneficiaries

This unusual and delightful garden will appeal to adults and children alike, with lots for each to explore including a secret garden. It extends to some three acres of hillside with a series of paths winding amongst a varied collection of trees, shrubs, bulbs and wild flowers. There are several small ponds, many wonderful wood carvings, an active visiting population of red squirrels and a viewpoint overlooking Loch Fyne to the Isle of Arran.

Directions: On the Tarbert side of Ardrishaig: entry to the garden is at the junction of Tarbert Road (A83) and Oakfield Road and immediately opposite the more southerly Scottish Water lay-by.

27 SEAFIELD

173 Marine Parade, Hunter's Quay, Dunoon PA23 8HJ
Scoular Anderson T: 01369 703107
E: scoulara9@gmail.com

Disabled Access:
None

Opening Times:
Saturday 27 June
2:00pm - 5:00pm
Sunday 28 June
2:00pm - 5:00pm

Admission:
£4.00, children free

Charities:
Children's Hospice
Association Scotland receives
40%, the net remaining to
SG Beneficiaries

Stunning seaside garden on a hillside with clever plantings, divided into separate smaller gardens including gravel garden, damp pond garden, heather garden, shady garden, herbaceous beds, shrubs, ferns and grasses.

Directions: Situated on the Cowal Peninsula at Hunter's Quay on A815 a few hundred yards south (Dunoon side) of the Western Ferries terminal. Parking on promenade.

STRACHUR HOUSE FLOWER & WOODLAND GARDENS
Strachur PA27 8BX
Sir Charles and Lady Maclean

Directly behind Strachur House the flower garden is sheltered by magnificent beeches, limes, ancient yews and Japanese maples. There are herbaceous borders, a burnside rhododendron and azalea walk and a rockery. Old fashioned and species roses, lilies, tulips, spring bulbs and Himalayan poppies make a varied display in this informal haven of beauty and tranquillity. The garden gives onto Strachur Park, laid out by General Campbell in 1782, which offers spectacular walks through natural woodland with two hundred-year-old trees, rare shrubs and a lochan rich in native wildlife.

Other Details: Teas available at the Post Office.

Directions: Turn off A815 at Strachur House Farm entrance. Park in farm square.

Disabled Access:
Full

Opening Times:
Saturday 23 May
1:00pm - 5:00pm
Sunday 24 May
1:00pm - 5:00pm

Admission:
£4.00

Charities:
CLASP receives 40%, the net remaining to SG Beneficiaries

TOROSAY CASTLE GARDENS
Craignure, Isle of Mull PA65 6AY
Duncan Travers T: 077389 33033
E: d.j.travers@btinternet.com

Magnificent Italianate terraced gardens surrounded by woodland and water gardens in dramatic setting with borrowed landscapes. Many fine specimens of rare and tender plants, walled gardens with vegetables and spectacular herbaceous borders, extensive collection of hydrangeas. Japanese garden under continuous development.

Other Details: The property changed ownership in 2012 and the castle is no longer open to the public.

Directions: One and a half miles from Craignure ferry terminal on A849, in the direction of Fionnphort.

Disabled Access:
Full

Opening Times:
Tuesday 3 March
10:00am - 5:00pm
Sunday 5 July
10:00am - 5:00pm
Sunday 6 September
10:00am - 5:00pm

Admission:
£3.00

Charities:
Lochdon School receives 40%, the net remaining to SG Beneficiaries

GLORIOUS GARDENS RHODODENDRON FESTIVAL 2015

The Glorious Gardens of Argyll and Bute are hosting the first Festival of Rhododendrons in April and May 2015.

Details of special events in all gardens and others close by are on **www.gardens-of-argyll.co.uk** and are available from any of the twenty gardens, most of which participate in Scotland's Gardens programme.

AYRSHIRE

District Organiser

Mrs R F Cuninghame	Caprington Castle, Kilmarnock KA2 9AA

Area Organisers

Mrs Glen Collins	Grougarbank House, Kilmarnock KA3 6HP
Mrs Michael Findlay	Carnell, By Hurlford, Kilmarnock KA1 5JS
Mrs John MacKay	Pierhill, Annbank KA6 5AW
Ms Ann Robinson	45 Bay Street, Fairlie KA29 0AL
Mrs A J Sandiford	Harrowhill Cottage, Kilmarnock KA3 6HX
Ms Heidi Stone	3 Noddsdale Cottage, Brisbane Glen Road, Largs KA30 8SL

Treasurer

Mrs T H P Donald	3 Brookfield Grove, Fenwick, Ayrshire KA3 6GD

Gardens open on a specific date

Caprington Castle, Kilmarnock	Sunday 15 February	1:00pm	-	4:00pm
Grougarbank House, Kilmarnock	Wednesday 29 April	11:00am	-	4:00pm
Kilmaurs Village Gardens, Kilmaurs	Sunday 10 May	1:30pm	-	5:00pm
Borlandhills, Dunlop	Sunday 24 May	2:00pm	-	5:00pm
1 Burnside Cottages, Coylton	Sunday 31 May	2:00pm	-	5:00pm
Holmes Farm, By Irvine	Saturday 6 June	1:00pm	-	5:00pm
Holmes Farm, By Irvine	Sunday 7 June	1:00pm	-	5:00pm
Gardens of West Kilbride and Seamill	Saturday 20 June	1:00pm	-	5:00pm
10 Grange Terrace and The Allotments of Annanhill Park, Kilmarnock	Sunday 28 June	2:00pm	-	5:00pm
Gardening Leave, SAC Auchincruive	Sunday 5 July	12:00pm	-	4:00pm
Carnell, By Hurlford	Sunday 12 July	2:00pm	-	5:00pm
Culzean, Maybole	Tuesday 14 July	9:30am	-	5:00pm
Cairnhall House, Mauchline Road, Ochiltree	Sunday 19 July	2:00pm	-	5:00pm
Girvan Community Garden, Girvan	Saturday 8 August	11:00am	-	4:00pm
Girvan Community Garden, Girvan	Sunday 9 August	11:00am	-	4:00pm

AYRSHIRE

Gardens open by arrangement

Burnside, Littlemill Road, Drongan	1 April - 30 September	01292 592445
High Fulwood, Stewarton	20 April - 6 September	01560 484705

Kilmaurs Gardens

Key to symbols

 New in 2015

 Teas

Cream teas

 Homemade teas

 Dogs on a lead allowed

 Wheelchair access

 Accommodation

 Plant stall

 Scottish Snowdrop Festival

Garden locations

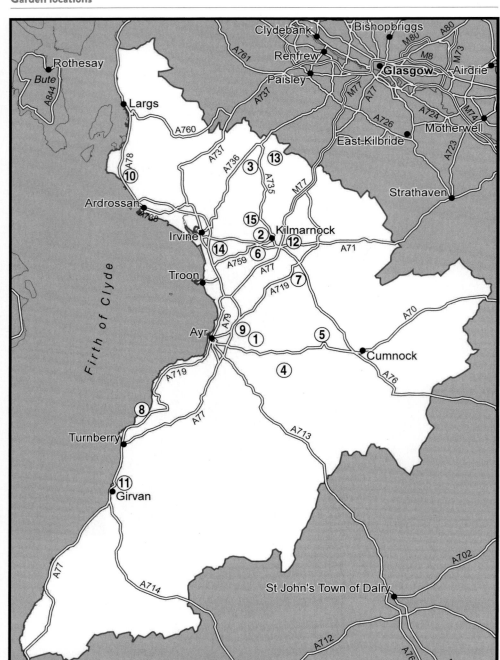

1 BURNSIDE COTTAGES
Sundrum, Coylton KA6 5JX
Carol Freireich

A sheltered cottage garden of 1.3 acres. Organically cultivated, native trees and many wild flowers encourage wide varieties of bird and insect life. A stream runs through a small wood, an old orchard with newer plantings of varieties chosen to tolerate northern conditions, a pond, vegetable garden and ornamental plantings all with plenty of places to sit.

Directions: A70 three miles from Ayr signed left at Sundrum Castle Caravan Park. Go up the road for ¾ mile and then left down dirt track where there is limited parking. Or continue to Coylton first left at Barclauch Drive round to the right, park at Woodhead Road and walk for five minutes to the garden. Look for signposts. Bus 45 or 48 Ayr/Cumnock to foot of Barclaugh Drive and follow signed route.

Disabled Access:
Partial

Opening Times:
Sunday 31 May
2:00pm - 5:00pm

Admission:
£4.00 children under 12 free

Charities:
Break the Silence receives 40%, the net remaining to SG Beneficiaries

2 10 GRANGE TERRACE AND THE ALLOTMENTS OF ANNANHILL PARK
Kilmarnock KA1 2JR
Mr and Mrs Iain Linton and The Annanhill Park Association

10 Grange Terrace: This south facing established garden has a diversity of well chosen shrubs and herbaceous borders. A vegetable plot with soft fruit and top fruit trees complete a delightful triangular garden. Featured in Amateur Gardening June 2014.

Annanhill Park Association Allotments: The former walled garden to Annanhill Park has been most successfully turned into allotments by the Annanhill Park Association in 2013. Well stocked plots are complemented by colourful huts.

Directions: From A77 Bellfield interchange take the A71 dual carriageway marked Irvine to first roundabout and take Crosshouse exit. Over a small roundabout directing to Hospital (B7081) and at T junction turn right to Kilmarnock Town Centre past Annanhill Park/Golf Course through set of lights to turn right off Irvine Road before filling station into Grange Terrace. Route will be yellow signposted to both gardens.

Disabled Access:
Partial

Opening Times:
Sunday 28 June
2:00pm - 5:00pm

Admission:
£4.00, children free

Charities:
Annanhill Allotments Society receives 40%, the net remaining to SG Beneficiaries

3 BORLANDHILLS
Brecknabraes Road, Dunlop KA3 4BU
Professor and Mrs Michael Moss

This is an exciting hilltop garden created over the last seventeen years, with hidden corners and magnificent views of Arran. It contains a surprising variety of habitats ranging from a bog garden with gunnera, primula and great clumps of irises to dry sheltered corners with fine displays of bulbs in late spring, magnolias, rhododendrons, azaleas and meconopsis. Roses and clematis scramble through hedges and over the buildings. There are herbaceous borders with many unusual Himalayan plants grown mostly from seed. In the heart of the garden there are large vegetable plots and two polytunnels with a great variety of produce that provide for the family throughout the year.

Directions: From the centre of Dunlop down Main Street, turn left at the Church into Brecknabraes Road (right is the B706 to Beith) and the garden is 0.7 miles on the left.

Disabled Access:
Partial

Opening Times:
Sunday 24 May
2:00pm - 5:00pm

Admission:
£4.00

Charities:
Send A Cow receives 40%, the net remaining to SG Beneficiaries

BURNSIDE
Littlemill Road, Drongan KA6 7EN
Sue Simpson and George Watt T: 01292 592445

This young 6½ acre garden was started in 2006. There is a wide range of plants from trees to alpines. Features include a 200 yard woodland border along the burn, herbaceous beds, screes, an ericaceous garden, an alpine house, a collection of alpine troughs and a pond. The informal arboretum is underplanted with groups of daffodils, camassia and fritillaries.

Other Details: Dogs on a lead please. Teas and light refreshments by prior arrangement.

Directions: From A77 Ayr bypass take A70 Cumnock for 5¼ miles at Coalhall, turn onto B730 Drongan(south) for 2½ miles. Burnside entrance immediately adjacent before black/white parapeted bridge. Survey grid reference: NS455162

Disabled Access:
Partial

Opening Times:
By arrangement
1 April - 30 September

Admission:
£4.00, children free

Charities:
Macmillan Nurses receives 40%, the net remaining to SG Beneficiaries

CAIRNHALL HOUSE
Mauchline Road, Ochiltree KA18 2QA
Ian and Sarah Hay

A nature lover's garden created over ten years from a thistle-filled field into an organic two acre garden of extensive flower beds (two new this year), large pond and vegetable plot, a clematis meadow and laburnum tunnel all designed to appeal to insects, butterflies, birds and people.

Other Details: Drop off onto gravel at the house for infirm and wheelchairs.

Directions: From A70 into Ochiltree where road forks to Cumnock, turn left up Mauchline Road. Drive is 150 yards on the left. Please note parking is limited but the cemetery car park nearby is an option. See drop off information above.

Disabled Access:
Partial

Opening Times:
Sunday 19 July
2:00pm - 5:00pm

Admission:
£4.00, children free

Charities:
MND Scotland receives 20%, Womankind receives 20%, the net remaining to SG Beneficiaries

CAPRINGTON CASTLE
Kilmarnock KA2 9AA
Mrs Robert Cuninghame and Mr William Cuninghame T: 01563 526157
E: caprington@googlemail.com

Open this year for snowdrops and woodland walks. Stout footwear suggested.

Directions: From M77 take the A71 to Irvine and exit at first roundabout to Gatehead, Dundonald, Troon. In Gatehead go over railway line and river bridge and take first left at Old Rome Farmhouse. The twin lodges are about half mile on. Yellow signposted from Ayr-Kilmarnock road after Bogend Toll.

Disabled Access:
Partial

Opening Times:
Sunday 15 February
1:00pm - 4:00pm

Admission:
£4.00, children free

Charities:
Holy Trinity Church Kilmarnock receives 40%, the net remaining to SG Beneficiaries

CARNELL

By Hurlford KA1 5JS

Mr John Findlay, Mr and Mrs Michael Findlay T: 01563 884236
E: carnellestates@aol.com   www.carnellestates.com

The 16th century Peel Tower looks down over a ten acre garden which has featured in the Beechgrove Garden, Country Life, The Good Gardens Guide as well as Suki Urquhart's book The Scottish Gardener. There is a traditional walled garden with a 100 yard long herbaceous border, as well as a rock and water garden, gazebo with Burmese statues, lawns and many other features of interest. Herbaceous, rose and phlox borders are in full bloom during July.

Directions: From A77 (Glasgow/Kilmarnock) take A76 (Mauchline/Dumfries) then right on to the A719 to Ayr for 1½ miles.

Disabled Access:
Partial

Opening Times:
Sunday 12 July
2:00pm - 5:00pm

Admission:
£5.00, children under 12 free

Charities:
Craigie Symington Parish Church of Scotland receives 20%, Motor Neurone Disease Scotland receives 20%, the net remaining to SG Beneficiaries

CULZEAN

Maybole KA19 8LE

The National Trust for Scotland T: 0165 588 4400
E: culzean@nts.org.uk   www.nts.org.uk

A major Scottish attraction and a perfect day out for all the family. Robert Adam's romantic 18th century masterpiece is perched on a cliff high above the Firth of Clyde. The Fountain Garden lies in front of the castle with terraces and herbaceous borders reflecting its Georgian elegance. The extensive country park offers beaches and rockpools, parklands, gardens, woodland walks and adventure playground. It contains fascinating restored buildings contemporary with the castle.

Other Details: Guided walk starts from the walled garden at 2:00pm and includes behind the scenes. There are also holiday cottages on site, a restaurant (with homemade wine from Culzean) and a shop. Castle and estate open - see NTS website for details.

Directions: On A719 twelve miles south of Ayr, four miles west of Maybole. Bus 60 Stagecoach, Ayr/Girvan via Maidens to entrance. One mile walk downhill from stop to Castle/Visitor Centre.

Disabled Access:
Partial

Opening Times:
Tuesday 14 July
9:30am - 5:00pm

Admission:
Normal admission applies, guided walk £3.00 (including NTS members)

Charities:
Donation to SG Beneficiaries

GARDENING LEAVE

c/o Gardens Unit, SAC Auchincruive KA6 5HW

Gardening Leave T: 01292 521444
E: admin@gardeningleave.org

Small, walled terrace garden located within the grounds of Auchincruive Estate in Ayrshire run by a charity which provides sessions of horticultural therapy to veterans of the Armed Forces. The garden houses vegetable beds, poppy collection and a quiet reflective corner. The charity is also in the process of restoring an 84 metre long Victorian greenhouse known as the 'Stovehouse'. Part of the Stovehouse is open for use.

Other Details: Teas and coffees will be served in the Stovehouse.

Directions: From Whitletts roundabout outside Ayr, follow B743 to Mauchline, bypass the signposted entrance to the Auchincruive Estate SAC. Continue for approximately ¾ mile and take next on right.

Disabled Access:
Partial

Opening Times:
Sunday 5 July
12:00pm - 4:00pm

Admission:
£4.00, children under 12 free

Charities:
Gardening Leave receives 40%, the net remaining to SG Beneficiaries

10 GARDENS OF WEST KILBRIDE AND SEAMILL
KA23
The Gardeners of West Kilbride and Seamill

A variety of gardens, well favoured by the usually mild coastal climate, will open on the Saturday only when the visitors will also be able to enjoy the excellent shopping facilities of the "Craft Town".

Other Details: Tickets, maps and refreshments all at the Village Hall.

Directions: Heading from Dalry take B781 for seven miles. Alternatively take the A78 south for eight miles from Largs or the A78 north for seven miles from Kilwinning. Signposted to Village Hall for tickets and maps marked with gardens opening, disabled access shown as applicable.

Disabled Access:
Partial

Opening Times:
Saturday 20 June
1:00pm - 5:00pm

Admission:
£4.00, children under 12 free

Charities:
North Ayrshire Cancer Care receives 40%,
the net remaining to
SG Beneficiaries.

11 GIRVAN COMMUNITY GARDEN
25 Knockcushan Street, Girvan KA26 9AG
The Gardeners of Girvan Community
E: secretary@girvancommunitygarden.com   www.girvancommunitygarden.com

Volunteers saved a space that was originally a kitchen garden. It also formed part of a bowling green and then became a nursery for the local council's plants before it was neglected for 30 years. The garden is surrounded by a ten foot sandstone wall. Inside is a magical mix of wildflowers, fruit trees, shrubs and many other plants. Volunteers look after modest rotational allotments and get a share of the produce. There are many surprises as recycling and upcycling is evident all around the garden. Learning is also a key element of the garden and we are always delighted to work with schools showing them the wonders of growing and cooking. What you will find is a rich environment for both people and wildlife.

Other Details: Please check our website for details of our events and workshops. Fully accessible compost toilet.

Directions: Just off A77 from Ayr to Stranraer travelling through Girvan.

Disabled Access:
Partial

Opening Times:
Saturday 8 August
11:00am - 4:00pm
Sunday 9 August
11:00am - 4:00pm

Admission:
£4.00, children free

Charities:
Girvan Community Garden
receives 40%, the net
remaining to SG Beneficiaries

12 GROUGARBANK HOUSE
Kilmarnock KA3 6HP
Mrs Glen Collins

A small garden created over the past seven years which includes borders, trees and shrubs, raised vegetable and fruit beds. A glorious bluebell walk runs down to the river Irvine through mature and newly planted trees.

Other Details: Teas/coffees light refreshments.

Directions: From A77 take A71 Edinburgh and Hurlford. At Hurlford Roundabout take B7073(Kilmarnock). From Crookedholm centre follow yellow signposts along Grougar Road to T junction then right for one mile to second house on right. Parking limited.

Disabled Access:
None

Opening Times:
Wednesday 29 April
11:00am - 4:00pm

Admission:
£3.50

Charities:
All proceeds to
SG Beneficiaries

HIGH FULWOOD
Stewarton KA3 5J2
Mr and Mrs Crawford T: 01560484705

One acre of mature garden, particularly fine in late spring with rhododendrons, azaleas, trillium, hellebore and other spring flowering plants and bulbs. One acre of developing garden with herbaceous borders, vegetable garden and orchard at its best during July and August. Two acres of native broadleaf woodland being created. No neat edges but lots to see at any time.

Directions: From Stewarton Cross take the B760 Old Glasgow Road one mile. Turn onto road marked to Dunlop. From Glasgow this turning is half a mile past Kingsford. Continue for two miles, turn right at T junction. High Fulwood short distance on right hand side.

Disabled Access:
None

Opening Times:
By arrangement
20 April - 6 September

Admission:
£4.00, children free

Charities:
Hessilhead Wildlife Rescue Trust receives 40%, the net remaining to SG Beneficiaries

HOLMES FARM
Drybridge, By Irvine KA11 5BS
Mr Brian A Young T: 01294 311210
E: yungi@fsmail.net

Plantaholic's paradise! A plantsman's garden created by a confirmed plantaholic. An ever evolving selection of perennials, bulbs, alpines and shrubs. Meandering paths guide the eye through plantings predominantly herbaceous, with small trees and shrubs. Some unusual plant collections are housed permanently in polytunnels. The garden opening will hopefully be timed for peak bloom of some of the 400 iris in the garden. Some areas of the garden are currently undergoing a partial replant and redesign. There is a plant nursery with a wide selection of plant treasures from the garden and a gift shop and gallery too!

Directions: Holmes is the only farm between Drybridge and Dreghorn on B730.

Disabled Access:
None

Opening Times:
Saturday 6 June
1:00pm - 5:00pm
Sunday 7 June
1:00pm - 5:00pm

Admission:
£4.00

Charities:
The Mackintosh Appeal receives 40%, the net remaining to SG Beneficiaries

KILMAURS VILLAGE GARDENS
Kilmaurs KA3 2QS
The Gardeners of Kilmaurs

Opening in the springtime this year , the gardeners of Kilmaurs will offer a variety of gardens at a different season which will be a great delight for visitors to this very attractive conservation village.

Other Details: Tickets, maps and teas at Maxwell Church Hall, Crosshouse Road KA3 2SA.

Directions: From M77 north take B751 turnoff at Fenwick for Kilmaurs. From A77 from east and south A71 Irvine and turn off to Crosshouse, Knockentiber on B751. Yellow signposted from A735 and B751.

Disabled Access:
Partial

Opening Times:
Sunday 10 May
1:30pm - 5:00pm

Admission:
£4.00, children free

Charities:
RNLI receives 20%, Glencairn Aisle receives 20%, the net remaining to SG Beneficiaries.

BERWICKSHIRE

Scotland's Gardens 2015 Guidebook is sponsored by **INVESTEC WEALTH & INVESTMENT**

District Organiser

Mrs F Wills	Anton's Hill, Coldstream TD12 4JD

Treasurer

Mr F Wills	Anton's Hill, Coldstream TD12 4JD

Gardens open on a specific date

Anton's Hill, Leitholm	Sunday 24 May	2:00pm	-	5:00pm
Lennel Bank, Leitholm	Sunday 5 July	10:30am	-	5:00pm
Netherbyres, Eyemouth	Sunday 5 July	2:00pm	-	5:30pm
Anton's Hill, Leitholm	Sunday 19 July	2:00pm	-	5:00pm
The Walled Garden, Leitholm	Sunday 19 July	2:00pm	-	5:00pm

Gardens open regularly

Bughtrig, Coldstream	1 June - 1 September	11:00am	-	5:00pm

Gardens open by arrangement

Anton's Hill, Leitholm	On request	01890 840203
Lennel Bank, Coldstream	On request	01890 882297
Netherbyres, Eyemouth	1 May - 31 August	01890 750337

Key to symbols

	New in 2015		Homemade teas		Accommodation
	Teas		Dogs on a lead allowed		Plant stall
	Cream teas		Wheelchair access		Scottish Snowdrop Festival

Garden locations

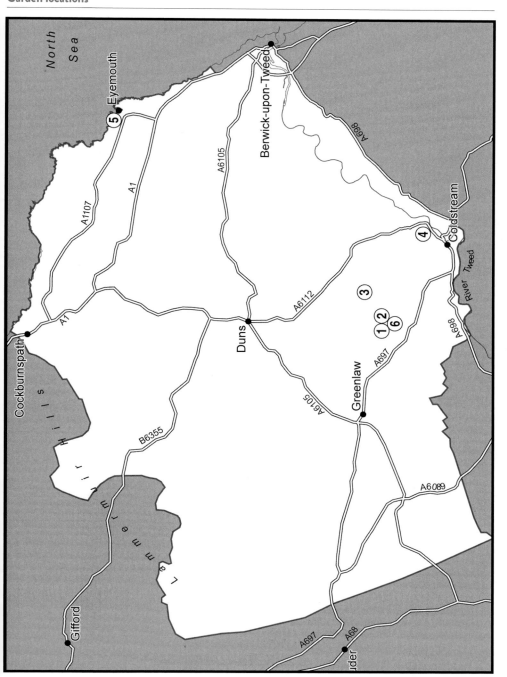

ANTON'S HILL
Leitholm, Coldstream TD12 4JD
Mr and Mrs F Wills T: 01890 840203
E: cillawills@antonshill.co.uk

A well treed mature garden which has been improved and added to since 1999. There are woodland walks and over 20 different varieties of oaks. The garden in spring has azaleas and rhododendrons, primroses and bluebells. There is a stumpery, a well planted pond, shrubberies and herbaceous borders, topiary elephant family of yew, shrub rose walk, leading to an acer glade with martagon lilies. There is a further pond planted with dogwood and gunnera with a hosta island.

Directions: Signposted off B6461, west of Leitholm.

Disabled Access:
Full

Opening Times:
Sunday 24 May
2:00pm - 5:00pm
Also by arrangement on request

Admission:
£4.00

Charities:
Christ Church, Duns receives 40%, the net remaining to SG Beneficiaries

ANTON'S HILL WITH THE WALLED GARDEN
Leitholm, Coldstream TD12 4JD
Mr and Mrs F. Wills T: 01890 840203
E: cillawills@antonshill.co.uk

As above.

Disabled Access:
Full

Opening Times:
Sunday 19 July
2:00pm - 5:00pm

Admission:
£5.00

Charities:
Oakfield Easton Maudit Ltd receives 40%, the net remaining to SG Beneficiaries

BUGHTRIG
Near Leitholm, Coldstream TD12 4JP
Mr and Mrs William Ramsay T: 01890 840777
E: ramsay@bughtrig.co.uk

A traditional hedged Scottish family garden with an interesting combination of herbaceous plants, shrubs, annuals and fruit. It is surrounded by fine specimen trees which provide remarkable shelter.

Directions: A quarter mile east of Leitholm on B6461.

Disabled Access:
Partial

Opening Times:
1 June - 1 September
11:00am - 5:00pm

Admission:
£4.00, children under 18 £1.00

Charities:
Donation to SG Beneficiaries

LENNEL BANK
Coldstream TD12 4EX
Mrs Honor Brown T: 01890 882297

Lennel Bank is a terraced garden overlooking the River Tweed, consisting of wide borders packed with shrubs and perennial planting, some unusual. The water garden, built in 2008, is surrounded by a rockery and utilises the slope ending in a pond. There is a small kitchen garden with raised beds in unusual shapes. Different growing conditions throughout the garden from dry, wet, shady and sun lend themselves to a variety of plants, which hopefully enhance interest in the garden.

Directions: On A6112 Coldstream to Duns road, one mile from Coldstream.

Disabled Access:
None

Opening Times:
Sunday 5 July
10:30am - 5:00pm
Also by arrangement on request

Admission:
£5.00

Charities:
British Heart Foundation receives 40%, the net remaining to SG Beneficiaries

NETHERBYRES
Eyemouth TD14 5SE
Col S J Furness T: 018907 50337

A unique 18th century elliptical walled garden. Annuals, roses, herbaceous borders, fruit and vegetables in summer.

Other Details: Plant sale on 5 July.

Directions: Half a mile south of Eyemouth on A1107 to Berwick.

Disabled Access:
Full

Opening Times:
Sunday 5 July
2:00pm - 5:30pm
Also by arrangement
1 May - 31 August

Admission:
£4.00, concessions £3.00, children under 12 free

Charities:
Gunsgreen House Trust receives 40%, the net remaining to SG Beneficiaries

THE WALLED GARDEN WITH ANTON'S HILL
Leitholm, Coldstream TD12 4JD
Alec West and Pat Watson

A restored one and three quarters acre garden in three distinct areas. The lower garden comprises formal vegetable plots, herbaceous and bedded out annual borders, a traditional 65 foot greenhouse and over 200 varieties of cordoned fruit trees. The upper walled garden contains a solardome with cacti collection. There are ponds in each area of the garden. The garden has recently featured in the "Great British Garden Revival" programme.

Other Details: A ride-on five inch gauge railway circles the outer garden.

Directions: Signposted off B6461 west of Leitholm.

Disabled Access:
Full

Opening Times:
Sunday 19 July
2:00pm - 5:00pm

Admission:
£5.00

Charities:
Oakfield Easton Maudit Ltd receives 40%, the net remaining to SG Beneficiaries

CAITHNESS, SUTHERLAND, ORKNEY & SHETLAND

Scotland's Gardens 2015 Guidebook is sponsored by **INVESTEC WEALTH & INVESTMENT**

District Organiser

Mrs Judith Middlemas	22 Miller Place, Scrabster, Thurso KW14 7UH

Area Organisers

Mrs Caroline Critchlow	The Quoy of Houton, Orphir, Orkney KW17 2RD
Mrs Mary Leask	VisitShetland, Market Cross, Lerwick ZE1 0LU
Mr Steve Mathieson	VisitShetland, Market Cross, Lerwick ZE1 0LU
Mrs Jonny Shaw	Amat, Ardgay, Sutherland IV24 3BS

Treasurer

Mr Chris Hobson	Braeside, Dunnet, Caithness KW14 8YD

Gardens open on a specific date

Amat, Ardgay	Saturday 6 June	2:00pm	-	5:00pm
Amat, Ardgay	Sunday 7 June	2:00pm	-	5:00pm
Duncan Street Gardens, Thurso	Sunday 14 June	1:00pm	-	5:00pm
Pentland Firth Gardens, Dunnet	Sunday 28 June	1:00pm	-	5:00pm
The Castle & Gardens of Mey	Wednesday 1 July	10:00am	-	5:00pm
Bighouse Lodge, by Melvich	Sunday 5 July	2:00pm	-	5:00pm
The Castle & Gardens of Mey	Wednesday 15 July	10:00am	-	5:00pm
House of Tongue, Lairg	Saturday 25 July	2:00pm	-	6:00pm
Langwell, Berriedale	Sunday 26 July	1:00pm	-	5:00pm
The Castle & Gardens of Mey	Saturday 15 August	10:00am	-	5:00pm
Millbank Gardens, Thurso	Sunday 16 August	2:00pm	-	5:00pm

Gardens open regularly

The Castle & Gardens of Mey	13 May - 26 July and		
	11 August - 30 September	10:00am	-	5:00pm

Key to symbols

 New in 2015

 Homemade teas

 Accommodation

 Teas

 Dogs on a lead allowed

 Plant stall

 Cream teas

 Wheelchair access

Scottish Snowdrop Festival

Garden locations

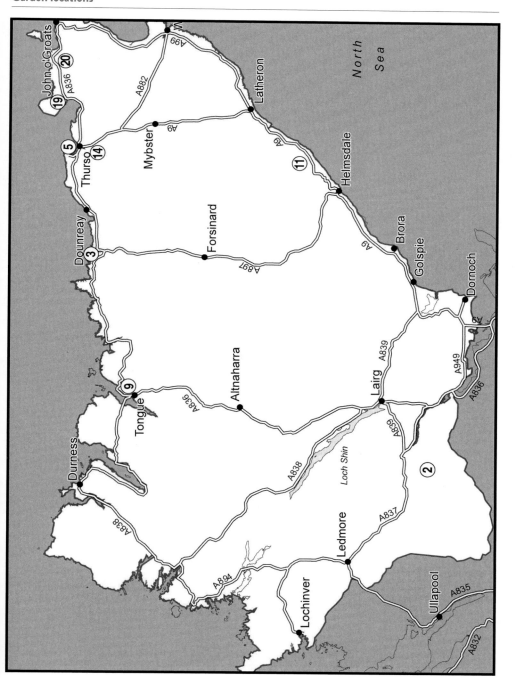

AMAT
Ardgay IV24 3BS
Jonny and Sara Shaw
E: sara.amat@aol.co.uk

Riverside garden set in Amat Forest. Herbaceous borders and rockery set in a large lawn looking onto a salmon pool. Old and new rhododendrons with woodland and river walk plus large specimen trees in policies.

Other Details: Teas £2.50

Directions: Take road from Ardgay to Croick nine miles. Turn left at the red phone box and the garden is 500 yards on the left.

Disabled Access:
Partial

Opening Times:
Saturday 6 June
2:00pm - 5:00pm
Sunday 7 June
2:00pm - 5:00pm

Admission:
£4.50

Charities:
Gardening Leave receives 20%, Croick Church receives 20%, the net remaining to SG Beneficiaries

---

BIGHOUSE LODGE
by Melvich KW14 7YJ
Bighouse Estate
E: info@bighouseestate.com   www.bighouseestate.com

Bighouse Lodge is situated on the north coast of Sutherland at the mouth of the River Halladale. The two acre walled garden, originally laid out in 1715, consists of a central axis leading to a charming bothy with lawn, herbaceous borders, a sunken garden and four separate conceptual gardens behind the hedgerows. Each garden contains a sculpture to reflect the aspects of the Bighouse Estate namely the River, the Forest, the Strath and the Hill. The garden has recently been restored and is now a most interesting place to visit.

Other Details: Gravelled paths. Teas £3.50.

Directions: Off A836 ½ mile East of Melvich.

Disabled Access:
Partial

Opening Times:
Sunday 5 July
2:00pm - 5:00pm

Admission:
£4.00, children under 12
£1.00

Charities:
RNLI receives 40%, the net remaining to SG Beneficiaries

DUNCAN STREET GARDENS
Thurso KW14 7HU
The Gardeners of Duncan Street

Three town gardens with their own micro climate, offering a good selection of interesting shrubs and trees, roses and herbaceous plants with landscaping on different levels. Each garden has its specialties including bonsai, alpines, cactus and succulents and water features.

Other Details: Start at 7 Duncan Street, Thurso. Wheelchair access is limited due to narrow paths and steps.

Disabled Access:
Partial

Opening Times:
Sunday 14 June
1:00pm - 5:00pm

Admission:
£4.00

Charities:
Caithness Samaritans receives 13⅓%, Thurso Pipe Band receives 13⅓%, Riding for the Disabled receives 13⅓%, the net remaining to SG Beneficiaries

LANGWELL
Berriedale KW7 6HD
Welbeck Estates T: 01593 751278/751237
E: macanson@hotmail.com

A beautiful and spectacular old walled garden with outstanding borders situated in the secluded Langwell Strath. Charming wooded access drive with a chance to see deer.

Directions: A9 for two miles from Berriedale.

Disabled Access:
Partial

Opening Times:
Sunday 26 July
1:00pm - 5:00pm

Admission:
£4.00, children under 12 free

Charities:
R.N.L.I. receives 40%, the net remaining to SG Beneficiaries

MILLBANK GARDENS
Millbank Road, Thurso KW14 8PS
The Millbank Gardens Gardeners

Millbank Road opens some beautiful cottage gardens. These include a terrace of small rear gardens with a range of trees, shrubs, perennials, roses and ground cover. Each garden shows its owners' approach to gardening in a small space and their varying and highly individual solutions.

Other Details: Start at the Rugby Pavilion for tickets and directions. Parking, toilets and teas at Pavilion. Children's I Spy sheet £0.50. Homemade tea £3.00.

Directions: The Rugby Pavilion is by Thurso Swimming Pool, Millbank Road. Entrance to rugby car park is between 12 and 14 Millbank Road.

Disabled Access:
Full

Opening Times:
Sunday 16 August
2:00pm - 5:00pm

Admission:
£4.00 includes all gardens

Charities:
Maggie's Cancer Caring Centre,Raigmore receives 40%, the net remaining to SG Beneficiaries

PENTLAND FIRTH GARDENS
Britannia Hall, Dunnet KW14 8YD
The Pentland Firth Gardeners T: 01847 851757

With panoramic views of the Pentland Firth, these gardens show what is possible when gardening on the exposed northern coast of Scotland. Two old favourites, one with a rock garden and herb wheel, greenhouse and container-grown vegetables, the other with a good selection of trees, a pond and a vegetable garden. The third new garden, recently started, shows how a bare site can be developed into a garden. All gardens have a good variety of hardy plants and shrubs to enjoy.

Other Details: Transport required in order to visit all gardens. Teas are available at Britannia Hall.

Directions: Start at Britannia Hall, Dunnet KW14 8YD where a map of gardens will be available on payment of admission fee.

Disabled Access:
Partial

Opening Times:
Sunday 28 June
1:00pm - 5:00pm

Admission:
£4.00

Charities:
Mary Ann's Cottage - Caithness Heritage Trust receives 40%, the net remaining to SG Beneficiaries

THE CASTLE & GARDENS OF MEY
Mey KW14 8XH
The Queen Elizabeth Castle of Mey Trust T: 01847 851473
E: enquiries@castleofmey.org.uk www.castleofmey.org.uk

Originally a Z plan castle bought by the Queen Mother in 1952 and then restored and improved. The walled garden and the East Garden were also created by the Queen Mother. An animal centre has been established over the last three years and is proving very popular with all ages. New herbaceous border for 2014, East facing, nestled under the West Wall contains Agapanthus, Phlox, Pink Aconitum, Sidalcea, Verbascum and Knautia among others.

Other Details: Tearoom, shop and animal centre. Castle opens 10:20am and last entries are at 4:00pm. Please check website for details as dates may be subject to change.

Directions: On A836 between Thurso and John O'Groats.

Disabled Access:
Partial

Opening Times:
Wednesdays 1 & 15 Jul, Sat 15 August 10:00am - 5:00pm
13 May - 26 July and
11 August - 30 September
10:00am - 5:00pm
Please check website for dates

Admission:
Gardens only £6.50, children £3.00, family £19.00.
Castle & Gardens £11, conc £9.75, children £6.50, family £29

Charities:
Donation to SG Beneficiaries

ORKNEY

Scotland's Gardens 2015 Guidebook is sponsored by **INVESTEC WEALTH & INVESTMENT**

Gardens open on a specific date

Orkney Garden Trail One	Sunday 7 June	11:00am	- 5:00pm
Orkney Garden Trail One	Sunday 14 June	11:00am	- 5:00pm
The Quoy of Houton, Orphir	Sunday 21 June	11:00am	- 5:00pm
The Herston Garden Trail	Sunday 28 June	11:00am	- 6:00pm
The Herston Garden Trail	Sunday 5 July	11:00am	- 6:00pm
Orkney Garden Trail Two	Sunday 12 July	11:00am	- 5:00pm
Orkney Garden Trail Two	Sunday 19 July	11:00am	- 5:00pm

SCOTLAND'S GARDENS BRIGHTWATER HOLIDAYS VISIT TO ORKNEY & THE NORTH 13 - 17 JULY

TAKE ADVANTAGE OF THE SCOTLAND'S GARDENS BRIGHTWATER HOLIDAYS TOUR PACKAGE AND SEE SOME OF THE GLORIOUS GARDENS IN ORKNEY AND THE NORTH OF SCOTLAND. SEE PAGE 40 FOR FURTHER DETAILS.

Quoy of Houton

Key to symbols

	New in 2015		Homemade teas		Accommodation
	Teas		Dogs on a lead allowed		Plant stall
	Cream teas		Wheelchair access		Scottish Snowdrop Festival

1 ORKNEY GARDEN TRAIL ONE
Various locations
The Gardeners of Orkney
E: c.kritchlow258@btinternet.com   www.orkneygardentrail.org.uk

1. 33 Hillside Road Stromness KW16 3HR (Mr David Walker)
An informal garden of approximately ½ an acre created from a field over the past 20 years. Situated on a gentle slope its features include dry stone walls and terracing, a pond, a large variety of trees and shrubs and many cottage garden perennials.
Directions: On Hillside Road approximately 100 yards past the swimming pool on the opposite side of the road.

2. Dalkeith Polytunnel Grimbister, Kirkwall KW15 1TT (Olive Robertson)
The main garden was a field 12 years ago: over our time living here we have transformed the area into a place the whole family can enjoy.The area now consists of a large lawn, various borders and a secluded patio area, a large vegetable plot and polytunnel. In good weather it can have three growing seasons over the summer months. A variety of vegetables flourish including cabbages, cauliflower, peas and tomatoes. 'I have enjoyed gardening and horticulture for over 25 years and have won most points in the East Mainland show for the past two years'.
Directions: A965 to Finstown, at Esson garage and turn up the old Finstown Road. Approximately one mile out of village, the polytunnel is clearly visible from the road.

3. Stenwood Finstown KW17 2JX (Mr and Mrs J Wood)
A garden of about one acre on a north facing slope. Starting at the bottom, visitors can wander through a number of interlinked areas featuring a wide range of perennial plants, primulas, roses, shrubs and rhododendrons.
Directions: Turn up the Heddle Road in the centre of Finstown (at the church) and the garden is situated approximately 300 metres on the left.

4. The Community Garden Finstown KW17 2JX
The garden has a stunning variety of features from miniature shrub and primula lined valleys and beautiful perennial flower bordered burns. There are large herbaceous flower beds around lawned areas. The public have access to this area at all times.
Directions: Almost directly opposite Stenwood up the land and first right.

5. Quoylanks Deerness Orkney KW172QQ (Chris Giles and Gillian Smee)
Mature garden created 25 years ago in 3/4 acre of farmland surrounding an old steading. Pathways wind through well established shelter belt and between raised beds, skirting the field edges with open views to the sea and the island of Copinsay. Informally planted with familiar shrubs and perennials and some more unusual species.
Directions: Head out from Kirkwall towards airport on A960. Pass over the causeway with sea and dunes on either side and head to top brow of hill. At this awkward junction two side roads join on the right. Second road has a large sign for Geo slipway but take the first! Continue straight for 200 yards to pink bungalow, here take first left signed Mussel Quoy. 100 yards further are two houses one a new bungalow ,the other a two storey house. We are on left immediately opposite up a long drive with a white gate at the top.

Other Details: Cream Teas at Quoylanks £5.00.

See also page 38 - 39 of this book.

Disabled Access:
Partial

Opening Times:
Sunday 7 June
11:00am - 5:00pm
Sunday 14 June
11:00am - 5:00pm

Admission:
£10.00 for entry into all gardens, £2.50 for a single garden, accompanied children under 12 free. Tickets available by cash or cheque from Quoy of Houton, Orphir, KW17 2RD, or Scapa Travel, 11 Bridge St, Kirkwall KW15 1HR. Tickets may be reserved in advance by emailing c.kritchlow258@btinternet.com or scapa@barrheadtravel.com Repeat visits to a garden £2.50

Charities:
Friends of the Neuro Ward ARI receives 40%, the net remaining to SG Beneficiaries

ORKNEY GARDEN TRAIL TWO
Various locations
The Gardeners of Orkney T: 01856811237
E: c.kritchlow258@btinternet.com

1. Kierfold Sandwick KW16 3JE (Mr and Mrs E Smith)
An established half acre walled Victorian garden with stunning views over Orkney's West Mainland. There has been a garden at Kierfold since the 1850s and the current design of the garden combines the historic influence of double borders with more informal planting. The garden is crammed with grasses, geraniums, iris and roses alongside some more unusual plants.
Directions: Leaving Stromness turn left onto A967/A966. Take B9056 signposted Skara Brae. On reaching Skaill Loch take the second right onto B9057 to Dounby. Kierfold is the first house on the right.

2. The Quoy of Houton Orphir, Orkney KW17 2RD (Mrs Caroline Critchlow)
An historic walled garden a stone's throw away from the sea and completely restored in 2008. The garden is planted to withstand winds in excess of 100 mph and features drystone walling features, raised beds and a 60 foot water rill. The planting reflects its coastal location and is planted in the cottage garden style with towering allium, many varieties of geranium and plants collected from around Europe. There are wild flower areas which encourage bees and butterflies. There is a separate walled vegetable garden and fruit cage which supplies the house and B&B and cottage guests. A new walled garden is planned for 2015.
Directions: A964 from Kirkwall to Houton. Take ferry turning, straight across at first junction following tarmac road to a two storey yellow house across the bay.

3. 14a Victoria Street Kirkwall, Orkney KW15 1DN
A small Victorian courtyard garden, with paved paths and secret garden rooms filled with interesting herbaceous, perennials and annuals. A little treasure tucked away behind the Earls Palace in the heart of Kirkwall. A real secret garden!
Directions: Go to the centre of Kirkwall behind the Bishops Palace and follow yellow signs.

4. Schoolquoy Orphir, Orkney KW17 2RF
The garden was established from an old school garden overgrown with weeds, wire grass and seed fuchsia. This secluded garden has been landscaped with terraced lawns, pathways,flower and shrub beds that wind up hill and appears like another garden as you come down hill. Visitors have been amazed at the plant varieties and inspired by the colours and layout design.
Directions: Follow A964 from Kirkwall to Orphir continue to next right turning to Scorrodale. The garden is on your right as you go up hill. **No dogs.**

5. Gyre Cottage Orphir, Orkney KW17 2RD
This pretty south easterly sloping croft garden surrounded on three sides by native trees has lofty spectacular views over Scapa Flow. It is a series of secret gardens with different planting in each. There is a lovely collection of grasses, alpines and some wonderful hydrangeas, spirea and hebe varieties.
Directions: Take A964 from Kirkwall to Orphir take left turning by the side of the Kirk and opposite the school follow lane down. Cottage is on right after the small wood.

6. The Bu Orphir, Orkney KW17 2RD
Located in a lovely rosa rugosa lined sheltered woodland dell just ¼ mile from Scapa Flow and a stone's throw away from a Viking church and drinking hall. This secluded garden has some real treasures. In summer the beds are crammed with home grown annuals and agapanthus flourish in large pots. Some lovely late flowering shrubs make this a good garden to visit in July. There is also a fascinating polytunnel where fruit trees thrive and a substantial pond which Jimmy will show you if you ask!
Directions: Continue down the lane from Gyre cottage past the farm and the garden is on the right.

Other Details: Cream teas at Quoy of Houton £5.00.
See also page 38 - 39 of this book.

Disabled Access:
Partial

Opening Times:
Sunday 12 July
11:00am - 5:00pm
Sunday 19 July
11:00am - 5:00pm

Admission:
£12.00 for entry to all gardens
£2.50 for a single garden. Accompanied children u12 free
Tickets available by cash or cheque from Quoy of Houton, Orphir, KW17 2RD, or Scapa Travel, 11 Bridge Street, Kirkwall KW15 1HR
Tickets may be reserved in advance by emailing c.kritchlow258@btinternet.com or scapa@barrheadtravel.com

Charities:
Friends of the Neuro Ward ARI receives 40%, the net remaining to SG Beneficiaries

3 **THE HERSTON GARDEN TRAIL**
St Margaret's Hope KW17 2RH
The Gardeners of Herston

The village of Herston is proud to open a collection of five seaside gardens, all different sizes and individual styles, but all coping with varying degrees of coastal exposure. In addition The Marengo Community Garden in neighbouring St Margaret's Hope will also be open.

1. Mucklejocks (Mr and Mrs Dalby)
A cottage garden next to the sea divided into different sections to afford seating areas, planted with perennials, annuals and coastal plants to encourage bees and butterflies.

2. Quoys of Herston (Carol and Steve Scott)
An enclosed drystone walled garden close to the sea in its fourth year of development. Planted in the cottage garden style to encourage wildlife.

3. South Banks (Mr and Mrs D Holt)
A semi-sheltered, east facing garden by the shore. If a garden plant wants to grow and survives, I let it do so.

4. Fiddlers Green (Mike and Sue Palmer)
A small seafront garden filled with traditional perennials and bulbs in the front and an ornamental vegetable garden with raised beds to the rear.

5. New House (Dave and Pauline Musson)
A sheltered informal garden, mainly perennials, regularly bathed in salt spray! It has evolved to flourish in sympathy with the local climate and wildlife, and is still evolving.

6. The Marengo Garden (Trish Spence)
Orkney's first community garden was created in 1997 with the help of national lottery funding and Tern Television who held a Community Corner Competition featured on The Beechgrove Garden programme. This beautiful mature cottage garden which had been abandoned for many years was re-created using many of the original trees and shrubs. The garden's unique sheltered position gives scope for interesting and unusual planting. The maintenance of the garden is continued today by volunteers within the Burray and South Ronaldsay communities. Situated within St. Margaret's Hope village the garden provides a much loved peaceful haven for all to enjoy.

Other Details: Cream teas will be available in the Marengo Centre in St Margaret's Hope on both Sundays, from 2:30pm to 4:00pm.

Directions: About a mile south of St Margarets Hope take the turning on the right signposted Herston three miles. Follow the single track road and it will take you right into the village where you will find five of the gardens. The Marengo Community Garden is in St Margaret's Hope itself. At the bottom of the Church Road, turn right and it's on the left hand side.

See also pages 38 - 39 of this book.

Disabled Access:
Partial

Opening Times:
Sunday 28 June
11:00am - 6:00pm
Sunday 5 July
11:00am - 6:00pm

Admission:
£12.00 includes entry to all six gardens

Charities:
Friends of the Neuro Ward at Aberdeen Royal Infirmary receives 40%, the net remaining to SG Beneficiaries

THE QUOY OF HOUTON
Orphir KW17 2RD
Kevin and Caroline Critchlow   T: 01856 811237
E: c.kritchlow258@btinternet.com

An historic walled garden a stone's throw away from the sea and completely restored in 2008. The garden is planted to withstand winds in excess of 100 mph and features drystone walling features, raised beds and a 60 foot water rill. The planting reflects its coastal location and is planted in the cottage garden style with towering allium, many varieties of geranium and plants collected from around Europe. There are wild flower areas which encourage bees and butterflies. There is a separate walled vegetable garden and fruit cage which supplies the house and B&B and cottage guests. A new walled garden is planned for 2015.

Other Details: Luxury cream teas £8.00, please book in advance.

Directions: A964 from Kirkwall to Houton. Take ferry turning, straight across at first junction following tarmac road to a two storey yellow house across the bay.

Disabled Access:
Partial

Opening Times:
Sunday 21 June
11:00am - 5:00pm

Admission:
£3.00

Charities:
Friends of the Neuro Ward
ARI receives 40%, the net
remaining to SG Beneficiaries

Finstown Community Garden

SHETLAND

Scotland's Gardens 2015 Guidebook is sponsored by **INVESTEC WEALTH & INVESTMENT**

Gardens open on a specific date

Frakkafield, Gott	Mons - Sats 18 May - 6 June	10:00am -	6:00pm
Frakkafield, Gott	Sundays 24 & 31 May	2:00pm -	6:00pm
Holmlea, Mid Yell	Sunday 12 July	10:00am -	7:00pm
Lea Gardens, Tresta	Sunday 12 July	2:00pm -	7:00pm
15 Linkshouse, Mid Yell	Thursdays 16, 23, 30 July	10:00am -	7:00pm
Holmlea, Mid Yell	Sundays 19, 26 July	10:00am -	7:00pm
Holmlea, Mid Yell	Sunday 2, 9, 16 August	10:00am -	7:00pm
15 Linkshouse, Mid Yell	Thursdays 6, 13, 20 August	10:00am -	7:00pm

Gardens open regularly

Highlands, Scalloway	1 May - 30 September	9:00am -	9:00pm
Lea Gardens, Tresta	1 April - 31 October closed Thursdays	2:00pm -	5:00pm
Nonavaar, Levenwick	1 March - 12 September Thursdays and Fridays only	2:00pm -	5:00pm
Norby, Sandness	1 January - 31 December	Dawn -	Dusk

Gardens open by arrangement

Cruisdale, Sandness	1 March - 31 October	01595 870739
Keldaberg, Cunningsburgh	1 June - 31 October	01950 477331
Lindaal, Tingwall	1 May - 30 September	01595 840420
Nonavaar, Levenwick	1 March - 12 September	01950 422447

Key to symbols

 New in 2015   Homemade teas   Accommodation

 Teas   Dogs on a lead allowed   Plant stall

 Cream teas   Wheelchair access   Scottish Snowdrop Festival

15 LINKSHOUSE
Mid Yell ZE2 9BP
Mr Charlie Inkster T: 01957 702049
E: cjinkster@btinternet.com

A small cottage garden with a greenhouse full of plants and colour, a pond complete with fountain and water lilies, and a small aviary with canaries and finches. The garden is well established with trees, bushes and a good variety of plants giving plenty of colour. Fuschias are a favourite providing a good selection of different varieties both in the garden and in the greenhouse. Also in the greenhouse are many varieties of streptocarpus adding to the colourful display.

Directions: In Yell head north on the A968, turn right to Mid Yell. Drive down through Mid Yell and turn towards Linkshouse Pier. The garden is at the far end of the row of white cottages.

Disabled Access:
None

Opening Times:
Thursdays 16, 23 and 30 July
10:00am - 7:00pm
Thursdays 6. 13 and 20
August 10:00am - 7:00pm

Admission:
£3.00

Charities:
Yell for Cancer Support receives 40%, the net remaining to SG Beneficiaries

CRUISDALE
Sandness ZE2 9PL
Alfred Kern T: 01595 870739

The garden is in a natural state with many willows, several ponds and a variety of colourful hardy plants that grow well in the Shetland climate. It is a work in progress, started about ten years ago and growing bigger over the years with more work planned.

Directions: From Lerwick head north on the A970, then at Tingwall take the A971 to Sandness, on the west side of Shetland. Opposite the school, on the right hand side with a wind generator in the field.

Disabled Access:
None

Opening Times:
By arrangement
1 March - 31 October
May be available at other times

Admission:
£3.00

Charities:
WRVS receives 40%, the net remaining to SG Beneficiaries

FRAKKAFIELD
Gott ZE2 9SB
Angus & Wendy Nicol T: 01595 840272

This is a long established wild garden with trees and rhododendrons the main attraction. There are two greenhouses; one is full of fruit trees: apple, cherry and plum. The other is filled with young plants to be sold for our business.

Other Details: Angus is also a beekeeper.
From 18 May to 6 June, if we're in, we're open, drop by or phone to check.

Directions: Head north from Lerwick. We are half way down the hill towards the Scalloway junction; take the track on right hand side. Opposite Dale Golf Course. Co-ordinates for sat nav N 60.16636 W 001.21604

Disabled Access:
None

Opening Times:
Monday to Saturday
18 May - 6 June
10:00am - 6:00pm
and Sundays 24 & 31 May
2:00pm - 6:00pm

Admission:
£3.00

Charities:
Brain Tumour Research
receives 40%, the net
remaining to SG Beneficiaries

HIGHLANDS
East Voe, Scalloway ZE1 0UR
Sarah Kay T: 01595 880526
E: info@easterhoull.co.uk www.easterhoull.co.uk

The garden is in two parts. The upper garden is mostly a rockery, with a large selection of plants, shallow pond, seating area and newly built 'polycrub' and green house. The lower garden is on a steep slope with a spectacular sea view over the village of Scalloway. There is a path to lead visitors around. The garden features a large collection of plants, vegetable patch, deep pond and pergola. It was awarded a 'Shetland Environmental Award' in 2014 for its strong theme of recycling.

Other Details: There is self catering accommodation available next to the garden. See website for details.

Directions: Follow A970 main road towards village of Scalloway. Near the top of the hill heading towards Scalloway take a sharp turn to the left, signposted Easterhoull Chalets. Follow road to chalets (painted blue with red roofs) and you will see the yellow SG sign for the garden.

Disabled Access:
None

Opening Times:
1 May - 30 September
9:00am - 9:00pm

Admission:
£3.50

Charities:
Yorkhill Childrens Charity
receives 40%, the net
remaining to SG Beneficiaries

HOLMLEA
Mid Yell ZE2 9BT
John and Sandra Robertson T: 01957 702062

The garden has a greenhouse, conservatory and drystane dyke, with a mixture of flowers, shrubs and vegetables. Enjoy wandering around admiring the variety of different shrubs and herbaceous plants interspersed with colourful annuals, then see the plot of mixed vegetables before moving on into the greenhouse where tomatoes, cucumbers and peppers grow.

Other Details: There is a large water wheel in the garden.

Directions: Once on the island of Yell, head for Mid Yell, going down to Linkshouse Pier. From there, go up past the shop about 150 yards. Holmlea is right on the corner with garage and basement.

Disabled Access:
Partial

Opening Times:
Sundays 12, 19 and 26 July
10:00am - 7:00pm
Sundays 2, 9 and 16 August
10:00am - 7:00pm

Admission:
£3.00

Charities:
Motor Neurone Disease receives 40%, the net remaining to SG Beneficiaries

KELDABERG
Cunningsburgh ZE2 9HG
Mrs L Johnston T: 01950 477331
E: linda.keldaberg@btinternet.com

A 'secret garden' divided into four areas. A beach garden of grasses, flowers and driftwood. The main area is a sloping perennial border leading down to a greenhouse, vegetable plot, up to a decked area with containers and exotic plants including agaves, pineapple lilies, cannas and gunneras. The new part has trees, raised vegetable beds, a rockery, retaining walls and an arbour in which to rest. There is a pond complete with goldfish, golden orf and koi plus aquatic plants, and a water lily.

Directions: On the A970 south of Lerwick is Cunningsburgh, take the Gord junction on the left after passing the village hall. Continue along the road to the first house past the Kenwood sign.

Disabled Access:
Partial

Opening Times:
By arrangement 1 June - 31 October - must phone first to avoid disappointment

Admission:
£3.00

Charities:
Chest Heart & Stroke Scotland receives 40%, the net remaining to SG Beneficiaries

LEA GARDENS
Tresta ZE2 9LT
Rosa Steppanova T: 01595 810454

Lea Gardens, started in the early 1980s, now covers almost two acres. The plant collection, the largest north of Inverewe Gardens, consists of 1,500 different species and cultivars from all over the world, including phyto-geographic elements of collections of plants from New Zealand, South Africa and South America. Planted to provide all year round interest it has been divided into a variety of habitats: woodland and shade, borders, wetland, raised beds, and acid and lime lovers. A winner of the 2011 Shetland Environmental Award.

Directions: From Lerwick take A970 north, turn left at Tingwall onto A971 past Weisdale along Weisdale Voe and up Weisdale hill. Coming down, Lea Gardens is on your right surrounded by trees.

Disabled Access:
Partial

Opening Times:
Sunday 12 July
2:00pm - 7:00pm
1 April - 31 October
2:00pm - 5:00pm
closed Thursdays

Admission:
£4.00

Charities:
20 July: All proceeds to SG Beneficiaries. All other dates donation to SG Beneficiaries

LINDAAL
Tingwall ZE2 9SG
Mr Adam Leslie T: 01595 840420
E: lindaal@btinternet.com

An established garden of almost one acre. Flat area around the house leading up a slope to a small woodland area with conifers and deciduous trees. In the garden there are four ponds and a well, tubs and hanging baskets with a mix of perennial plants and annuals. Good for wildlife with frogs and birds.

Directions: Go north from Lerwick to Tingwall taking the Laxfirth junction on your right past the local hall and school, round the end of the loch and straight up the hill to first wooden house on the right.

Disabled Access:
Partial

Opening Times:
By arrangement
1 May - 30 September
Please phone first

Admission:
£3.00

Charities:
MS Society Shetland Branch receives 40%, the net remaining to SG Beneficiaries

NONAVAAR
Levenwick ZE2 9HX
James B Thomason T: 01950 422447

This is a delightful country garden, sloping within drystone walls, overlooking magnificent coastal views. It contains ponds, terraces, trees, bushes, varied perennials, annuals, vegetable garden and greenhouse.

Other Details: Arts & Crafts studio.

Directions: Head south from Lerwick. Turn left at Levenwick sign soon after Bigton turnoff. Follow road to third house on left after Midway stores. Park where there is a 'Garden Open' sign.

Disabled Access:
None

Opening Times:
1 March - 12 September
2:00pm - 5:00pm
Thursdays and Fridays only
Also by arrangement
during this time Saturday -
Wednesday, please phone first

Admission:
£3.00

Charities:
Cancer Research receives 40%, the net remaining to SG Beneficiaries

NORBY
Burnside, Sandness ZE2 9PL
Mrs Gundel Grolimund T: 01595 870246
E: gislinde@tiscali.co.uk

A small but perfectly formed garden and a prime example of what can be achieved in a very exposed situation. Blue painted wooden pallets provide internal wind breaks and form a background for shrubs, climbers and herbaceous plants, while willows provide a perfect wildlife habitat. There are treasured plants such as chionocloa rubra, pieris, Chinese tree peonies, and a selection of old-fashioned shrub roses, lilies, hellebores, grasses from New Zealand etc.

Directions: Head north on the A970 from Lerwick then west on the A971 at Tingwall. At Sandness, follow the road to Norby, turn right at the Methodist Church, 'Burnside' at end of road.

Disabled Access:
None

Opening Times:
1 January - 31 December
Dawn - Dusk
If no one is in please feel free to wander around

Admission:
£3.00

Charities:
Survival International receives 40%, the net remaining to SG Beneficiaries

DUMFRIESSHIRE

Scotland's Gardens 2015 Guidebook is sponsored by **INVESTEC WEALTH & INVESTMENT**

District Organiser

Mrs Sarah Landale	Dalswinton House, Dalswinton, Auldgirth DG2 0XZ

Area Organisers

Mrs Fiona Bell-Irving	Bankside, Kettleholm, Lockerbie DG11 1BY
Mrs Liz Mitchell	Drumpark, Irongray, Dumfriesshire DG2 9TX

Treasurer

Mr Harold Jack	The Clachan, Newtonairds DG2 0JL

Gardens open on a specific date

Craig, Langholm	Sunday 15 February	12:00pm	-	4:00pm
Portrack House, Holywood	Sunday 3 May	12:00pm	-	5:00pm
Peilton, Moniaive	Friday 8 May	12:00pm	-	4:00pm
Capenoch, Thornhill	Sunday 10 May	2:00pm	-	5:00pm
Peilton, Moniaive	Friday 15 May	12:00pm	-	4:00pm
Dalswinton House, Dalswinton	Sunday 17 May	2:00pm	-	5:00pm
Dabton, Thornhill	Sunday 24 May	2:00pm	-	5:00pm
Leap Cottage, West Cluden	Sunday 31 May	2:00pm	-	5:00pm
Newtonairds Lodge, Newtonairds	Sunday 7 June	2:00pm	-	5:00pm
Westerhall, Langholm	Sunday 7 June	2:00pm	-	5:00pm
Dunesslin, Dunscore	Sunday 14 June	2:00pm	-	5:00pm
Cowhill Tower, Holywood	Sunday 21 June	2:00pm	-	5:00pm
Westwater Farm, Langholm	Sunday 19 July	12:00pm	-	5:00pm

Gardens open regularly

Newtonairds Lodge, Newtonairds	7 May - 13 August	10:00am	-	6:00pm

Key to symbols

	New in 2015		Homemade teas		Accommodation
	Teas		Dogs on a lead allowed		Plant stall
	Cream teas		Wheelchair access		Scottish Snowdrop Festival

CAPENOCH
Penpont, Thornhill DG3 4TZ
Mr and Mrs Robert Gladstone

There are rare trees throughout the grounds and the main garden is the remnants of the garden laid out in Victorian times. There is a pretty little raised knot garden called the Italian garden and a lovely old Victorian conservatory. Parking is available at the house but you may prefer to park in Penpont Village and walk up the drive to Capenoch, as there are lovely bluebells and wild flowers in the oak woods on either side of the drive.

Other Details: Homemade teas are available in Penpoint Tearoom (one mile from the house). There is a good variety of plants for sale in the old Walled Garden where Morag has the garden centre.

Directions: Take the A702 west from Thornhill, drive through Penpont and the entrance to the house is at the lodge on the left hand side, just at the speed restriction sign.

Disabled Access:
Partial

Opening Times:
Sunday 10 May
2:00pm - 5:00pm
for bluebells

Admission:
£4.00, children £0.50

Charities:
The Jo Walters Trust receives 40%, the net remaining to SG Beneficiaries

COWHILL TOWER
Holywood DG2 0RL
Mr and Mrs P Weatherall T: 01387 720304

This is an interesting walled garden. There are topiary animals, birds and figures and a beautiful woodland walk. Splendid views can be seen from the lawn right down the Nith valley. There are also a variety of statues from the Far East.

Directions: Holywood 1½ miles off A76, five miles north of Dumfries.

Disabled Access:
Partial

Opening Times:
Sunday 21 June
2:00pm - 5:00pm

Admission:
£4.00, children £0.50

Charities:
Maggie's Cancer Caring Centres receives 40%, the net remaining to SG Beneficiaries

CRAIG
Langholm DG13 0NZ
Mr and Mrs Neil Ewart T: 013873 70230
E: nmlewart@googlemail.com

Craig snowdrops have evolved over the last 30 or so years. First around the house and policies, a large variety have been planted with a varied flowering season stretching from the start of January until April and peaking mid-February. Large drifts of Leucojum Vernum (Winter Snowflake) have started to naturalise here and, secondly, along the riverbank, a variety of snowdrops swept down by the river have naturalised in the adjacent woodland, known as the Snowdrop Walk.

Other Details: Each walk takes about 20 minutes. Wellies are essential. Wheelchair access down by the river is not possible but easier around the house. Teas will be available in the nearby Bentpath Village Hall.

Directions: Craig is three miles from Langholm on the B709 towards Eskdalemuir. The Village Hall is at Bentpath, one mile further towards Eskdalemuir.

Disabled Access:
Partial

Opening Times:
Sunday 15 February
12:00pm - 4:00pm
for the Snowdrop Festival

Admission:
£4.00, children £0.50

Charities:
Kirkandrews Church receives 40%, the net remaining to SG Beneficiaries

DABTON
Thornhill DG3 5AR
The Duke and Duchess of Buccleuch T: 01848 330467
E: phunter@buccleuch.com

19th century house built of pink stone. Extensive walled garden. Ninety-five yards long herbaceous border, roses, island beds and shrubs, ponds with azaleas and primulas, woodland walk, vegetable garden and greenhouses.

Directions: Entrance off A76 between Thornhill and Carronbridge.

Disabled Access:
Partial

Opening Times:
Sunday 24 May
2:00pm - 5:00pm

Admission:
£4.00, children free

Charities:
Legion Scotland receives 40%, the net remaining to SG Beneficiaries

DALSWINTON HOUSE
Dalswinton DG2 0XZ
Mr and Mrs Peter Landale T: 01387 740220

Late 18th century house sits on top of a hill surrounded by herbaceous beds and well established shrubs, including rhododendrons and azaleas overlooking the loch. Attractive walks through woods and around the loch. It was here that the first steamboat in Britain made its maiden voyage in 1788 and there is a life-size model beside the water to commemorate this. Over the past year, there has been much clearing and development work around the loch, which has opened up the views considerably.

Other Details: A recently established small but very good plant centre is now in the old walled garden.

Directions: Seven miles north of Dumfries off A76.

Disabled Access:
Partial

Opening Times:
Sunday 17 May
2:00pm - 5:00pm

Admission:
£4.00, children £0.50

Charities:
Kirkmahoe Parish Church receives 40%, the net remaining to SG Beneficiaries

DUNESSLIN
Dunscore DG2 0UR
Iain and Zara Milligan T: 01387 820345

Set in the hills with good views, the principal garden consists of a series of connecting rooms filled with herbaceous plants. There is a substantial rock garden with alpines and unusual plants and a hill walk to view three cairns by Andy Goldsworthy.

Directions: From Dunscore, follow the road to Corsock. Approximately 1½ miles further on, turn right at the post box, still on the road to Corsock and at small crossroads ½ mile on, turn left.

Disabled Access:
None

Opening Times:
Sunday 14 June
2:00pm - 5:00pm

Admission:
£4.00

Charities:
Alzheimer Scotland receives 40%, the net remaining to SG Beneficiaries

LEAP COTTAGE
West Cluden, Dumfries DG2 9UW
Mr Raymond Nelson
E: nelson_nomad@yahoo.com.au

Leap Cottage sits on the site of a former mill dating back to the 1600s and is situated in the most amazing setting, right down on the banks of the Cluden Water, a tributary of the the River Nith with wonderful views of the river's twists and turns. The tiny and enchanting garden is filled to the brim with a variety of plants and colour and there is a lovely walk through the trees right down to the river's edge, just beside the cottage.

Other Details: Access and parking to the cottage is awkward and limited so parking is at the farm. Walk to T-Junction, turn right and keep going to end of the road. Walk about 150 yards.

Directions: Take A76 Dumfries /Thornhill Road. Turn left to Lochside Industrial Estate on outskirts of Dumfries. Follow Irongray Road, past all houses until barn on right. Turn in here and park and then follow the signs.

Disabled Access:
None

Opening Times:
Sunday 31 May
2:00pm - 5:00pm

Admission:
£3.00

Charities:
All proceeds to
SG Beneficiaries

NEWTONAIRDS LODGE
Newtonairds DG2 0JL
Mr and Mrs J Coutts
www.newtonairds-hostasandgarden.co.uk

An interesting 1.2 acre plantsman's garden punctuated with topiary, trees and shrubs, surrounding a 19th century listed baronial lodge. The National Collection is integrated with a further 150 other hosta varieties on a natural terraced wooded bank.

Other Details: National Plant Collection®: Hosta Plantaginea hybrids and cultivars. The plants, of which there is a great variety, are of exceptional quality and all grown and brought on in situ at Newtonairds Lodge.

Directions: From Dumfries take A76 north. At Holywood take B729 (Dunscore). After one mile turn left (Morrinton). After three miles red sandstone lodge is on right, behind black iron railings.

Disabled Access:
Partial

Opening Times:
Sunday 7 June
2:00pm - 5:00pm
7 May - 13 August
10:00am - 6:00pm
Thursdays only

Admission:
£4.00

Charities:
Peter Pan Moat Brae Trust receives 20%, Dumfries North West Free Meals Project receives 20%, the net remaining to SG Beneficiaries

---

PEILTON
Moniaive DG3 4HE
Mrs A Graham T: 01848 200363

This really very special and attractive woodland garden has a great variety of rhododendrons, shrubs and flowering trees. Peilton is of particular interest for the real plantsman.

Other Details: Teas are available in nearby Moniaive in the Green Tea Room.

Directions: Off A702 between Kirkland of Glencairn and Moniaive.

Disabled Access:
None

Opening Times:
Friday 8 May
12:00pm - 4:00pm
Friday 15 May
12:00pm - 4:00pm

Admission:
£4.00

Charities:
Progressive Supranuclear Palsy (PSP) receives 40%, the net remaining to SG Beneficiaries

PORTRACK HOUSE
Holywood DG2 0RW
Charles Jencks
www.charlesjencks.com

Original 18th century manor house with Victorian addition; octagonal folly library. Twisted undulating landforms and terraces designed by Charles Jencks as "The Garden of Cosmic Speculation"; lakes designed by Maggie Keswick; rhododendrons, large new greenhouse in a geometric kitchen garden of the Six Senses; Glengower Hill plantation and view; woodland walks with Nonsense Building (architect: James Stirling); Universe cascade and rail garden of the Scottish Worthies; interesting sculpture including that of DNA and newly completed Comet Bridge.

Other Details: There are no pre-sale tickets available.

Directions: Holywood one and a half miles off A76, five miles north of Dumfries.

Disabled Access:
Partial

Opening Times:
Sunday 3 May
12:00pm - 5:00pm

Admission:
£6.00

Charities:
Maggie's Cancer Caring Centres receives 40%, the net remaining to SG Beneficiaries

WESTERHALL
Bentpath, Langholm DG13 0NQ
Mrs Peter Buckley

An extensive collection of azaleas, rhododendrons, rare shrubs and mature trees set in a landscape of follies, sculpture and stunning vistas. The redesigned walled garden contains a glasshouse with some exotic plants which have been collected from around the world.

Other Details: Selling plants this year are Allan Clark, a Rhododendron Specialist and Helen Knowles from Tinnisburn Nursery and award winner at many shows.

Directions: From Langholm take B709 towards Eskdalemuir. After approximately five miles in village of Bentpath, turn right by white house. Go down through village, over small/narrow bridge and turn right by church. Carry on this road for approximately one mile. Parking at farm, signed.

Disabled Access:
Partial

Opening Times:
Sunday 7 June
2:00pm - 5:00pm

Admission:
£4.00, children free

Charities:
Westerkirk Parish Trust receives 40%, the net remaining to SG Beneficiaries

WESTWATER FARM
Langholm DG13 0LU
Mr and Mrs Charlie Clapperton T: 01387 381004

In a wonderful, remote and romantic setting, the interesting walled garden adjacent to the house has both herbaceous plants and shrubs. There is also a woodland garden with a variety of bamboos and interesting trees. Dotted around the house and steadings are some fabulous pots .

Other Details: The beautifully restored steadings around the house, house some very special donkeys amongst other farm animals.

Directions: Thirteen miles from Lockerbie on the B7068 Lockerbie to Langholm road (five miles from Langholm). Entrance is signed Westwater on the left coming from Lockerbie. Keep to left fork for house.

Disabled Access:
Partial

Opening Times:
Sunday 19 July
12:00pm - 5:00pm

Admission:
£4.00

Charities:
All proceeds to SG Beneficiaries

Garden locations

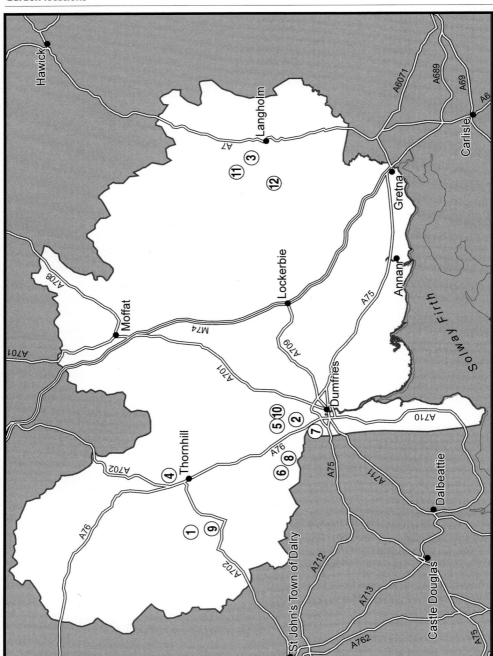

DUNBARTONSHIRE

Scotland's Gardens 2015 Guidebook is sponsored by **INVESTEC WEALTH & INVESTMENT**

District Organiser

Mrs Tricia Stewart	High Glenan, 24a Queen Street, Helensburgh G84 9LG

Area Organisers

Ms C Fennell	29 Oxhill Place, Dumbarton G82 4EX
Mrs J Goel	33 West Argyle Street, Helensburgh G84 8XR
Mrs M Greenwell	Avalon, Shore Road, Mambeg Garelochhead G84 0EN
Mrs R Lang	Ardchapel, Shandon, Helensburgh G84 8NP
Mrs R Macaulay	Denehard, Garelochhead G84 0EL
Mrs M Rogers	Station House, Station Road, Tarbet G83 7DA

Treasurer

Mrs K Murray	7 The Birches, Shandon, Helensburgh G84 8HN

Gardens open on a specific date

Kilarden, Rosneath	Sunday 26 April	2:00pm	- 5:00pm
Ross Priory, Gartocharn	Sunday 17 May	2:00pm	- 5:00pm
Brandon Grove with Milton Cottage, Helensburgh	Sunday 31 May	2:00pm	- 5:00pm
Milton Cottage with Brandon Grove, Helensburgh	Sunday 31 May	2:00pm	- 5:00pm
Geilston Garden, Cardross	Sunday 7 June	1:00pm	- 5:00pm
Glebeside House with Rowanan, Rhu	Sunday 2 August	2:00pm	- 5:00pm
Rowanan with Glebeside House, Rhu	Sunday 2 August	2:00pm	- 5:00pm

GARDEN PICTURES AND LOCAL MAPS ARE AVAILABLE ON OUR WEBSITE:
www.scotlandsgardens.org

DUNBARTONSHIRE

Gardens open regularly

Glenarn, Rhu	21 March - 21 September	Dawn - Dusk

Gardens open by arrangement

8 Laggary Park, Rhu	1 August - 30 September	01436 821314

Plant sales

Hill House Plant Sale, Helensburgh	Sunday 6 September	11:00am - 4:00pm

8 Laggary Park

Key to symbols

 New in 2015   Homemade teas   Accommodation

 Teas   Dogs on a lead allowed   Plant stall

 Cream teas   Wheelchair access   Scottish Snowdrop Festival

Garden locations

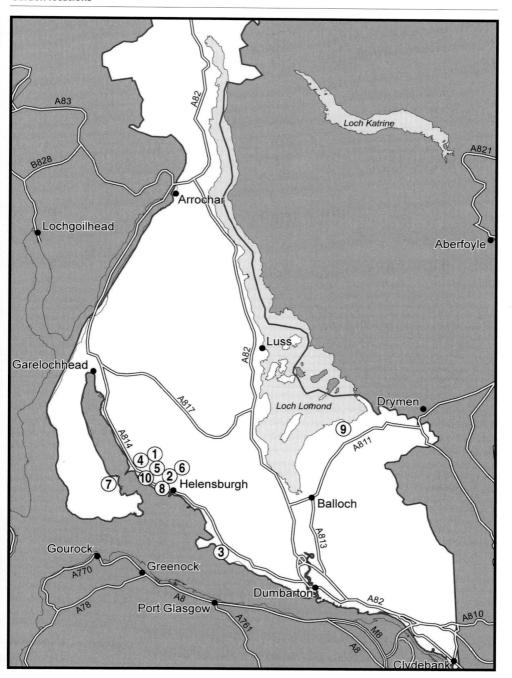

8 LAGGARY PARK
Rhu, Helensburgh G84 8LY
Susan Miller T: 01436 821314
E: susan.miller17@btinternet.com

This half acre garden features a collection of over 80 hydrangea species and cultivars, which will be at their best at this time. Also flowering shrubs and specimen trees. Clematis arbour, pergola and mixed beds featuring penstemons, salvias, lobelias, agastache and violas, all offering late summer colour.

Other Details: Hydrangeas will be offered for sale.

Directions: Take A814 shore road from Helensburgh to Rhu Marina. Turn right into Pier Road and take second turn right (signposted) into Laggary Park and bear right. Please park in Pier Road.

Disabled Access:
Partial

Opening Times:
By arrangement
1 August - 30 September

Admission:
£4.00

Charities:
SSPCA receives 40%, the net remaining to SG Beneficiaries

BRANDON GROVE WITH MILTON COTTAGE
119 West Princes Street, Helensburgh G84 8EX
Margery Osborne

Brandon Grove, one of the earliest farm houses (circa 1780), was formerly known as Shore Farm in the small fishing town of Helensburgh. Today its secluded south-facing walled garden is totally hidden from public view. Winding paths and stepping stones meander through flower beds and grassed areas. Mature trees and shrubs include a range of acers, rhododendrons, azaleas, camellias, hydrangea, a magnificent magnolia, an outstanding dogwood, various flowering cherries along with much more.

Directions: At Commodore Hotel on A814, turn into Glasgow Street and first left onto West Princes Street. Garden is opposite Helensburgh Tennis Club. Please park on West Princes Street.

Disabled Access:
Partial

Opening Times:
Sunday 31 May
2:00pm - 5:00pm

Admission:
£4.00 includes entrance to Milton Cottage Garden, children free

Charities:
St Andrew's Church Hall Development Fund receives 40%, the net remaining to SG Beneficiaries

GEILSTON GARDEN
Main Road, Cardross G82 5HD
The National Trust for Scotland T: 0844 4932219
E: jgough@nts.org.uk www.nts.org.uk

Geilston Garden has many attractive features including the walled garden with the herbaceous border providing summer colour, the tranquil woodland walks and a large working kitchen garden. This is the ideal season for viewing the Siberian Iris in flower along the Geilston Burn and the Japanese Azaleas. During the summer months, July to September, there is a range of fresh fruit and vegetables for sale from the large kitchen garden.

Other Details: There will be a plant stall selling Geilston-grown perennials together with some early produce to include rhubarb, spinach and asparagus. Teas and homebaking will also be available.

Directions: On the A814, one mile from Cardross towards Helensburgh.

Disabled Access:
Partial

Opening Times:
Sunday 7 June
1:00pm - 5:00pm

Admission:
£5.00, children under 12 free

Charities:
Donation to SG Beneficiaries

GLEBESIDE HOUSE WITH ROWANAN
Spy's Lane, Rhu G84 8RA
Mr and Mrs Peter Proctor

Traditional Scottish house built in 1834 with a third of an acre of ground. A small garden surrounds the house and comprises a natural rockery, shrubs at the rear, an old wash house recently renovated, laburnum arch and four or five "rooms" in the larger garden. To the front and side there are mixed herbaceous islands and borders, mature shrubs, lawn and greenhouse.

Other Details: Homemade teas available at Rowanan.

Directions: Take A814 from Helensburgh to Rhu Marina. Turn right into Pier Road. Spy's Lane is up the hill on the left. Park on Pier Road.

Disabled Access:
Partial

Opening Times:
Sunday 2 August
2:00pm - 5:00pm

Admission:
£4.00, includes Rowanan,
children free

Charities:
Motor Neurone Disease
Scotland receives 20%, Riding
for the Disabled receives
20%, the net remaining to
SG Beneficiaries

GLENARN
Glenarn Road, Rhu, Helensburgh G84 8LL
Michael and Sue Thornley T: 01436 820493
E: masthome@btinternet.com www.gardens-of-argyll.co.uk

Glenarn survives as a complete example of a ten acre garden which spans from 1850 to the present day. There are winding paths through glens under a canopy of oak and lime, sunlit open spaces, a vegetable garden with beehives, and a rock garden with views over the Gareloch. It is famous for its collection of rare and tender rhododendrons but horticulturally there is much more besides.

Other Details: Catering for groups by prior arrangement.

Directions: On A814, two miles north of Helensburgh, up Pier Road. Cars to be left at gate unless passengers are infirm.

Disabled Access:
Partial

Opening Times:
21 March - 21 September
Dawn - Dusk

Admission:
£4.00

Charities:
Donation to SG Beneficiaries

HILL HOUSE PLANT SALE
Helensburgh G84 9AJ
The National Trust for Scotland/SG T: 01436 673900
E: gsmith@nts.org.uk www.nts.org.uk

The Plant Sale is held in the garden of The Hill House which has fine views over the Clyde estuary and is considered Charles Rennie Mackintosh's domestic masterpiece. The gardens continue to be restored to the patron's planting scheme with many features that reflect Mackintosh's design. The sale includes a wide selection of nursery grown perennials and locally grown trees, shrubs, herbaceous, alpine and house plants.

Other Details: Teas will be served inside Hill House and the garden will also be open.

Directions: Follow signs to The Hill House.

Disabled Access:
Full

Opening Times:
Sunday 6 September
11:00am - 4:00pm
Admission:
Free

Charities:
All proceeds to
SG Beneficiaries

KILARDEN
Rosneath G84 0PU
Jimmy and Carol Rowe

Sheltered hilly ten acre woodland with notable collection of species and hybrid rhododendrons gathered over a period of fifty years by the late Neil and Joyce Rutherford as seen on the "Beechgrove Garden".

Other Details: Homemade teas served in the church hall. The church will be open; organ music.

Directions: A quarter of a mile from Rosneath off B833.

Disabled Access:
Partial

Opening Times:
Sunday 26 April
2:00pm - 5:00pm

Admission:
£3.00, children free

Charities:
Friends of St Modan's
receives 40%, the net
remaining to SG Beneficiaries

GLORIOUS GARDENS RHODODENDRON FESTIVAL 2015

The Glorious Gardens of Argyll and Bute are hosting the first Festival of Rhododendrons in April and May 2015.

Details of special events in all gardens and others close by are on **www.gardens-of-argyll.co.uk** and are available from any of the twenty gardens, most of which participate in Scotland's Gardens programme.

MILTON COTTAGE WITH BRANDON GROVE
125 West Princes Street, Helensburgh G84 8EX
Michael & Mary Louden

The garden has been created by Michael and Mary Louden over the past 28 years. Located on a raised beach, 200 yards from the Clyde estuary, it benefits from the Gulf Stream. This ⅓ to ½ acre has vegetables, fruit, herbaceous and unusual shrubs. It is walled on two sides with a hedge on the third. Split into "rooms", there are rare trees such as Cersis Silliquastrum (Judas Tree), Magnolia Wilsonii, Eucryphia Nymanensis, Saphora Tetraptera and lovely tree peonies.

Directions: At Commodore Hotel on the A814, turn into Glasgow Street and first left onto West Princes Street. Garden is opposite the Helensburgh Tennis Club. Please park on West Princes Street.

Disabled Access:
Partial

Opening Times:
Sunday 31 May
2:00pm - 5:00pm

Admission:
£4.00 includes entry to Brandon Grove, children free

Charities:
St Andrew's Church Hall Development Fund receives 40%, the net remaining to SG Beneficiaries

---

ROSS PRIORY
Gartocharn G83 8NL
University of Strathclyde

An 1812 Gothic addition by James Gillespie Graham to the 1693 house with glorious views over Loch Lomond. A good selection of rhododendrons, azaleas, selected shrubs and trees can be seen along with an extensive walled garden with glasshouses, pergola and ornamental plantings. There is a family burial ground as well as garden trails.

Other Details: Teas are served in the house. Please note that the house is not open to view. There is also a putting green.

Directions: Gartocharn 1½ miles off A811. Bus: Balloch to Gartocharn leaves Balloch at 1:00pm and 3:00pm.

Disabled Access:
Partial

Opening Times:
Sunday 17 May
2:00pm - 5:00pm

Admission:
£5.00, children under 12 free

Charities:
CHAS receives 40%, the net remaining to SG Beneficiaries

ROWANAN WITH GLEBESIDE HOUSE
Pier Road, Rhu G84 8LH
Mrs Patricia Buchanan

A sheltered south facing garden sensitively created by the present owner who, in 2005, built a modern home in the grounds of her former property where in the 1920s Sir James Guthrie, artist, lived in retirement. There are stunning views across the Clyde Estuary. The two acre garden has mature trees and shrubs, lawns, mixed borders and walls clothed in wisteria and clematis. A fine terrace with extensive raised beds has colour through the seasons. Beautiful container planting.

Directions: Take A814 shore road from Helensburgh to Rhu Marina. Turn right into Pier Road. Rowanan is 300 yards uphill on left. Please park on Pier Road.

Disabled Access:
Partial

Opening Times:
Sunday 2 August
2:00pm - 5:00pm

Admission:
£4.00 includes Glebeside House, children free

Charities:
Motor Neurone Disease Scotland receives 20%, Riding for the Disabled receives 20%, the net remaining to SG Beneficiaries

EAST LOTHIAN

District Organiser

Frank Kirwan	Humbie Dean, Humbie, East Lothian EH36 5PW

Area Organisers

Bill Alder	Granary House, Kippielaw, Haddington EH41 4PY
Simon Edington	Meadowside Cottage, Strathearn Road, North Berwick EH39 5BZ
Mark Hedderwick	Gifford Bank, Gifford EH41 4JE
Christian Lindsay	Kirkland, Whittingehame, East Lothian EH41 4QA
Julie Parker	Steading Cottage, Stevenson, Haddington EH41 4PU
Judy Riley	The Old Kitchen, Tyninghame House, Tyninghame EH42 1XW
Beryl McNaughton	Macplants Berrybank Nursery, 5 Boggs Holdings, Pencaitland EH34 5BA
June Tainsch	Amisfield Walled Garden, Haddington EH41 3TE

Treasurer

Mike Traynor	Symmar's Cottage, Humbie EH36 5PA

Gardens open on a specific date

Shepherd House, Inveresk	Saturday 21 February	11:00am	-	4:00pm
Shepherd House, Inveresk	Sunday 22 February	11:00am	-	4:00pm
Winton House, Pencaitland	Sunday 19 April	12:00pm	-	4:30pm
Shepherd House, Inveresk	Saturday 25 April	11:00am	-	4:00pm
Shepherd House, Inveresk	Sunday 26 April	11:00am	-	4:00pm
Tyninghame House and The Walled Garden, Dunbar	Sunday 10 May	1:00pm	-	5:00pm
Broadwoodside, Gifford	Saturday 16 May	2:00pm	-	6:00pm
Humbie Garden Circle, Humbie	Wednesday 20 May	2:00pm	-	6:00pm
Belhaven Hill School, Dunbar	Sunday 24 May	2:00pm	-	5:00pm
Belhaven House, Dunbar	Sunday 24 May	2:00pm	-	5:00pm
St Mary's Pleasance, Haddington	Mon to Fri 1 to 5 June	9:00am	-	5:00pm
Humbie Garden Circle, Humbie	Wednesday 3 June	2:00pm	-	6:00pm
Hopefield, Gladsmuir	Sunday 7 June	2:00pm	-	6:00pm
St Mary's Pleasance, Haddington	Mon to Fri 8 to 12 June	9:00am	-	5:00pm
Humbie Garden Circle, Humbie	Wednesday 17 June	2:00pm	-	6:00pm
Amisfield Walled Garden, Haddington	Sunday 21 June	2:00pm	-	5:00pm
Tyninghame House and The Walled Garden, Dunbar	Sunday 28 June	1:00pm	-	5:00pm

EAST LOTHIAN

Gardens open regularly

Inwood, Carberry, Musselburgh	1 May - 30 September Tuesdays and Thursdays	2:00pm - 5:00pm
Shepherd House, Inveresk, Musselburgh	10 February to 26 February and 14 April - 9 July Tuesdays and Thursdays	2:00pm - 4:00pm

The Walled Garden, Tyninghame © Ray Cox

Key to symbols

	New in 2015		Homemade teas		Accommodation
	Teas		Dogs on a lead allowed		Plant stall
	Cream teas		Wheelchair access		Scottish Snowdrop Festival

Garden locations

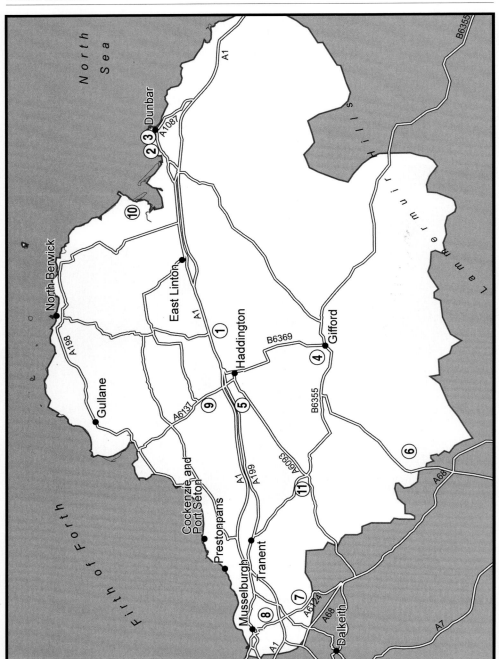

AMISFIELD WALLED GARDEN
Haddington EH41 4PU
Amisfield Preservation Trust
www.amisfield.org.uk

18th century walled garden, abandoned for many years. The garden, which has an area of approximately eight acres, is completely enclosed by 16 foot high walls of dressed stone. Each corner features a stone pavilion, all of which the domed roofs have been lost. Over the last five years, herbaceous borders, vegetable plots and fruit trees have been planted and new paths laid. A hornbeam walk was planted in 2010 and is maturing well. Apple trees were planted on the diagonal pathways and small orchards have been introduced within the last two years, and willow beds planted in the Winter Garden. A wild flower meadow has been introduced as a further step in our bio-diversity plan. Archaeologists are starting to uncover the former 'pinery vinery' glasshouse.

Directions: Follow the A199 from Haddington; turn south about one mile east of Haddington at the Stevenson/Hailes Castle junction. Garden is on right just after the bridge over the River Tyne.

Disabled Access:
Full

Opening Times:
Sunday 21 June
2:00pm - 5:00pm

Admission:
£4.00

Charities:
Amisfield Preservation Trust receives 40%, the net remaining to SG Beneficiaries

BELHAVEN HILL SCHOOL WITH BELHAVEN HOUSE
Belhaven Road, Dunbar EH42 1NN
Mr Innes MacAskill

Originally called Winterfield House, the School has retained the formal garden in front of the walled garden which is accessed through an ornate gate and archway and is laid to lawn with box-edged borders, some containing wild flowers. A gate from the playing field leads to the Belhaven House garden.

Directions: Approaching Dunbar from A1 on A1087 Belhaven House is opposite Brewery Lane on the junction with Duke Street and the school entrance is a further 300 yards past a high stone wall.

Disabled Access:
Partial

Opening Times:
Sunday 24 May
2:00pm - 5:00pm

Admission:
£4.00.children under 12 free
(includes admission to
Belhaven House)

Charities:
East Lothian Special Needs Playscheme receives 40%, the net remaining to SG Beneficiaries

BELHAVEN HOUSE WITH BELHAVEN HILL SCHOOL
Belhaven Road, Dunbar EH42 1NN
Mr and Mrs Jon Bruneau

Approached from the School playing field Belhaven House has four acres of formal Georgian gardens, walled vegetable and fruit garden and woodland. Owned for a while by Sir George Taylor, a former director of Kew gardens and famous botanist.

Other Details: Champion Trees: Arbutus Unedo, Davidia Involucrata, Eucryphia Nymansensis and more. Teas available at the school.

Directions: Approaching Dunbar from A1 on A1087 Belhaven House is opposite Brewery Lane on the junction with Duke Street.

Disabled Access:
Partial

Opening Times:
Sunday 24 May
2:00pm - 5:00pm

Admission:
£4.00 children under 12 free
(includes entry to Belhaven
Hill School)

Charities:
East Lothian Special Needs Play Schemes receives 40%, the net remaining to SG Beneficiaries

Belhaven House

 BROADWOODSIDE
Gifford EH41 4JQ
Anna and Robert Dalrymple
www.broadwoodside.co.uk

The garden at Broadwoodside is planted in and around a farm steading, rescued from dereliction. Two sheltered courtyards are encircled by the old buildings; outside the planting extends into the surrounding farmland and woods on an ambitious scale. "This is one of Scotland's finest contemporary private gardens, with excellent structure, imaginative use of objects, and some of the most eye-catching planting in Scotland … who could ask for more." Scotland for Gardeners, 2014

Directions: On B6355 going out of Gifford towards Pencaitland, at the Golf Course junction.

Disabled Access:
Partial

Opening Times:
Saturday 16 May
2:00pm - 6:00pm

Admission:
£5.00, children free

Charities:
Cancer Research Scotland
receives 40%, the net
remaining to SG Beneficiaries

 HOPEFIELD
Gladsmuir EH33 2AL
Kate & Teddy Tulloch

Hopefield is a pantiled farmhouse built around a courtyard, where the walls feature rambling roses, plum trees and wisteria. Herbaceous borders by the house are enclosed with pergolas covered with roses, clematis and wisteria. The garden, where heavy clay is a huge challenge, has been extended over 18 years with 'rooms' created from reclaimed fields. A lochan, made ten years ago and approached through standard Elaeagnus mop heads and a lime walk, has been planted to encourage wildlife, creating a wonderful backdrop to the house and garden and stunning views over the Lammermuirs.

Other Details: Cream teas will be provided in the barn by Save the Children.

Directions: Turn south off the A199 at Gladsmuir, signposted for Hopefield and Butterdean Wood. Hopefield is the second house on the left.

Disabled Access:
Partial

Opening Times:
Sunday 7 June
2:00pm - 6:00pm

Admission:
£5.00, children free

Charities:
Save the Children receives
40%, the net remaining to
SG Beneficiaries

6 **HUMBIE GARDEN CIRCLE**
Humbie EH36 5PW
The Gardeners of Humbie T: 07768 996382
E: frank.kirwan@which.net

1. Stobshiel House (Mr Maxwell and Lady Sarah Ward)
A large garden to see for all seasons. Walled garden adjacent to the house,
box-edged borders filled with bulbs, roses and lavender beds. There is also a
rustic summerhouse, glasshouse, formal lily pond and castellated yew hedge.
The shrubbery has rhododendrons, azaleas and bulbs. Growing in the water and
woodland garden are meconopsis and primulas. Enjoy the beautiful woodland walks.
Other Details: Teas available. Plant stall. No dogs allowed. No disabled access.
Directions: One mile north east of Humbie off the B6368, signed Stobshiel.

2. Humbie Dean (Mr Frank Kirwan)
A two acre ornamental and woodland garden at 600 feet under single-handed
renovation and major extension since 2008 - tree clearance; creation of light and
access to the woodland; replanting; construction of paths, steps, and an elevated
walkway/bridge. A limited palette of plants with extensive primula, meconopsis
and spring bulbs; bluebell meadow; mature and recent azalea and rhododendron
planting.
Other Details: Plant stall. No dogs allowed. No disabled access.
Directions: Enter Humbie from A68, pass school and village hall on left then
immediately turn right into lane. Take second left.

3. Symmar's Cottage (Mike and Ann Traynor)
A fully enclosed southwest-facing garden extending to just over a third acre which
has been a work in progress over the past three years. The planting is informal,
featuring herbaceous borders providing flower and foliage interest throughout the
year. These borders also include a wide range of shrubs, ornamental trees, climbers
and spring bulbs. Early June normally sees many different species of Iris in flower.
Numerous seating areas have been created both to view the different planting areas
in the garden and to enjoy the open outlook over the East Lothian countryside.
Other Details: Dogs on lead allowed. Disabled access.
Directions: One mile north west of Humbie on the B6371.

4. Old Windymains Cottage (Nicola and John Bolton)
A semi-formal garden of just under an acre which, starting as a typical farm cottage
plot with a newly planted Scots Pine sapling to one side, has evolved and expanded
over the years. Having acquired a piece of the adjacent field and woodland (felling
22 of the by then large pines), creation of herbaceous and other beds, a pond, water
feature, and a summerhouse was commenced. There is a large area of lawn; a small
vegetable plot and a strawberry bed. Extensive views over some of East Lothian's
farmland give a spacious feel.
Other Details: Dogs on lead allowed. Disabled access.
Directions: One mile north west of Humbie on the B6371.

5. Lammerlaw House (Gina and John Rutherford)
Facing predominately south and extends to over an acre, with spectacular
uninterrupted views of the Lammermuir Hills. The garden steps down from the
house through parterre rose beds onto an extensive lawn, terminating at a large
pond. A deep shrubaceous border includes a large number of rhododendrons. The
southern and western flanks are laid out with evergreen shrubs along with coniferous
and deciduous trees at various stages of maturity. There is a patio backed by a
smaller but no less interesting perennial border adjacent to the house.
Other Details: Dogs on lead allowed. Disabled access.
Directions: One mile north west of Humbie on the B6371.

Additional Details: Groups of 10 or more must pre-book.

See also page 37 of this book.

Disabled Access:
Partial

Opening Times:
Wednesday 20 May
2:00pm - 6:00pm
Wednesday 3 June
2:00pm - 6:00pm
Wednesday 17 June
2:00pm - 6:00pm

Admission:
£15.00 for unlimited access
to all five gardens over the
three days.
£5.00 per garden for day
tickets to Stobshiel House or
Humbie Dean
£5.00 for a day ticket to
the combined three gardens
at Symmar's Cottage, Old
Windymains Cottage and
Lammerlaw House

Charities:
Circle receives 40%, the net
remaining to SG Beneficiaries

7 INWOOD
Carberry, Musselburgh EH21 8PZ
Mr and Mrs I Morrison T: 0131 665 4550
E: lindsay@inwoodgarden.com www.inwoodgarden.com

Created from scratch, Inwood Garden sits snugly around the house, with a fine cloud pruned Chamaecyparis pisifera Boulevard at the entrance and a sheltering backdrop of mature woodland. This acre enthusiast's garden is packed with interesting plants in generously proportioned island beds. It's worth a visit at any time during the season with massed tulips and rhododendrons in spring, rambling roses and clematis in high summer and hydrangeas and late flowering perennials in early autumn. Greenhouses with begonias and streptocarpus collections and a pond invite further exploration. An "RHS Partner Garden".

Other Details: Teas served in the tearoom. Toilet available.

Directions: From the A1 take A6094 exit signed Wallyford and Dalkeith. At roundabout turn left on A6124. Continue uphill for 1½ miles.

Disabled Access:
Partial

Opening Times:
1 May - 31 August
2:00pm - 5:00pm
Tuesdays and Thursdays
Groups welcome by prior
arrangement

Admission:
£4.00, children free

Charities:
Donation to SG Beneficiaries

8 SHEPHERD HOUSE
Inveresk, Musselburgh EH21 7TH
Sir Charles and Lady Fraser T: 0131 665 2570
E: annfraser@talktalk.net www.shepherdhousegarden.co.uk

Shepherd House and its one acre garden form a walled triangle in the middle of the 18th century village of Inveresk. The main garden is to the rear of the house where the formality of the front garden is continued with a herb parterre and two symmetrical potagers. A formal rill runs the length of the garden, beneath a series of rose and clematis arches and connects the two ponds. The snowdrops are mainly grown in beds and borders. However, there is a growing collection of "specialist snowdrops" around 50 different cultivars some of which will be displayed in our "Snowdrop Theatre".

An addition to the garden in 2013 was a Shell House, designed by Lachie Stewart. Charles and Ann have also published a book 'Shepherd House Garden' which is for sale at Open Days, by application to Shepherd House or the web site.

Other Details: Prints and cards by Ann Fraser will be on sale at weekend openings. Some plants for sale on 21 and 22 February.

Directions: Near Musselburgh. From A1 take A6094 exit signed Wallyford and Dalkeith and follow signs to Inveresk.

Disabled Access:
Partial

Opening Times:
Saturday & Sunday
21 - 22 February
11:00am - 4:00pm
for the Snowdrop Festival
Saturday & Sunday
25 - 26 April
11:00am - 4:00pm
Tuesdays and Thursday
10 February - 26 February
and 14 April - 9 July
2:00pm - 4:00pm

Admission:
£4.00, children free via our
honesty box

Charities:
The Teapot Trust receives
40%, the net remaining to SG
Beneficiaries

ST MARY'S PLEASANCE
28 Sidegate, Haddington EH41 4BO
Haddington Garden Trust

Behind Haddington House, which dates from 1648, lies a Jacobean garden which was created in the 1970s with trees, shrubs and plants known to have been in cultivation in Scotland in the 17th century. The area has a range of features common at that time including a mount and a sunken garden. Most spectacular at the beginning of June is the long walkway of pleached Laburnum which will be in full flower. The restoration of the garden by the Trust is now well under way with the rose beds recently replanted.

Other Details: There will be a conducted tour of the garden on each day at 2.00pm. The garden opening is one of the events of the final day of the annual Haddington Festival.

Directions: From the centre of Haddington take the B6368 for Gifford. The gated entrance to the garden is beside Haddington House. It adjoins St Mary's Churchyard.

Disabled Access:
Full

Opening Times:
Monday to Friday
1 June to 5 June
and 8 June to 12 June
9:00am - 5:00pm

Admission:
By donation

Charities:
The Haddington Garden Trust receives 40%, the net remaining to SG Beneficiaries

---

TYNINGHAME HOUSE AND THE WALLED GARDEN
Dunbar EH42 1XW
Tyninghame Gardens Ltd and Mrs C.Gwyn

Splendid 17th century pink sandstone Scottish baronial house, remodelled in 1829 by William Burn, rises out of a sea of plants. The gardens include herbaceous border, formal rose garden, Lady Haddington's Secret Garden with old fashioned roses and an extensive "wilderness" spring garden with magnificent rhododendrons, azaleas, flowering trees and bulbs. Grounds also include a one mile beech avenue to the sea. The formal walled garden combines the lawn, sculpture and yew hedges, an "apple walk", extensive herbaceous planting including roses and peonies with an informal arboretum. The Romanesque ruin of St Baldred's Church commands views across the Tyne Estuary and Lammermuir Hills. Tyninghame has been awarded 'Outstanding' for every category in the Inventory of Gardens and Designed Landscapes of Scotland.

Directions: Gates on A198 at Tyninghame Village.

Disabled Access:
Full

Opening Times:
Sunday 10 May
1:00pm - 5:00pm
Sunday 28 June
1:00pm - 5:00pm

Admission:
£5.00, children free

Charities:
Leuchie House receives 40% 10th May opening,
The Project Trust receives 40% 28th June opening;
the net remaining to SG Beneficiaries

WINTON HOUSE
Pencaitland EH34 5AT
Sir Francis Ogilvy Winton Trust T: 01875 340222
www.wintonhouse.co.uk

The gardens continue to develop and improve. In addition to the natural areas around Sir David's Loch and the Dell, extensive mixed borders are taking shape for the terrace borders and walled garden. In spring a glorious covering of daffodils makes way for cherry and apple blossoms. Enjoy an informative tour of this historic house and walk off delicious lunches and home baking around the estate.

Directions: Entrance off B6355 Tranent/Pencaitland Road.

Disabled Access:
Full

Opening Times:
Sunday 19 April
12:00pm - 4:30pm

Admission:
£4.00
Guided House Tours
£5.00/£3.00, children under 10 free

Charities:
Bethany Christian Trust receives 40%, the net remaining to SG Beneficiaries

EDINBURGH & WEST LOTHIAN

Scotland's Gardens 2015 Guidebook is sponsored by **INVESTEC WEALTH & INVESTMENT**

District Organiser

Victoria Reid Thomas	Riccarton Mains Farmhouse, Currie EH14 4AR

Area Organisers

Nicky Lowe	2/17 Powderhall Rigg, Edinburgh EH7 4GA
Michael Pearson	42 Pentland Avenue, Edinburgh EH13 0HY
Caroline Pearson	42 Pentland Avenue, Edinburgh EH13 0HY

Treasurer

Charles Welwood	Kirknewton House, Kirknewton EH27 8DA

Gardens open on a specific date

61 Fountainhall Road, Edinburgh	Sunday 5 April	2:00pm	-	5:00pm
61 Fountainhall Road, Edinburgh	Sunday 12 April	2:00pm	-	5:00pm
Redcroft, Edinburgh	Sunday 19 April	2:00pm	-	5:00pm
Gilmour Road Gardens, Edinburgh	Sunday 26 April	2:00pm	-	5:00pm
41 Hermitage Gardens, Edinburgh	Saturday 2 May	2:00pm	-	5:00pm
41 Hermitage Gardens, Edinburgh	Sunday 3 May	2:00pm	-	5:00pm
Dean Gardens, Edinburgh	Sunday 10 May	2:00pm	-	5:00pm
101 Greenbank Crescent, Edinburgh	Sunday 17 May	2:00pm	-	5:00pm
61 Fountainhall Road, Edinburgh	Sunday 17 May	2:00pm	-	5:00pm
Redcroft, Edinburgh	Sunday 17 May	2:00pm	-	5:00pm
Dr Neil's Garden, Duddingston Village	Saturday 23 May	2:00pm	-	5:00pm
20 Blackford Road, Edinburgh	Sunday 24 May	2:00pm	-	5:00pm
61 Fountainhall Road, Edinburgh	Sunday 24 May	2:00pm	-	5:00pm
Dr Neil's Garden, Duddingston Village	Sunday 24 May	2:00pm	-	5:00pm
The Glasshouses at the Royal Botanic Garden Edinburgh	Sunday 7 June	10:00am	-	5:30pm
Rocheid Garden, Edinburgh	Saturday 13 June	2:00pm	-	6:00pm
61 Fountainhall Road, Edinburgh	Sunday 21 June	2:00pm	-	5:00pm
Merchiston Cottage, Edinburgh	Sunday 21 June	2:00pm	-	5:00pm
Hunter's Tryst, Edinburgh	Sunday 19 July	2:00pm	-	5:00pm
45 Northfield Crescent, Bathgate	Saturday 25 July	2:00pm	-	5:00pm
45 Northfield Crescent, Bathgate	Sunday 26 July	2:00pm	-	5:00pm
61 Fountainhall Road, Edinburgh	Sunday 6 September	2:00pm	-	5:00pm
61 Fountainhall Road, Edinburgh	Sunday 13 September	2:00pm	-	5:00pm

EDINBURGH & WEST LOTHIAN

Gardens open regularly

Newliston, Kirkliston	1 May - 4 June except Mons and Tues	2:00pm - 6:00pm
The Glasshouses at the Royal Botanic Garden Edinburgh	2 January - 31 December Feb and Oct Jan, Nov and Dec	10:00am - 6:00pm 10:00am - 5:00pm 10:00am - 4:-00pm

Gardens open by arrangement

101 Greenbank Crescent, Edinburgh	1 March - 31 October	0131 447 6492
Hunter's Tryst, Edinburgh	On request	0131 477 2919
Redcroft, Edinburgh	8 - 30 September	0131 337 1747
Rocheid Garden, Edinburgh	On request	anna@afguest.co.uk

Merchiston Cottage

Key to symbols

New in 2015	Homemade teas	Accommodation
Teas	Dogs on a lead allowed	Plant stall
Cream teas	Wheelchair access	Scottish Snowdrop Festival

Garden locations

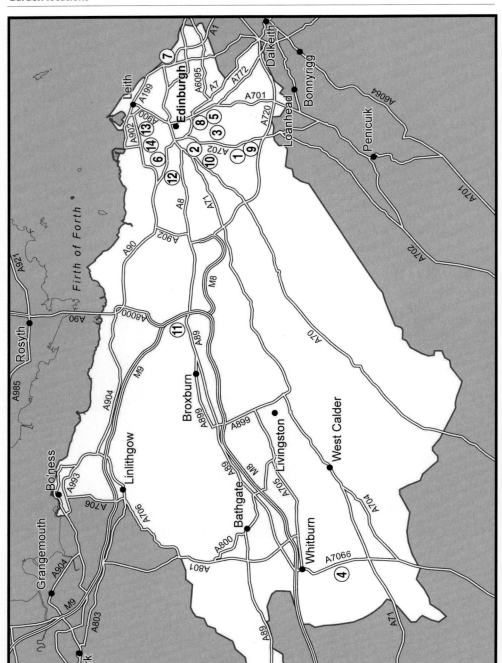

101 GREENBANK CRESCENT
Edinburgh EH10 5TA
Mr and Mrs Jerry and Christine Gregson T: 0131 447 6492
E: jerry_gregson@yahoo.co.uk

The front of the house is on a busy town bus route, but the back of the house is in the country. This is a terraced garden including a water feature, a variety of shrubs and trees, and wandering paths and steps with fine views of nearby hills and the neighbouring Braidburn Valley Park.

Directions: From Edinburgh centre, take A702 via Morningside Station. Turn right at Greenbank Church crossing. On 5 and 16 bus routes: ask for stop opposite Greenbank Row.

Disabled Access:
None

Opening Times:
Sunday 17 May
2:00pm - 5:00pm
Also by arrangement
1 March - 31 October

Admission:
£3.00

Charities:
Macmillan Cancer Support receives 40%, the net remaining to SG Beneficiaries

20 BLACKFORD ROAD
Edinburgh EH9 2DS
John and Tricia Wood

Victorian walled garden designed for all year colour, structure and interest. Mature trees and box-hedging with wide range of mixed beds of shrubs and herbaceous plants.

Directions: Buses: 41 (Monkwood Court / Kilgraston Road) 5 and 24 (Strathearn Road / Marchmont Road - three mins walk)

Disabled Access:
Full

Opening Times:
Sunday 24 May
2:00pm - 5:00pm

Admission:
£4.00

Charities:
Retired Greyhound Trust, Edinburgh Branch receives 40%, the net remaining to SG Beneficiaries

41 HERMITAGE GARDENS
Edinburgh EH10 6AZ
Dr and Mrs Tony Toft
E: toft41@hotmail.com

This relatively large city garden on the corner of Hermitage Gardens and Drive is at its best in spring with its rock garden, rhododendrons, camellias, acers, tulips and mature trees.

Other Details: Plant Stall run by Binny Plants. Parking is not restricted at weekends and there is disabled access from Hermitage Drive.

Directions: Buses 5, 11, 15, 16 and 23.

Disabled Access:
Partial

Opening Times:
Saturday 2 May
2:00pm - 5:00pm
Sunday 3 May
2:00pm - 5:00pm

Admission:
£4.00

Charities:
Chest Heart and Stroke receives 40%, the net remaining to SG Beneficiaries

45 NORTHFIELD CRESCENT
Longridge, Bathgate   EH47 8AL
Mr Jamie Robertson T: 07885 701642
E: jamierobertson04@hotmail.co.uk

A delightful garden with a wide variety of shrubs, herbaceous, bedding and dozens of dahlia plants. Large pond with a small waterfall and a colourful decked area with an attractive selection of bedding plants.
There is a vegetable patch with raised bed. A twelve foot by eight foot feature greenhouse showing award winning pot plants. The garden is the current holder of the Oatridge College award and has won several gold medals. The owner has won the "West Lothian Gardener of the Year" prize three times and is chairman of the Livingston and District Horticultural Society.

Directions: From A71: turn right after Breith at traffic lights, go about a mile and turn right into the Crescent. From Whitburn: take A706 Longridge Road to Longridge and last left into the Crescent.

Disabled Access:
Partial

Opening Times:
Saturday 25 July
2:00pm - 5:00pm
Sunday 26 July
2:00pm - 5:00pm

Admission:
£3.00

Charities:
World Cancer Research receives 40%, the net remaining to SG Beneficiaries

61 FOUNTAINHALL ROAD
Edinburgh EH9 2LH
Mrs Annemarie Hammond T: 0131 667 6146
E: froglady@blueyonder.co.uk   www.froglady.pwp.blueyonder.co.uk

Large walled town garden in which trees and shrubs form an architectural backdrop to a wide variety of flowering plants. The growing collection of hellebores and trilliums and a large variety of late blooming flowers provide interest from early March to late October. In addition, there are now several alpine beds which include a large collection of Sempervivums. Three ponds, with and without fish, have attracted a lively population of frogs.

Directions: See website for details.

Disabled Access:
Full

Opening Times:
Sundays 5 and 12 April
Sundays 17 and 24 May
Sunday 21 June
Sundays 6 and 13 September
2:00pm - 5:00pm

Admission:
£4.00

Charities:
Froglife receives 40%, the net remaining to SG Beneficiaries

DEAN GARDENS
Edinburgh EH4 1QE
Dean Gardens Management Committee
www.deangardens.org

Nine acres of semi-woodland garden with spring bulbs on the steep banks of the Water of Leith in central Edinburgh. Founded in the 1860s by local residents, the Dean Gardens contains part of the great structure of the Dean Bridge, a Thomas Telford masterpiece of 1835. Lawns, paths, trees, and shrubs with lovely views to the weir in the Dean Village and to the St Bernard's Well. There is also a children's play area.

Directions: Entrance at Ann Street or Eton Terrace.

Disabled Access:
Partial

Opening Times:
Sunday 10 May
2:00pm - 5:00pm

Admission:
£3.00, children free

Charities:
All proceeds to
SG Beneficiaries

DR NEIL'S GARDEN
Duddingston Village EH15 3PX
Dr Neil's Garden Trust
E: info@drneilsgarden.co.uk   www.drneilsgarden.co.uk

Wonderful secluded, landscaped garden on the lower slopes of Arthur's Seat including conifers, heathers, alpines, physic garden, herbaceous borders and ponds. Thompson's Tower with the Museum of Curling and beautiful views across Duddingston Loch.

Directions: Kirk car park on Duddingston Road West and then follow signposts through the Manse Garden.

Disabled Access:
Partial

Opening Times:
Saturday 23 May
2:00pm - 5:00pm
Sunday 24 May
2:00pm - 5:00pm

Admission:
£3.00

Charities:
Dr Neil's Garden Trust receives 40%, the net remaining to SG Beneficiaries

GILMOUR ROAD GARDENS
Gilmour Road EH16 5NB
Mrs Rae Renwick T: 0131 622 0728
E: rae_renwick@yahoo.com

Gilmour Road is a quiet residential street on the south side of Edinburgh, near Cameron Toll. There will be seven gardens open, ranging from small to large some being well established and others newly designed. In spring there is an excellent display of magnolias, rhododendrons and azaleas as well as an array of spring bulbs. One of our gardens hosts a volunteer from The Garden Sharing Scheme. Craigmillar Bowling Club, 34 Gilmour Road will be the focus for tickets, maps, teas and a plant sale.

Other Details: Teas £2.50.

Directions: Buses 3 and 31 from Princes Street and 7 and 8 from the top of Leith.

Disabled Access:
Partial

Opening Times:
Sunday 26 April
2:00pm - 5:00pm

Admission:
£5.00 for entrance to all seven gardens.

Charities:
Alzheimer Scotland receives 40%, the net remaining to SG Beneficiaries

HUNTER'S TRYST
95 Oxgangs Road, Edinburgh EH10 7BA
Jean Knox T: 0131 477 2919
E: jean.knox@blueyonder.co.uk

Well stocked, mature, medium-sized town garden comprising herbaceous/shrub beds, lawn, vegetables and fruit, water feature, seating areas and trees.

Directions: From Fairmilehead crossroads head down Oxgangs Road to Hunter's Tryst roundabout, last house on the left. Take buses 4, 5, 18 or 27. The bus stop is at Hunter's Tryst and the garden is opposite Hunter's Tryst.

Disabled Access:
Partial

Opening Times:
Sunday 19 July
2:00pm - 5:00pm
Also by arrangement on request

Admission:
£3.00

Charities:
Lothian Cat Rescue receives 40%, the net remaining to SG Beneficiaries

MERCHISTON COTTAGE
16 Colinton Road, Edinburgh EH10 5EL
Esther Mendelssohn

Small, walled, urban, wildlife friendly and organic bee keeper's garden. This eco friendly tapestry of wildlife habitats encourages birds, insects and frogs as pest control. In addition, the bees not only provide honey, but also act as pollinators for the many fruit plants including blueberries and mulberries. When possible, the bees can be seen at close quarters in an observation hive.

Directions: Near Holy Corner, opposite Watson's College School. Take Lothian buses 11 or 16.

Disabled Access:
Partial

Opening Times:
Sunday 21 June
2:00pm - 5:00pm

Admission:
£4.00

Charities:
Alyn Children's Hospital receives 40%, the net remaining to SG Beneficiaries

---

NEWLISTON
Kirkliston EH29 9EB
Mr and Mrs R C Maclachlan T: 0131 333 3231
E: mac@newliston.fsnet.co.uk

Eighteenth century designed landscape with good rhododendrons and azaleas. The house, designed by Robert Adam, is also open.

Directions: Four miles from Forth Road Bridge, entrance off B800.

Disabled Access:
Partial

Opening Times:
1 May - 4 June
2:00pm - 6:00pm
except Mondays and Tuesdays

Admission:
£3.00

Charities:
Children's Hospice Association receives 40%, the net remaining to SG Beneficiaries

---

REDCROFT
23 Murrayfield Road, Edinburgh EH12 6EP
James and Anna Buxton T: 0131 337 1747
E: annabuxtonb@aol.com

A walled garden surrounding an Arts and Crafts villa which provides an unexpected haven off a busy road. Planted and maintained with form and texture in mind. Open in April for daffodils, fritillaries and other early spring bulbs, blossom and rhododendrons; in May for a fine display of other flowering shrubs and tulips; and in September for autumn crocuses, nerines, dahlias and usually plentiful apples.

Other Details:
April - Fresh Start (Edinburgh) receives 40%.
May - New Caledonian Woodlands receives 40%.
September - Fresh Start (Edinburgh) and New Caledonian Woodlands both receive 20%.

Directions: Murrayfield Road runs north from Corstorphine Road to Ravelston Dykes. Easy parking, free. Buses 26, 31 and 38.

Disabled Access:
Full

Opening Times:
Sunday 19 April
and Sunday 17 May
2:00pm - 5:00pm
Also by arrangement 8 to 30 September

Admission:
£4.00

Charities:
Fresh Start Edinburgh & New Caledonian Woodlands share 40% , the net remaining to SG Beneficiaries. (See Other Details for breakdown)

ROCHEID GARDEN
Rocheid House, 20 Inverleith Terrace, Edinburgh EH3 5NS
Mrs Anna Guest
E: anna@afguest.co.uk

A young but rapidly maturing garden with an impressive diversity of plants, shrubs, trees, including native, exotic and rare, providing a tranquil retreat in the midst of the city. The transition from Eastern leads one through ribbons of bamboo and ornamental grasses into the Mediterranean. The natural swimming pond forms a dramatic focus and is surrounded by rich planting and overlooked by olive trees. The planted tunnel leads to the woodland by the river. Mature trees above an exciting variety of planting, creating a mosaic of colour, diversity and interest. Award-winning compost shed with a roof creating waves of ornamental grasses.

Other Details: Teas, weather permitting.

Directions: The garden is on the southern side of the Royal Botanic Garden, Edinburgh.

Disabled Access:
Partial

Opening Times:
Saturday 13 June
2:00pm - 6:00pm
Also by arrangement on request for groups only

Admission:
£4.50

Charities:
Alzheimer Scotland receives 40%, the net remaining to SG Beneficiaries

THE GLASSHOUSES AT THE ROYAL BOTANIC GARDEN EDINBURGH
20A Inverleith Row, Edinburgh EH3 5LR
Royal Botanic Gardens T: 0131 248 2909
www.rbge.org.uk

The Glasshouses with ten climatic zones are a delight all year round. The Orchids and Cycads House brings together primitive cycads which dominated the land flora some 65 million years ago, and a diverse range of orchids, the most sophisticated plants in the world. In summer, giant water lilies, Victoria amazonica, are the star attraction in the Tropical Aquatic House. Plants with vibrant flowers and fascinating foliage thrive in the Rainforest Riches House and the complex ecosystems of life in the world's deserts are explored in the Arid Lands House. A large collection of gingers (Zingiberaceae), one of the largest collections of vireya rhododendrons in the world and a case housing carnivorous plants are among other attractions.

Directions: Located off the A902, one mile north of city centre. Entrances at Inverleith Row and Arboretum Place. Lothian Buses 8, 23 and 27 stop close to the East Gate entrance on Inverleith Row. The Majestic Tour Bus stops at Arboretum Place.

Disabled Access:
Full

Opening Times:
Sunday 7 June
10:00am - 5:30pm
2 Jan - 31 Dec 10am - 6pm
Closed 25 December
Closes 5:00pm Feb & Oct,
4:00pm Jan, Nov & Dec

Admission:
£5.00, conc £4.00, children u16 free (includes donation to the RBGE, for prices without donation check rbge.org.uk)

Charities:
Donation to SG Beneficiaries

41 Hermitage Gardens, Edinburgh

ETTRICK & LAUDERDALE

Scotland's Gardens 2015 Guidebook is sponsored by **INVESTEC WEALTH & INVESTMENT**

Area Organisers

Mrs M Kostoris	Wester Housebyres, Melrose TD6 9BW
Mrs P Litherland	Laidlawstiel House, Clovenfords, Galashiels TD1 1TJ
Mrs D Warre	Peace Cottage, Synton Parkhead, Ashkirk TD7 4PB

Treasurer

Mrs D Muir	Torquhan House, Stow TD1 2RX

Gardens open on a specific date

Bemersyde, Melrose	Sunday 26 April	2:00pm	- 5:00pm
Laidlawstiel House, Galashiels	Sunday 31 May	2:00pm	- 5:00pm
Harmony Garden, Melrose	Sunday 21 June	1:00pm	- 4:00pm
Priorwood Gardens, Melrose	Sunday 21 June	1:00pm	- 4:00pm
Carolside, Earlston	Friday 3 July	11:00am	- 5:00pm
Carolside, Earlston	Saturday 4 July	11:00am	- 5:00pm
Carolside, Earlston	Friday 10 July	11:00am	- 5:00pm
Carolside, Earlston	Saturday 11 July	11:00am	- 5:00pm
Carolside, Earlston	Friday 17 July	11:00am	- 5:00pm
Carolside, Earlston	Saturday 18 July	11:00am	- 5:00pm

Plant sales

Borders Plant and Produce Sale, Melrose	Saturday 16 May	10:30am	- 4:00pm

BORDERS PLANT AND PRODUCE SALE
MELROSE SATURDAY 16 MAY

Stock up on all sorts of goodies for your garden
at our mega charity plant sale.

See page 174 or 238 for more details.

**PLANT
DONATIONS
WELCOME**

Key to symbols

	New in 2015		Homemade teas		Accommodation
	Teas		Dogs on a lead allowed		Plant stall
	Cream teas		Wheelchair access		Scottish Snowdrop Festival

Garden locations

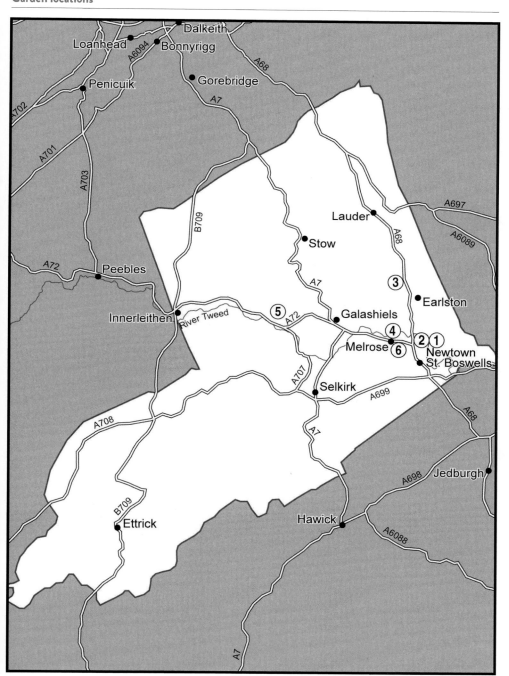

BEMERSYDE
Melrose TD6 9DP
The Earl Haig

Sixteenth century peel tower reconstructed in the seventeenth century with added mansion house. Glorious show of daffodils around the house. Woodland garden and walks along the River Tweed. Good footwear required.

Other Details: Discover the 800 year old Covin tree.

Directions: From A68 follow signs to Scott's View and then follow the yellow Scotland's Gardens signs to Bemersyde.

Disabled Access:
Partial

Opening Times:
Sunday 26 April
2:00pm - 5:00pm

Admission:
£3.00, children free

Charities:
Poppy Scotland receives 40%, the net remaining to SG Beneficiaries

BORDERS PLANT AND PRODUCE SALE
Broomhill Steading, Melrose TD6 9DF
Scotland's Gardens

Stock up on all sorts of goodies for your garden, larder or freezer at our mega charity plant sale. Vegetable plants, herbaceous, annuals, shrubs, trees, etc. Produce, second hand potting shed tools and **much more.** If you would like to "bring" as well as "buy" we would be grateful for **ANY** contributions, please bring goods labelled and priced or drop off at one of the collection points prior to day of the sale.   For your nearest collection point or further information contact **Victoria Kostoris** E: vakost@aol.com, T: 01896 822151 / 07778 343842
Georgina Seymour E: georgina.stobo@gmail.com, T: 01721 760245 / 07977 464504
Arabella Lewis E: arabella.lewis@btinternet.com, T: 01835 870357 / 07980 073274

Other Details: Refreshments available all day. Cash or cheque sales only.

Directions: Off Melrose bypass, close to A68.

Disabled Access:
Full

Opening Times:
Saturday 16 May
10:30am - 4:00pm

Admission:
Free

Charities:
Scotland's Gardens, Marie Curie (Borders) and Samaritans (Borders) each receives a third of proceeds

CAROLSIDE
Earlston TD4 6AL
Mr and Mrs Anthony Foyle T: 01896 849272
E: info@carolside.com www.carolsidegardens.com

A traditional and romantic garden set in a beautiful 18th century landscape, comprising lawns, shrubberies, mixed borders, a secret garden, a winter garden and an oval walled garden containing herbaceous borders, fruits, vegetables, parterres and a historically important collection of roses that has been carefully assembled over 24 years. Kenneth Cox in his book "Scotland for Gardeners" describes Carolside as "one of Scotland's finest private gardens".

Other Details: National Plant Collection®: A National Collection of pre 1900 Gallica Roses.

Directions: One mile north of Earlston on A68. Entrance faces south.

Disabled Access:
Full

Opening Times:
Fri & Sat 3 - 4 July
Fri & Sat 10 - 11 July
Fri & Sat 17 - 18 July
11:00am - 5:00pm

Admission:
£5.00, children free

Charities:
Marie Curie Cancer Care receives 40%, the net remaining to SG Beneficiaries

HARMONY GARDEN WITH PRIORWOOD GARDEN
St Mary's Road, Melrose TD6 9LJ
The National Trust for Scotland T: 01896 822493
E: ggregson@nts.org.uk www.nts.org.uk

Wander through this tranquil garden, wonderful herbaceous borders, lawns, fruit and vegetable plots, and enjoy fine views of the Abbey and Eildon Hills.

Other Details: Seasonal fruits and vegetable sales on trolley at entrance. Plant Stall and dried flowers are available at Priorwood.

Directions: Road: Off A6091, in Melrose, opposite the Abbey.
Bus: First from Edinburgh and Peebles.

Disabled Access:
Full

Opening Times:
Sunday 21 June
1:00pm - 4:00pm

Admission:
£6.50 for both gardens. N.B. Price correct at time of going to print.

Charities:
Donation to SG Beneficiaries

LAIDLAWSTIEL HOUSE
Clovenfords, Galashiels TD1 1TJ
Mr and Mrs P Litherland

Walled garden containing herbaceous border, fruit, and vegetables in raised beds. Colourful rhododendrons and azaleas. There are splendid views down to the River Tweed.

Directions: A72 between Clovenfords and Walkerburn, turn up the hill signposted for Thornielee. The house is on the right at the top of the hill.

Disabled Access:
None

Opening Times:
Sunday 31 May
2:00pm - 5:00pm

Admission:
£4.00, children free

Charities:
CLIC Sargent receives 40%, the net remaining to SG Beneficiaries

PRIORWOOD GARDENS WITH HARMONY GARDEN
Abbey Road, Melrose TD6 9PX
The National Trust for Scotland T: 01896 822493
E: ggregson@nts.org.uk www.nts.org.uk

In Melrose, overlooked by the Abbey ruins, this unique garden produces plants for a superb variety of dried flower arrangements made and sold here. The orchard contains many historic apple varieties.

Other Details: Plant stall and dried flowers available. Seasonal fruits and vegetable sales on trolley at Harmony Garden entrance.

Directions: Road: Off A6091, in Melrose opposite the Abbey. Bus: First from Edinburgh and Peebles.

Disabled Access:
Full

Opening Times:
Sunday 21 June
1:00pm - 4:00pm

Admission:
£6.50 for both gardens. N.B. Price correct at time of going to print.

Charities:
Donation to SG Beneficiaries

FIFE

District Organiser

Lady Erskine	Cambo House, Kingsbarns KY16 8QD

Area Organisers

Mrs Jeni Auchinleck	2 Castle Street, Crail KY10 3SQ
Mrs Lisa Bremner	Grey Craig House, Bridge Street, Saline KY12 9TS
Mrs Jayne Clarke	Marine House, Ordnance Road, Crombie KY12 8JZ
Mrs Evelyn Crombie	Keeper's Wood, Over Rankeilour, Cupar KY15 4NQ
Mrs Lisa Hall	Old Inzievar House, Oakley, Dunfermline KY12 8HA
Mrs Lindsay Murray	Craigfoodie, Dairsie KY15 4RU
Ms Louise Roger	Chesterhill, Boarhills, St Andrews KY16 8PP
Mrs April Simpson	The Cottage, Boarhills, St Andrews KY16 8PP
Mrs Fay Smith	37 Ninian Fields, Pittenweem, Anstruther KY10 2QU
Mrs Julia Young	South Flisk, Blebo Craigs, Cupar KY15 5UQ

Treasurer

Mrs Sally Lorimore	Willowhill, Forgan, Newport-on-Tay DD6 8RA

Gardens open on a specific date

Lindores House, By Newburgh	Sunday 1 March	2:00pm	-	6:00pm
Balcarres, Colinsburgh	Sunday 5 April	2:00pm	-	5:30pm
Cambo House Spring Plant and Craft Fair, Kingsbarns	Sunday 19 April	11:00am	-	4:00pm
Earlshall Castle, Leuchars	Sunday 3 May	2:00pm	-	5:00pm
Northwood Cottage, Newport-on-Tay	Sunday 17 May	1:00pm	-	5:00pm
Tayfield, Newport-on-Tay	Sunday 17 May	1:00pm	-	5:00pm
Willowhill, Newport-on-Tay	Sunday 17 May	1:00pm	-	5:00pm
Kirklands, Saline	Sunday 24 May	2:00pm	-	5:00pm
Earlshall Castle, Leuchars	Sunday 7 June	2:00pm	-	5:00pm
Greenhead Farmhouse, Greenhead of Arnot	Sunday 14 June	2:00pm	-	5:00pm
Culross Palace Garden, Culross	Sunday 21 June	11:00am	-	5:00pm
Kinghorn Village Gardens	Sunday 21 June	12:00pm	-	4:30pm
Pittenweem: Gardens in the Burgh	Sunday 21 June	11:00am	-	5:00pm
Gilston House, Leven	Saturday 27 June	1:00pm	-	5:00pm
Strathmiglo Village Gardens, Fife	Sunday 28 June	1:00pm	-	5:00pm
Crail: Small Gardens in the Burgh	Saturday 18 July	1:00pm	-	5:00pm
Crail: Small Gardens in the Burgh	Sunday 19 July	1:00pm	-	5:00pm

FIFE

Balcaskie with Kellie Castle, Pittenweem	Sunday 26 July	12:00pm	- 5:00pm
Falkland Palace, Cupar	Sunday 26 July	1:00pm	- 5:00pm
Glassmount House, By Kirkcaldy	1 April - 30 September	12:00pm	- 4:00pm
Kellie Castle with Balcaskie, Pittenweem	Sunday 26 July	12:00pm	- 5:00pm
Hill of Tarvit	Sunday 4 October	10:30am	- 4:00pm

Gardens open regularly

The Angus and Fife Garden Trail	5 May - 25 June	10:00am	- 8:00pm
Willowhill, Forgan, Newport-on-Tay	11 June - 29 August Thurs, Fris and Sats	2:00pm	- 7:00pm

Gardens open by arrangement

Barham, Bow of Fife	1 April - 31 July	01337 810227
Earlshall Castle, Leuchars	1 January - 31 December	01334 839205
Logie House, Dunfermline	1 April - 31 October	07510 654812
South Flisk, Cupar	15 April - 31 May	01334 850859
Strathairly House, Leven	1 April - 31 August	01333 352936/360422 or 07594 097052
The Tower, Wormit	1 April - 30 September	01382 541635 or 07768 406946
Willowhill, Newport-on-Tay	1 May - 29 August	01382 542890
Wormistoune House, Crail	1 April - 30 September	01333 450356

Plant sales

Hill of Tarvit Plant Sale and Autumn Fair, Cupar	Sunday 4 October	10:30am	- 4:00pm

Key to symbols

	New in 2015		Homemade teas		Accommodation
	Teas		Dogs on a lead allowed		Plant stall
	Cream teas		Wheelchair access		Scottish Snowdrop Festival

Garden locations

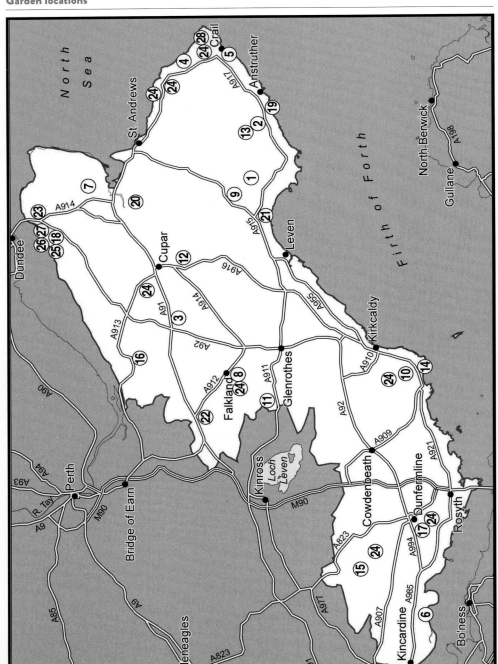

BALCARRES
Colinsburgh KY9 1HN
The Earl and Countess of Crawford and Balcarres

Superb 19th century formal and extensive woodland gardens with a wide variety of plants.

Directions: Half a mile north of Colinsburgh off A942.

Disabled Access:
None

Opening Times:
Sunday 5 April
2:00pm - 5:30pm

Admission:
£5.00, children free

Charities:
Colinsburgh Town Hall Restoration Projects receives 40%, the net remaining to SG Beneficiaries

BALCASKIE WITH KELLIE CASTLE
Pittenweem KY10 2RD
The Anstruther Family

In 1905 George Elgood wrote that Balcaskie was 'one of the best and most satisfying gardens in the British Isles'. Over the centuries the gardens have seen input from Gilpin, Bryce & Nesfield. Today the gardens are at the start of a period of restoration with help from the National Trust for Scotland.

Directions: Access is via Kellie Castle only and transport will take visitors from Kellie Castle to Balcaskie. Road: B9171, three miles NNW of Pittenweem. Bus: Flexible from local villages by pre-booking.

Disabled Access:
Partial

Opening Times:
Sunday 26 July
12:00pm - 5:00pm

Admission:
£8.00 for entrance to both gardens

Charities:
Donation to SG Beneficiaries

BARHAM
Bow of Fife KY15 5RG
Sir Robert & Lady Spencer-Nairn T: 01337 810227

A small woodland garden with snowdrops, spring bulbs, trilliums, rhododendrons and ferns. Also a summer garden with rambler roses, herbaceous borders, island beds and a well stocked vegetable garden.

Other Details: Small nursery of rare and unusual plants grown from seed collected or plants divided from the garden.

Directions: A914 miles west of Cupar.

Disabled Access:
None

Opening Times:
By arrangement
1 April - 31 July

Admission:
£4.00, OAP's £3.00, children free.

Charities:
Pain Association Scotland receives 40%, the net remaining to SG Beneficiaries

CAMBO HOUSE SPRING PLANT AND CRAFT FAIR
Kingsbarns KY16 8QD
Sir Peter and Lady Erskine T: 01333 450313
E: cambo@camboestate.com   www.camboestate.com

Invited nurseries will join Cambo to provide a wide ranging and interesting plant sale. Local craft and food stalls have also been invited. The gardens and woodland walks will be open.

Other Details: Champion Trees: Bundle Beech. 40% of funds raised on this day will go towards the Cambo Stables Project to provide a training and education centre on the estate.

Directions: A917 between Crail and St Andrews.

Disabled Access:
Full

Opening Times:
Sunday 19 April
11:00am - 4:00pm

Admission:
£2.50

Charities:
Cambo Stables Project receives 40%, the net remaining to SG Beneficiaries

CRAIL: SMALL GARDENS IN THE BURGH
KY10 3SQ
The Gardeners of Crail

A number of small gardens in varied styles: cottage, historic, plantsman's and bedding.

Other Details: Tickets and maps available from Mrs Auchinleck, 2 Castle Street, Crail and Kathleen and Jim Main, 17 Marketgate North, Crail.

Directions: Approach Crail from either St Andrews or Anstruther by A917. Park in the Marketgate.

Disabled Access:
None

Opening Times:
Saturday 18 July
1:00pm - 5:00pm
Sunday 19 July
1:00pm - 5:00pm

Admission:
£5.00

Charities:
1st Crail Brownies receives 10%, Crail Preservation Society receives 30%, the net remaining to SG Beneficiaries

CULROSS PALACE GARDEN
Culross KY12 8JH
The National Trust for Scotland T: 0844 493 2189
E: mjeffery@nts.org.uk   www.nts.org.uk

Relive the domestic life of the 16th and 17th centuries amid the old buildings and cobbled streets of this Royal Burgh on the River Forth. A model 17th century garden has been recreated behind Culross Palace to show the range of plants available and includes vegetables, culinary and medicinal herbs, soft fruits and ornamental shrubs. Don't miss the adorable Scots Dumpy chickens!

Other Details: Fruit and vegetable stalls from produce grown at Culross Palace. Admission includes tea/coffee and cakes. Tours with Head Gardener at 12:00pm, 2:00pm, and 4:00pm.

Directions: Off A985, three miles east of Kincardine Bridge, six miles west of Dunfermline. Stagecoach, Stirling to Dunfermline or First, Edinburgh to Dunfermline. Falkirk station twelve miles, Dunfermline station six miles.

Disabled Access:
Partial

Opening Times:
Sunday 21 June
11:00am - 5:00pm

Admission:
£6.00 including NTS members. N.B. Prices correct at time of going to print.

Charities:
Donation to SG Beneficiaries

EARLSHALL CASTLE
Leuchars KY16 0DP
Paul & Josine Veenhuijzen T: 01334 839205

Extensive and interesting garden designed by Sir Robert Lorimer. Fascinating topiary lawn, for which Earlshall is renowned, rose terrace, croquet lawn with herbaceous borders, shrub border, box garden, orchard, kitchen and herb garden.

Directions: On Earlshall road, three quarters of a mile east of Leuchars Village (off A919).

Disabled Access:
Partial

Opening Times:
Sunday 3 May
2:00pm - 5:00pm
Sunday 7 June
2:00pm - 5:00pm Also by arrangement on request

Admission:
£5.00, children free.

Charities:
May: RAF Benevolent Fund receives 40%, **June: St Athernase Church, Leuchars** receives 40%, the net remaining to SG Beneficiaries

FALKLAND PALACE AND GARDEN
Falkland, Cupar KY15 7BU
The National Trust for Scotland T: 0844 493 2186
E: falklandpalace&garden@nts.org.uk www.nts.org.uk

Set in a medieval village, the Royal Palace of Falkland is a superb example of Renaissance architecture. Garden enthusiasts will appreciate the work of Percy Cane, who designed the gardens between 1947 and 1952.

Other Details: Champion Trees: Acer platanoides 'Crimson King'. The open day, will be dedicated to the herbs we grow in the palace's physic garden. This garden was inspired by Mary Queen of Scots and planted with 16th century herbs.

Directions: Road: A912, ten miles from M90, junction 8, eleven miles north of Kirkcaldy. Bus: Stagecoach Fife stops in High Street (100 metres). OS Ref: NO252075.

Disabled Access:
Partial

Opening Times:
Sunday 26 July
1:00pm - 5:00pm

Admission:
£12.50, concessions £9.00, family £29.50, one parent: £23.00, NTS members: free. N.B. Prices correct at the time of going to print.

Charities:
Donation to SG Beneficiaries

GILSTON HOUSE
By Largoward, Leven KY8 5QP
Mr and Mrs Edward Baxter T: 01333 360245
E: catherine@cathbrown.com www.eastneukestates.co.uk

Large mature garden surrounding Gilston House (not open) including revamped terrace garden. Established shrubs mixed with gorgeous perennials. Specimen trees, wide lawns and extensive parkland. Pond walk and woodland walk.

Other Details: Children are very welcome, there is plenty of space to run around. Bring a picnic. Dogs on leads please. 40% of the day's proceeds go to RHET which promotes bringing farmers into classrooms and children onto farms. Free car parking (at owner's risk).

Directions: Signposted on A915 between Largoward and Upper Largo.

Disabled Access:
Full

Opening Times:
Saturday 27 June
1:00pm - 5:00pm

Admission:
£5.00, children free.

Charities:
RHET receives 40%, the net remaining to SG Beneficiaries

GLASSMOUNT HOUSE
By Kirkcaldy KY2 5UT
James and Irene Thomson T: 01592 890214
E: peterlcmclaren@yahoo.co.uk

Densely planted walled garden with surrounding woodland. An A-listed sun dial, Mackenzie & Moncur greenhouse and historical doocot are complemented by newer built structures. Daffodils are followed by a mass of candelabra and cowslip primula, meconopsis and Cardiocrinum giganteum. Hedges and topiary form backdrops for an abundance of bulbs, clematis, rambling roses and perennials, creating interest through the summer into September.

Other Details: Artists studio, gallery, wood store. Featured in *Country Living*, *The English Garden* 2012, *The Scottish Field* 2013. Winner of The Times/Fetzer Back Gardens of the Year 2008 Green garden category.

Directions: West from Kirkcaldy on B9157 turn left after two miles for Kinghorn. Turn right uphill at crossroads. Drive is 200 yards on right. From Kinghorn on the B923 follow signs past EcoCentre for a mile to the crossroads. Turn left uphill; drive is 200 yards on right.

Disabled Access:
None

Opening Times:
1 April - 30 September
12:00pm - 4:00pm
Monday to Friday.
Other dates by arrangement
Also part of the Angus & Fife
Garden Trail, see page 188.

Admission:
£3.50

Charities:
Parkinsons UK receives
40%, the net remaining to
SG Beneficiaries

GREENHEAD FARMHOUSE
Greenhead of Arnot KY6 3JQ
Mr and Mrs Malcolm Strang Steel T: 01592 840459
www.fife-bed-breakfast-glenrothes.co.uk

The south facing garden combines a sense of formality in its symmetrical layout with an informal look of mixed herbaceous borders planted "cottage" style. There are roses, fruit and a small vegetable plot. The polytunnel is in its third year of use.

Other Details: Dogs on leads.

Directions: A911 between Auchmuir Bridge and Scotlandwell.

Disabled Access:
None

Opening Times:
Sunday 14 June
2:00pm - 5:00pm

Admission:
£4.00

Charities:
Perth College Altzheimer
Project receives 40%, the net
remaining to SG Beneficiaries

HILL OF TARVIT PLANT SALE AND AUTUMN FAIR
Hill of Tarvit, Cupar KY15 5PB
The National Trust for Scotland/Scotland's Gardens Fife
E: catherine@camboestate.com or hilloftarvit@nts.org.uk   www.nts.org.uk

Hill of Tarvit is one of Scotland's finest Edwardian mansion houses with superb paintings by Sir Henry Raeburn, Allan Ramsay and eminent Dutch artists. Surrounding the mansion house are spectacular gardens designed by Robert Lorimer, woods, open heath and parkland to explore. For the energetic, a walk to the monument situated on the hill behind the house is rewarded with spectacular views over the Fife countryside. Monument at the top of the hill.

Other Details: House open (reduced entry fee) 1:00pm-5:00pm. Garden Tearoom open 11:00am-5:00pm. The spectacular gardens designed by Robert Lorimer will also be open, normal entrance fee applies. In addition there are woodlands, open heath and parkland to explore.

Directions: Two miles south of Cupar off A916.

Disabled Access:
Partial

Opening Times:
Sunday 4 October
10:30am - 4:00pm

Admission:
Plant sale £2.50, children under 16 free

Charities:
All proceeds to
SG Beneficiaries

KELLIE CASTLE GARDEN WITH BALCASKIE
Pittenweem KY10 2RF
The National Trust for Scotland T: 0844 493 2184
E: marmour@nts.org.uk www.nts.org.uk

This superb garden, around 400 years old, was sympathetically restored by the Lorimer family in the late 19th century. The Arts and Crafts style garden has a selection of old-fashioned roses and herbaceous plants, cultivated organically and hosts an amazing 30 varieties of rhubarb and 75 different types of apple.

Other Details: Access to Balcaskie and Kellie Castle via Kellie Castle only, a free minibus will transport visitors between the gardens. There will be an exciting mix of artist and craft stalls on offer.

Directions: Road- B9171, three miles NNW of Pittenweem.
Bus- Flexible from local villages by pre-booking.

Disabled Access:
Partial

Opening Times:
Sunday 26 July
12:00pm - 5:00pm

Admission:
£8.00 includes both gardens

Charities:
Donation to SG Beneficiaries

KINGHORN VILLAGE GARDENS
KY3
The Gardeners of Kinghorn Village

Kinghorn is a large coastal village boasting an interesting variety of gardens, some directly on the sea front and some hidden treasures. Kinghorn in Bloom is a community gardening group which strives to make Kinghorn a greener,cleaner, more attractive place. We have been awarded Gold by Beautiful Fife for the last two consecutive years.

Other Details: Tickets and maps from Carousel Coffee Shop, Pettycur Road, Kinghorn KY3 9RN.

Directions: Kinghorn village is between Kirkcaldy and Burntisland.

Disabled Access:
None

Opening Times:
Sunday 21 June
12:00pm - 4:30pm

Admission:
£4.00

Charities:
Kinghorn in Bloom receives 40%, the net remaining to SG Beneficiaries

15 KIRKLANDS

Saline KY12 9TS
Peter & Gill Hart T: 01383 852737
E: gillhart@globalnet.co.uk   www.kirklandshouseandgarden.co.uk

Kirklands was built in 1832 on the site of an older house. Peter and Gill came to Kirklands 38 years ago and began creating a garden which is still a work in progress. The garden is made up of herbaceous borders, bog garden, extended woodland garden with bluebells, rhododendrons, terraced walled vegetable garden with raised beds, greenhouse and espalier fruit trees. Saline Burn divides the garden from the ancient woodland and the woodland walk.

Other Details: Operation Ollie is a cerebral palsy charity that raises funds for our nephew's son to receive treatment in the USA. Also part of The Angus & Fife Garden Trail, see page 188.

Directions: Junction 4, M90, then B914. Parking in the centre of the village, then a short walk to the garden. Limited disabled parking at Kirklands.

Disabled Access:
Partial

Opening Times:
Sunday 24 May
2:00pm - 5:00pm
Also part of the Angus & Fife
Garden Trail, see page 188.

Admission:
£4.00, children free

Charities:
Operation Ollie - Let's
Get Him Walking receives
40%, the net remaining to
SG Beneficiaries

---

16 LINDORES HOUSE

By Newburgh KY14 6JD
Mr and Mrs R Turcan

Stunning lochside position with snowdrops, leucojums, rhododendrons, trilliums and herbaceous borders. Woodland walks and amazing 17th century yew believed to be the largest in Fife.

Other Details: Champion Trees: Yew. Soup and home made bread served in the conservatory. Snowdrops, leucojum and tender abutilon for sale.

Directions: Off A913 two miles east of Newburgh.

Disabled Access:
Partial

Opening Times:
Sunday 1 March
2:00pm - 6:00pm

Admission:
£3.00, children free

Charities:
Newburgh Scout Group
receives 40%, the net
remaining to SG Beneficiaries

---

17 LOGIE HOUSE

Crossford, Dunfermline KY12 8QN
Mrs John Hunt T: Karl 07510 654812
E: sarah@logiehunt.co.uk

Central to the design of this walled garden is a path through a double mixed border. Long rows of vegetables, and fruit, also contribute to colour and design when seen from the house and terrace. A long border of repeat flowering roses, and rose and annual beds contribute to an extended season of colour and interest. There is a magnificent and very productive Mackenzie & Moncur greenhouse in excellent condition with fully working vents and original benches and central heating system. The garden is surrounded by a belt of mixed woodland with walks.

Other Details: Group refreshments are available by arrangement. Dogs welcome outwith the walled garden. Also part of the Angus & Fife Garden Trail, see page 188.

Directions: M90 exit 1 for Rosyth and Kincardine Bridge (A985). After about two miles turn right to Crossford. At traffic lights, turn right and the drive is on the right at the end of the village main street.

Disabled Access:
Full

Opening Times:
By arrangement
1 April - 31 October
Also part of the Angus & Fife
Garden Trail, see page 188.

Admission:
£5.00

Charities:
Type 1 Juvenile Diabetes
Research Fund receives
40%, the net remaining to
SG Beneficiaries

18 NORTHWOOD COTTAGE WITH TAYFIELD AND WILLOWHILL
St Fort Farm, Newport-on-Tay DD6 8RE
Mr and Mrs Andrew Mylius T: 07974083110
www.stfort.co.uk

A visit to Ruskins house and woodland garden at Brantwood, was the inspiration for creating a woodland garden here. Paths were formed in a natural and informal way. Azaleas and specimen rhododendrons are the principal plants in the garden as the acid soil within the wood makes them ideal along with ability to withstand browsing from roe deer. The rhododendrons comprise a wide selection of both specimen and hybrids. Most of the azaleas are Azalea ponticum chosen for their excellent scent and good autumn colour. The Northwood is about 30 acres and is home to a colony of red squirrels, some of the paths lead to view points overlooking the fields with the river Tay and Tay rail bridge as a backdrop. In addition to over 200 rhododendrons some other plants of interest include Eucryphia, Cerdiphyllum pendulara, tulip tree, various red acers, a wide selection of rowans, liquidambar, metasequoia, magnolias and so on.

Other Details: The garden is approached with a woodland walk of about 400m from the car park and garden entrance. A garden plan is available at the entrance hut.

Directions: One and three quarters miles south of the Tay Road Bridge off the A92, between the Forgan and Five Roads roundabouts.

Disabled Access:
None

Opening Times:
Sunday 17 May
1:00pm - 5:00pm

Admission:
£5.00

Charities:
Forgan Arts Centre receives 40%, the net remaining to SG Beneficiaries

19 PITTENWEEM: GARDENS IN THE BURGH
KY10 2PQ
The Gardeners of Pittenweem T: 01333 311988

A great variety in garden design: from well-established traditional, to open aspect landscaped and from organic permaculture to conventional allotment gardens, plus one or two surprises in this compact circuit of about 11 gardens.

Other Details: Tickets and maps obtainable at 3 Seaview Row, Pittenweem (near West Braes Car Park), and from several gardens. Plant and book stalls. Refreshments are available in pubs, coffee shops and some gardens. Disabled access for some gardens.

Directions: On the A917 coast road enter Pittenweem following the signs to the West Braes Car Park at the west side of town.

Disabled Access:
Partial

Opening Times:
Sunday 21 June
11:00am - 5:00pm

Admission:
£5.00

Charities:
Fife Women's Aid receives 20%, Local RNLI receives 20%, the net remaining to SG Beneficiaries

SOUTH FLISK
Blebo Craigs, Cupar KY15 5UQ
Mr and Mrs George Young T: 01334 850859
E: julia@standrewspottery.co.uk www.standrewspottery.co.uk

A flooded former quarry forms the centrepiece of the enchanting three acre garden at South Flisk. The pond itself supports toads, frogs, newts, dragonflies and hundreds of golden orfe while water lilies and marginal plants add colour throughout the season. There are spectacular views of north Fife, Highland Perthshire and Angus. Boulders, cliffs and the many big, mature trees form a backdrop for all manner of spring bulbs, rhododendrons, magnolias, azaleas, and carpets of colourful primulas while the woodland area sports meconopsis, trilliums, podophyllums and some beautiful hellebores. At the front of the house (a former smiddy) is a charming, mature walled garden with traditional cottage garden planting. This garden is at its best in spring and early summer.

Other Details: South Flisk is home to a working pottery where you can meet George Young and watch him at work.

Directions: Six miles west of St Andrews off the B939 between Strathkinness and Pitscottie. There is a small stone bus shelter opposite the road into the village and a small sign saying Blebo Craigs. Or check out the map on our website.

Disabled Access:
Partial

Opening Times:
By arrangement
15 April - 31 May

Admission:
£4.00, children free

Charities:
RUDA receives 40%,
the net remaining to
SG Beneficiaries.

STRATHAIRLY HOUSE
Upper Largo, Leven KY8 6ED
Mr and Mrs Andrew Macgill   01333 360422 / 01333 352936 / 07594 097052
E: elaine@strathairly.com

A recently restored walled garden. Herbaceous and mixed planting schemes. Parkland and woodlands with views over Largo Bay.

Directions: Located outside the village of Upper Largo on the A917 Leven to Elie coast road.

Disabled Access:
Partial

Opening Times:
By arrangement
1 April - 31 August

Admission:
£4.00, children under 16 free

Charities:
SSAFA Forces Help receives
40%, the net remaining to
SG Beneficiaries

STRATHMIGLO VILLAGE GARDENS
Fife KY14 7PR
The Gardeners of Strathmiglo

A selection of lovely village and walled gardens including open aspect, vegetables, topiary and courtyard gardens. The river Eden runs through the village which lies just below the beautiful West Lomond Hill.

Other Details: Parking is available at the village hall where tickets and maps are also provided. Homemade teas will be available at the village hall throughout the afternoon.

Directions: Off the A91, 2 miles west of Auchtermuchty, enter village from either the east or west end. Follow signs in the High Street to parking area and ticket sales.

Disabled Access:
Partial

Opening Times:
Sunday 28 June
1:00pm - 5:00pm

Admission:
£5.00

Charities:
Cystic Fibrosis Trust receives 20%, Macmillan Cancer Support receives 20%, the net remaining to SG Beneficiaries

TAYFIELD WITH NORTHWOOD COTTAGE AND WILLOWHILL
Forgan, Newport-on-Tay DD6 8RA
William and Elizabeth Berry

A wide variety of shrubs and fine trees, many to mark celebrations of the family who have lived here for over 200 years. Some trees are of great age and Tayfield has the tallest beech tree recorded in Scotland at 39 metres. A picturesque approach to Tayfield House is enhanced by wonderful large tree rhododendrons in May and views across the Tay all year round. The grounds are wildlife rich and contain two large ponds. Look out for red squirrels which are often seen.

Other Details: Champion Trees: Beech.

Directions: One and a half miles south of Tay Road Bridge. Take the B995 to Newport off the Forgan roundabout.

Disabled Access:
Partial

Opening Times:
Sunday 17 May
1:00pm - 5:00pm

Admission:
£5.00

Charities:
Forgan Arts Centre receives 40%, the net remaining to SG Beneficiaries

Logie House,

24 THE ANGUS AND FIFE GARDEN TRAIL
Various locations in Angus and Fife
The Gardeners of Fife and Angus
www.angusfifetrail.org.uk

ANGUS

1. The Herbalist's Garden at Logie
Tuesdays 26 May - 23 June   1:00pm - 6:00pm   Teas and plant sale.

2. Kirkside of Lochty
Tuesdays 19 May - 23 June   11:00am - 5:00pm

3. Kirkton House
Tuesdays 5 May - 23 June   11:00am - 5:00pm

4. The Garden Cottage
Tuesdays 5 May - 23 June   1:00pm - 7:00pm

SOUTH/CENTRAL FIFE

5. Glassmount House
Wednesdays 6 May - 24 June   12noon - 4:00pm

6. Kirklands
Wednesdays 20 May - 10 June   11:00am - 4:00pm   Plant sale.

7. Logie House
Wednesdays 6 May - 24 June   11:00am - 3:00pm   Plant sale.

8. Millfield House
Wednesdays 20 May - 24 June   4:00pm - 8:00pm

EAST/CENTRAL FIFE

9. Kenlygreen House
Thursdays 14 May - 4 June   10:00am - 4:00pm

10. Kenly Green Farm
Thursdays 21 May - 25 June   3:00pm - 7:00pm

11. St Mary's Farm
Thursdays 21 May - 25 June   4:00pm - 8:00pm

12. Wormistoune
Thursdays 7 May - 25 June   11:00am - 4:00pm   Plant sale.

Disabled Access:
Partial

Opening Times:
5 May - 25 June
10:00am - 8:00pm
Times and dates vary for all
gardens.

Admission:
£25.00 (plus £1.00 p&p) for
entrance to all gardens.
Early Bird Price £20.00 (plus
£1.00 p&p) available until
28 February 2015.
Accompanied children free.

Charities:
Macmillan Cancer Support
receives 20%, Worldwide
Cancer Research receives
20%, the net remaining to
SG Beneficiaries

Other Details: A limited number of tickets are available and may be purchased by debit/credit card at www.angusfifetrail.org.uk or by cheque payable to Scotland's Gardens from S. Lorimore, Willowhill, Forgan, Newport on Tay, Fife DD6 8RA. A brochure giving full descriptions and directions to all gardens will be supplied with tickets.

See also pages 34 - 36 of this book.

25 THE TOWER
1, Northview Terrace, Wormit DD6 8PP
Peter and Angela Davey T: 01382 541635 M: 07768 406946

Situated four miles south of Dundee, this one acre Edwardian landscaped garden has panoramic views over the River Tay. Features include a rhododendron walk, rockeries, informal woodland planting schemes with native and exotic plants, offering year round interest. Original raised paths lead to a granite grotto with waterfall pool. Also of interest are raised vegetable beds made from granite sets.

Other Details: Garden is on a hillside with steep paths, therefore unsuited to those with poor mobility.

Directions: From B946 park on Naughton Road outside Spar shop and walk up path left following signs.

Disabled Access:
None

Opening Times:
By arrangement
1 April - 30 September

Admission:
£3.50

Charities:
Barnados receives 40%, the net remaining to SG Beneficiaries

26 WILLOWHILL
Forgan, Newport-on-Tay DD6 8RA
Eric Wright and Sally Lorimore T: 01382 542890
E: e.g.wright@dundee.ac.uk

An evolving three acre garden featured in Scotland for Gardeners and Scotland on Sunday. The house is surrounded by a series of mixed borders designed with different vibrant colour combinations for effect all season and a vegetable plot. Newly developed area containing borders of bulbs, roses and perennials. A stepped terrace of alpines leads to a wildlife pond in grassland planted with trees, bulbs and herbaceous perennials through which wide sweeping paths are mown.

Other Details: Garden is on a hillside with steep paths, therefore unsuited to those with poor mobility.

Directions: One and a half miles south of Tay Road Bridge. Take the B995 to Newport off the Forgan roundabout. Willowhill is the first house on the left hand side next to the Forgan Arts Centre.

Disabled Access:
Partial

Opening Times:
11 June - 29 Aug
2:00pm - 7:00pm
Thurs, Fri & Sats
Also by arrangement
1 May - 29 August

Admission:
£4.00, season ticket £10.00

Charities:
RIO Community Centre receives 40%, the net remaining to SG Beneficiaries

27 WILLOWHILL WITH NORTHWOOD COTTAGE AND TAYFIELD

Forgan, Newport-on-Tay DD6 8RA
Eric Wright and Sally Lorimore T: 01382 542890
E: e.g.wright@dundee.ac.uk

See details under Willowhill above.

Disabled Access:
Partial

Opening Times:
Sunday 17 May
1:00pm - 5:00pm
Admission:
£5.00

Charities:
Forgan Arts Centre receives
40%, the net remaining to
SG Beneficiaries

28 WORMISTOUNE HOUSE

Crail KY10 3XH
Baron and Lady Wormiston T: 01333 450356
E: ktaylor.home@googlemail.com (Head Gardener)

This 17th century Scots tower house and gardens have been painstakingly restored over the last 20 years. The charming 1.5 acre walled garden is a series of 'rooms', each one with its own individual enchantment. These include a wildlife meadow, productive potager, intricate formal parterre, magical Griselinia garden and recently planted late-season perennial borders. The garden's backbone is the splendid midsummer herbaceous border – as featured on the cover of Kenneth Cox's *Scotland for Gardeners*. The walled garden also contains two award-winning Georgian style garden pavilions. Outside the walled garden enjoy woodland walks around the newly re-landscaped lochan.

Other Details: Owing to building works, this year Wormistoune will be opening by arrangement to individuals and groups. You are welcome to contact us in advance, when planning your visit, to find out what's looking good in the garden. Also part of the Angus & Fife Garden Trail, see page 188.

Directions: One mile north of Crail on the A917 Crail to St Andrews road.

Disabled Access:
None

Opening Times:
By arrangement
1 April - 30 September
Also part of the Angus & Fife
Garden Trail, see page 188.

Admission:
£5.00, children free

Charities:
CHAS receives 40%, the net
remaining to SG Beneficiaries

GLASGOW & DISTRICT

Scotland's Gardens 2015 Guidebook is sponsored by **INVESTEC WEALTH & INVESTMENT**

District Organiser

Ms Lynn A Harris | 46 Lauderdale Gardens, Glasgow G12 9QT

Area Organisers

Mrs Pauline Bell	26 Norwood Drive, Giffnock, Glasgow G46 7LS
Mrs Mandy Colin	12a Belhaven Terrace, Glasgow
Mrs S Elliot	46 Corrour Road, Newlands G43 2DX
Mrs C Hamilton	12a Belhaven Terrace, Glasgow G12 0TG
Mrs A Murray	44 Gordon Road, Netherlee G44 3TW
Mrs Sandra Wilson	Robinsfield Gatehouse, Bardowie G62 6ER

Treasurer

Mr J Murray | 44 Gordon Road, Netherlee G44 3TW

Gardens open on a specific date

Holmwood, Cathcart	Saturday 4 April	12:00pm - 4:00pm
Holmwood, Cathcart	Sunday 5 April	12:00pm - 4:00pm
Ardlinnhe, Glasgow	Sunday 31 May	11:00am - 5:00pm
Aeolia with Blackmill, Kilsyth	Sunday 7 June	2:00pm - 5:00pm
Blackmill with Aeolia, Kilsyth	Sunday 7 June	2:00pm - 5:00pm
53 Dalziel Drive, Glasgow	Saturday 13 June	2:00pm - 5:00pm
Kamares, Newton Mearns	Sunday 5 July	12:00pm - 5:00pm
Greenbank Garden, Clarkston	Saturday 19 September	11:00am - 5:00pm
Greenbank Garden, Clarkston	Sunday 20 September	11:00am - 5:00pm

Gardens open by arrangement

Aeolia with Blackmill, Kilsyth	1 April - 30 September	01236 821983
Blackmill with Aeolia, Kilsyth	1 April - 30 September	01236 821667

Key to symbols

	New in 2015	Homemade teas		Accommodation	
	Teas	Dogs on a lead allowed		Plant stall	
	Cream teas	Wheelchair access		Scottish Snowdrop Festival	

Garden locations

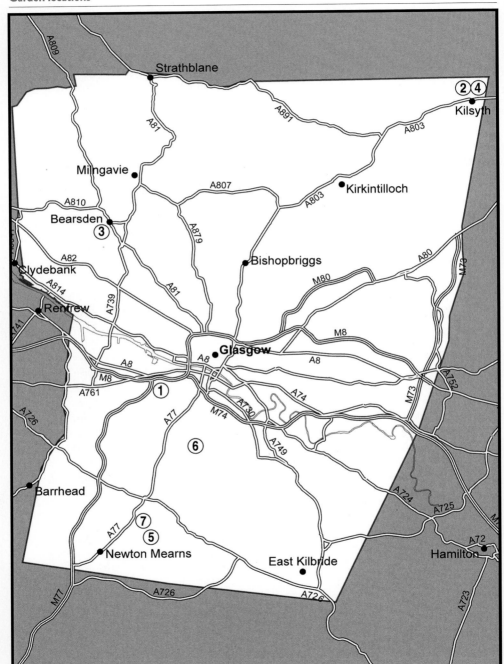

53 DALZIEL DRIVE
Pollokshields, Glasgow G41 4NY
Catherine Henderson T: 0141 427 2476

Delightful south-facing walled garden in Europe's first Garden Suburb. Lovely mixed shrub and herbaceous borders, small pond with water feature. All year interest with bursts of colour and interest in spring, high summer and late summer. Highlights include lavenders, hydrangeas, verbena and Japanese anemones.

Directions: From M77 south, take J1 signposted Pollokshields. From Haggs Road take first left into St Andrews Drive. First left into Terregles Avenue, first right on to Albert Drive and then fifth road on the left is Dalziel Drive.

Disabled Access:
Full

Opening Times:
Saturday 13 June
2:00pm - 5:00pm

Admission:
£6.00 including tea and home baking

Charities:
Kidsout receives 40%, the net remaining to SG Beneficiaries

AEOLIA WITH BLACKMILL
Allanfauld Road, Kilsyth G65 9DE
Mr and Mrs George Murdoch T: 01236 821983

A third of an acre garden developed since 1960 by the owners. Mature specimen trees and shrubs, a large variety of rhododendrons, primulas, hardy geraniums and herbaceous plants.

Directions: A803 to Kilsyth, through main roundabout. Turn left into Parkburn Road up to the crossroads. Short walk up Allanfauld Road. Buses 27, 24, and X86.

Disabled Access:
Partial

Opening Times:
Sunday 7 June
2:00pm - 5:00pm
Also by arrangement
1 April - 30 September

Admission:
£6.50 includes entry to both gardens and homemade teas

Charities:
Strathcarron Hospice receives 40%, the net remaining to SG Beneficiaries

ARDLINNHE
20 Lochend Road, Bearsden, Glasgow G61 1DX
John Nicolson
E: johnnynicolson@aol.com

Ardlinnhe is an Arts and Crafts house, originally laid out in farmland at the turn of the 20th century for Sandeman, the port wine family. The garden was restored in 2009 by the landscape architect Luis Buitrago, MLArch. Designed to compliment the Arts and Crafts house, the garden surrounds the house on four sides and has a natural stream feeding into the loch, a Scottish native species woodland area, as well as interesting trees and borders planted with species popular in the early 20th century. Also in the garden is an original Second World War Anderson shelter which visitors may explore.

Directions: From A809 Drymen Road, turn into Station Road. Turn first left into Pendicle Road. Lochend Road is second on left at top of hill. On street parking available. Walking distance from Bearsden Railway Station.

Disabled Access:
Partial

Opening Times:
Sunday 31 May
11:00am - 5:00pm

Admission:
£5.00 including tea and biscuits

Charities:
Scottish Association for Mental Health receives 20%, LGBT Youth Scotland receives 20%, the net remaining to SG Beneficiaries

BLACKMILL WITH AEOLIA
Allanfauld Road, Kilsyth G65 9DE
Mr and Mrs Alan Patrick T: 01236 821667

Across the road from Aeolia is an acre of mature specimen trees, rhododendrons and shrubs on the site of an old mill. There is an ornamental pond and rock pool built into the remains of an old mill building. A further two acres of woodland glen and interesting rock formation on the cliff face. Paths along the Garrel Burn with views to many cascading waterfalls. A micro hydro scheme is on view along with many different types of dry stone walls.

Directions: A803 to Kilsyth, through main roundabout. Turn left into Parkburn Road up to the crossroads. Short walk up Allanfauld Road. Buses 27, 24, X86.

Disabled Access:
Partial

Opening Times:
Sunday 7 June
2:00pm - 5:00pm
Also by arrangement
1 April - 30 September

Admission:
£6.50 includes entry to both gardens and homemade tea

Charities:
Strathcarron Hospice receives 40%, the net remaining to SG Beneficiaries

GREENBANK GARDEN
Flenders Road, Clarkston G76 8RB
The National Trust for Scotland T: 0844 493 2201
E: dferguson@nts.org.uk www.nts.org.uk

A unique walled garden with plants and designs of particular interest to suburban gardeners. There are also fountains and a woodland walk.

Other Details: National Plant Collection®: Bergenia cvs. & spp.
Our annual bulb fair will be held on both days (11:00am-4:00pm).
On Saturday the Head Gardener will lead a guided walk at 2:30pm.
Greenbank House will be open on Sunday between 2:00pm-4:00pm.
There is no disabled access to Greenbank House but full access to the garden.

Directions: Flenders Road, off Mearns Road, Clarkston. Off M77 and A727, follow signs for East Kilbride to Clarkston Toll. Bus - 44a, Glasgow to Newton Mearns. Rail - Clarkston station 1¼ miles.

Disabled Access:
Full

Opening Times:
Saturday 19 September
11:00am - 5:00pm
Sunday 20 September
11:00am - 5:00pm

Admission:
£6.50, concessions £5.00, family £16.50, one parent £11.50. NTS members free. N.B. Prices are correct at time of publication.

Charities:
Donation to SG Beneficiaries

HOLMWOOD

61-63 Netherlee Road, Cathcart G44 3YU
The National Trust for Scotland T: 0844 493 2204
E: holmwood@nts.org.uk   www.nts.org.uk

Kitchen garden planted with a range of Victorian fruits, herbs and vegetables. There are five acres of landscaped grounds to explore.

Other Details: Lots of Easter family fun and games. See NTS website for full details.

Directions: Netherlee Road, off Clarkston Road, B767 or Rhannan Road four miles south of Glasgow city centre. Frequent bus service from city centre.

Disabled Access:
Partial

Opening Times:
Saturday 4 April
12:00pm - 4:00pm
Sunday 5 April
12:00pm - 4:00pm

Admission:
By donation.

Charities:
Donation to SG Beneficiaries

KAMARES

18 Broom Road, Newton Mearns, Glasgow G77 5DN
Derek and Laura Harrison E: laurah6367@gmail.com

Sitting in ⅔ of an acre, Kamares is a hacienda-style house surrounded on all sides by matures trees and a lovely beech hedge. The garden has much of interest for the visitor, including a well-established pond, a collection of acers, well-established and colourful mixed shrub and herbaceous borders, rare US sequoias and a living sculptural arbour. There are also several patio gardens, including a delightful courtyard with rockery. There are many sculptures and other artworks in the garden, particularly some fun topiary and cloud pruned pines. The owner is an artist and uses the garden as an alternative canvas, as well as drawing inspiration from it for her beautiful still life paintings

Other Details: Fun garden treasures trail/quiz. Teas and home baking £3.00

Directions: From the A77 heading south, turn left into Broom Estate and sharp left again into Broom Road. Kamares is the last house on the left near the top of the hill. On road parking is available beyond the house on Broom Road, Broomcroft Road, Sandringham Road and Dunvegan Avenue.

Disabled Access:
Full

Opening Times:
Sunday 5 July
12:00pm - 5:00pm

Admission:
£4.00

Charities:
Jewish Care Scotland receives
40%, the net remaining to
SG Beneficiaries

ISLE OF ARRAN

Scotland's Gardens 2015 Guidebook is sponsored by **INVESTEC WEALTH & INVESTMENT**

District Organiser

Mrs S C Gibbs   Dougarie, Isle of Arran KA27 8EB

Treasurer

Mrs E Adam   Bayview, Pirnmill, Isle of Arran KA27 8HP

Gardens open on a specific date

Brodick Castle & Country Park, Brodick	Thursday 14 May	7:00pm
The Glades, Whiting Bay	Sunday 7 June	2:00pm - 5:00pm
Brodick Castle & Country Park, Brodick	Thursday 18 June	7:00pm
Dougarie	Wednesday 1 July	2:00pm - 5:00pm
Brodick Castle & Country Park, Brodick	Thursday 16 July	7:00pm

Dougarie, Isle of Arran © Arran in Focus

Key to symbols

New in 2015	Homemade teas	Accommodation
Teas	Dogs on a lead allowed	Plant stall
Cream teas	Wheelchair access	Scottish Snowdrop Festival

BRODICK CASTLE & COUNTRY PARK
Brodick, Isle of Arran KA27 8HY
The National Trust for Scotland T: 0844 493 2152
E: brodickcastle@nts.org.uk www.nts.org.uk

At any time of year the gardens are well worth a visit, though especially in spring when the internationally acclaimed rhododendron collection bursts into full bloom. There are exotic plants and shrubs, a walled garden and a woodland garden to be enjoyed by garden enthusiasts, families and children. Venture out into the country park and discover wildflower meadows where Highland cows graze, woodland trails and tumbling waterfalls. There is something for everyone.

Other Details: National Plant Collection®: three rhododendron collections. Champion Trees: Embothrium coccineum.

Directions: Brodick two miles. Service buses from Brodick Pier to Castle. Regular sailings from Ardrossan and Claonaig (Argyll). Information from Caledonian MacBrayne, Gourock, 01475 650100.

Disabled Access:
Partial

Opening Times:
Thursdays 14 May, 18 June and 16 July 7:00pm
for tours with Head Gardener

Admission:
£6.00 (including NTS members) for tour

Charities:
Donation to SG Beneficiaries

DOUGARIE
KA27 8EB
Mr and Mrs S C Gibbs
E: office@dougarie.com

Most interesting terraced garden in castellated folly built in 1905 to celebrate the marriage of the 12th Duke of Hamilton's only child to the Duke of Montrose. Good selection of tender and rare shrubs, herbaceous border, kitchen garden. Small woodland area with interesting trees including Azara, Abutilon, Eucryphia, Hoheria and Nothofagus.

Other Details: Teas in 19th century boathouse.

Directions: Blackwaterfoot five miles. Regular ferry sailing from Ardrossan and Claonaig (Argyll). Information from Caledonian MacBrayne, Gourock (Tel 01475 650100).

Disabled Access:
None

Opening Times:
Wednesday 1 July
2:00pm - 5:00pm

Admission:
£3.50

Charities:
Pirnmill Village Association receives 40%, the net remaining to SG Beneficiaries

THE GLADES
Whiting Bay KA27 8QS
Mrs Susan Marriott

A recently developed garden with sweeping lands surrounded by shrubs and herbaceous borders in the heart of Glenashdale. Whispering grasses lead to a rose and laburnum entwined pergola, banked by woodland plants and tree ferns. Spectacular gunnera edge a large spring pond.

Directions: As parking is limited it is suggested cars are left in the village. The garden is a ten minute walk from there. The garden will be well signposted.

Disabled Access:
None

Opening Times:
Sunday 7 June
2:00pm - 5:00pm

Admission:
£3.50

Charities:
Whiting Bay Improvements and the Village Hall receive 40%, the net remaining to SG Beneficiaries

KINCARDINE & DEESIDE

Scotland's Gardens 2015 Guidebook is sponsored by **INVESTEC WEALTH & INVESTMENT**

District Organisers

Tina Hammond	7 Watson Street, Banchory AB31 5UB
Julie Nicol	Bogiesheil, Ballogie, Aboyne AB34 5DU

Area Organisers

Mrs Andrea Bond	Rosebank, Crathes, Banchory AB31 5JE
Mrs Wendy Buchan	Inneshewen, Dess, Aboyne AB31 5BH
Mr Gavin Farquhar	Ecclesgreig Castle, St Cyrus DD10 0DP
Mrs Helen Jackson	
Mrs Catherine Nichols	Bridge of Canny, Banchory AB31 4AT
Mr and Mrs David Younie	Bealltainn, Ballogie, Aboyne AB34 5DL

Treasurer

To be advised

Gardens open on a specific date

Crathes Castle Garden, Banchory	Saturday 21 February	10:00am		
Ecclesgreig Castle, St Cyrus	Sunday 1 March	1:00pm	-	4:00pm
Crathes Castle Garden, Banchory	Saturday 18 April	2:00pm		
Inchmarlo House Garden, Banchory	Sunday 24 May	1:30pm	-	4:30pm
Woodend House, Banchory	Sunday 31 May	1:30pm	-	4:30pm
Kincardine, Kincardine O'Neil	Sunday 14 June	1:30pm	-	5:00pm
Ecclesgreig Castle, St Cyrus	Sunday 21 June	1:00pm	-	5:00pm
Drum Castle Garden, Banchory	Wednesday 1 July	2:00pm	-	3:30pm
Findrack, Torphins	Sunday 5 July	2:00pm	-	5:00pm
Drum Castle Garden, by Banchory	Wednesday 15 July	2:00pm	-	3:30pm
Drum Castle Garden, by Banchory	Wednesday 22 July	2:00pm	-	3:30pm
Drum Castle Garden, by Banchory	Wednesday 29 July	2:00pm	-	3:30pm
Glenbervie House, Stonehaven	Sunday 2 August	2:00pm	-	5:00pm
Fasque House, Laurencekirk	Sunday 9 August	2:00pm	-	5:00pm

KINCARDINE & DEESIDE

Gardens open regularly

Drum Castle Garden, by Banchory   1 April - 31 October   11:00am - 5:00pm

Gardens open by arrangement

14 Arbeadie Avenue, Banchory   1 May - 31 July   01330 823615

Glenbervie

Key to symbols

 New in 2015   Homemade teas   Accommodation

 Teas   Dogs on a lead allowed   Plant stall

 Cream teas   Wheelchair access   Scottish Snowdrop Festival

Garden locations

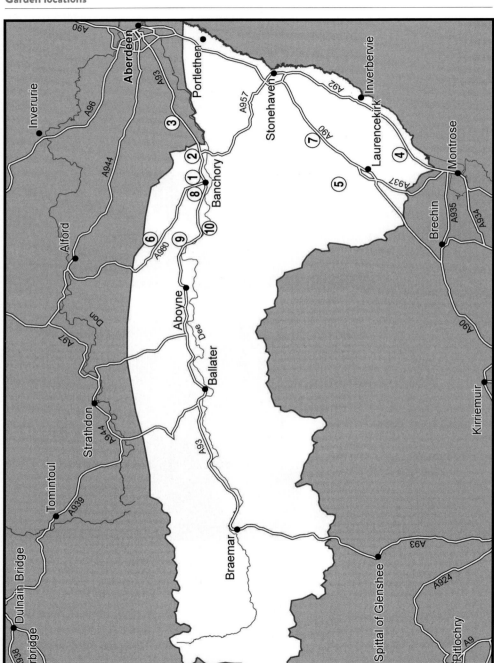

14 ARBEADIE AVENUE
Banchory AB31 4EL
Mr and Mrs Alisdair Harrison T: 01330 823615
E: alisdair.harrison@btinternet.com

A delightful small garden designed to be maintenance free. The garden includes water features and a traditional Japanese garden with a wooden walkway, pergolas, ponds and running stream. The use of slate, natural stones and lighting features all add to the atmosphere and interest.

Other Details: Groups of up to twelve people welcome as are evening visits. Alasdair is more than happy to discuss and give advice to anyone considering transforming their own garden, building a water feature or installing garden lighting.

Directions: From Station Road, Banchory (main road) go up Arbeadie Road and Arbeadie Avenue is on the left near the top of the hill.

Disabled Access:
None

Opening Times:
By arrangement
1 May - 31 July

Admission:
£3.50

Charities:
Forget Me Not (Banchory) receives 40%, the net remaining to SG Beneficiaries

CRATHES CASTLE GARDEN
Banchory AB31 5QJ
The National Trust for Scotland T: 0844 493 2166
E: crathes@nts.org.uk www.nts.org.uk

21 February: Join our expert Head Gardener for a full day to learn about the principles of pruning within the beautiful setting of the gardens at Crathes Castle. This practical, hands on workshop will cover general formative pruning as well as looking at how to prune most roses, trees and shrubs.
18 April: Members of the garden team will lead you through some of the finer points of planning, designing and maintaining an herbaceous border. This practical, hands on session will cover general techniques including the division and growing on of your own plants.

Other Details: National Plant Collection®: Dianthus (Malmaison).
February Pruning Workshop: Price includes tea/coffee and a light lunch.
April Event: Price includes some free plant material. Booking essential via NTS website www.nts.org.uk for both events. Places are limited.

Directions: On A93, 15 miles west of Aberdeen and three miles east of Banchory.

Disabled Access:
Full

Opening Times:
Saturday 21 February
10:00am
Saturday 18 April 2:00pm

Admission:
**February event: £50.00 (includes lunch)
April event: £20.00.
Admission also applicable to NTS members**

Charities:
Donation to SG Beneficiaries

DRUM CASTLE GARDEN
Drumoak, by Banchory AB31 5EY
The National Trust for Scotland T: 0844 493 2161
E: drum@nts.org.uk www.nts.org.uk

Each Wednesday at 2:00pm in July join the Head Gardener for a walk through the historic rose garden. The Trust has established a collection of old-fashioned roses, at its peak for blossom and colour during July. Other garden areas include a pond and bog garden, wildlife meadow and new wildlife garden and a cutting garden. Open to visitors April to October. Evening guided tours available on request.

Other Details: Advance booking is essential for guided walks. Plant sales including home grown herbaceous. Garden Workshops throughout the year - see website for details.

Directions: On A93 three miles west of Peterculter. Ten miles west of Aberdeen and eight miles east of Banchory.

Disabled Access:
Partial

Opening Times:
Wednesdays 1, 15, 22 and 29 July 2:00pm - 3:30pm for guided walk
1 April - 31 October
11:00am - 5:00pm daily.

Admission:
£4.00, concessions £2.00, NTS members free, guided walks £5.00 (all participants)

Charities:
Donation to SG Beneficiaries

ECCLESGREIG CASTLE
St Cyrus DD10 0DP
Mr Gavin Farquhar T: 01224 214301
E: enquiries@ecclesgreig.com www.ecclesgreig.com

Ecclesgreig Castle, Victorian Gothic on a 16th century core, is internationally famous as an inspiration for Bram Stoker's Dracula. The snowdrop walk starts at the castle, meanders around the estate, along woodland paths and the pond, ending at the garden. The woodlands contain some very interesting trees and shrubs. Herbaceous borders 10 feet wide and 140 feet long are in the Italian balustraded gardens. The garden has classical statues and stunning shaped topiary with views across St Cyrus to the sea. Started from a derelict site, development continues.

Directions: Ecclesgreig will be signposted from the A92 Coast Road and from the A937 Montrose / Laurencekirk Road.

Disabled Access:
Partial

Opening Times:
Sunday 1 March
1:00pm - 4:00pm
for the Snowdrop Festival
Sunday 21 June
1:00pm - 5:00pm

Admission:
£4.00, accompanied children free

Charities:
Scottish Civic Trust receives 20%, Montrose Guides receives 20%, the net remaining to SG Beneficiaries

FASQUE HOUSE
Fettercairn, Laurencekirk AB30 1DN
Mr and Mrs Douglas Dick-Reid
www.fasquehouse.co.uk

Fasque House is situated within the finely landscaped Fasque House Estate with the foothills of the Grampians behind and rolling parkland to the front. The house remained in the ownership of the Gladstone family until 2007. The current owners purchased it in 2010 and are currently restoring the house and gardens to their former glory. Landscaping of the West Garden took place in 2013 with a sunken terrace garden containing a formal pond and a mixture of formal and herbaceous plants. There are some magnificent trees and beautiful walks in the surrounding woodlands. The grandiose walled garden and old Apple Store are also being restored but the planting has not yet begun.

Other Details: Self catering accommodation is available.

Directions: Off B974 Cairn O'Mount road 1¼ miles north of Fettercairn.

Disabled Access:
Partial

Opening Times:
Sunday 9 August
2:00pm - 5:00pm

Admission:
£4.00, children free

Charities:
Fettercairn Community Allotments receives 20%, Home Start Stonehaven receives 20%, the net remaining to SG Beneficiaries

FINDRACK
Torphins AB31 4LJ
Mr and Mrs Andrew Salvesen

The gardens of Findrack are set in beautiful wooded countryside and are a haven of interesting plants and unusual design features. There is a walled garden with circular lawns and deep herbaceous borders, a stream garden leading to a wildlife pond, vegetable garden and woodland walk.

Directions: Leave Torphins on A980 to Lumphanan after ½ mile turn off, signposted Tornaveen. There is a stone gateway one mile up on the left.

Disabled Access:
Partial

Opening Times:
Sunday 5 July
2:00pm - 5:00pm

Admission:
£4.50, children under 12
£1.00

Charities:
The Breadmaker receives
40%, the net remaining to
SG Beneficiaries

GLENBERVIE HOUSE
Drumlithie, Stonehaven AB39 3YA
Mr and Mrs A Macphie

Nucleus of present day house dates from 15th century with additions in 18th and 19th centuries. A traditional Scottish walled garden on a slope with roses, herbaceous and annual borders along with fruit and vegetables. One wall is taken up with a Victorian style greenhouse with many species of pot plants and climbers including peach and figs. A woodland garden by a burn is punctuated with many varieties of plants, primula to name but one.

Other Details: Partial disabled access but please note some steep pathways and tree roots can make walking difficult in places. **No dogs please.**

Directions: Drumlithie one mile. Garden one and a half miles off A90.

Disabled Access:
Partial

Opening Times:
Sunday 2 August
2:00pm - 5:00pm

Admission:
£4.50, children under 12 free

Charities:
Friends of Anchor
(Haematology and Oncology
Dept ARI) receives 40%,
the net remaining to
SG Beneficiaries

INCHMARLO HOUSE GARDEN
Inchmarlo, Banchory AB31 4AL
Skene Enterprises (Aberdeen) Ltd T: 01330 826242
E: info@inchmarlo-retirement.co.uk   www.inchmarlo-retirement.co.uk

An ever-changing five acre Woodland Garden, featuring ancient Scots pines, Douglas firs and silver firs, some over 42 metres tall, beeches and rare and unusual trees, including pindrow firs, Pere David's maple, Erman's birch and a mountain snowdrop tree. The Oriental Garden features a Kare Sansui, a dry slate stream designed by Peter Roger, a RHS Chelsea gold medal winner. The Rainbow Garden, within the keyhole-shaped purple Prunus cerasifera hedge, has been designed by Billy Carruthers, an eight times gold medal winner at the RHS Scottish Garden Show.

Directions: From Aberdeen via North Deeside Road on A93, one mile west of Banchory turn right at the main gate to the Inchmarlo Estate.

Disabled Access:
Full

Opening Times:
Sunday 24 May
1:30pm - 4:30pm

Admission:
£5.00, OAP £4.00, children
14 and under free

Charities:
Alzheimer Scotland receives
20%, Forget Me Not receives
20%, the net remaining to
SG Beneficiaries

9

KINCARDINE
Kincardine O'Neil AB34 5AE
Mr and Mrs Andrew Bradford

A woodland or wilderness garden in development with some mature rhododendrons and azaleas and new planting amongst mature trees. Sculpture by Lyman Whittaker of Utah. A walled garden with a mixture of herbaceous and shrub borders, a sensational laburnum walk, vegetables and fruit trees. Extensive lawns and wildflower meadows and a thought-provoking Planetary Garden. All with a background of stunning views across Royal Deeside.

Other Details: Children's treasure trail and excellent plant stall.

Directions: Kincardine O'Neil on A93. Gates and lodge are opposite the village school.

Disabled Access:
Partial

Opening Times:
Sunday 14 June
1:30pm - 5:00pm

Admission:
£5.00, children £2.00
(including entry to the
treasure trail)

Charities:
Children 1st receives 20%,
Kincardine O'Neil Village
Hall receives 20%, the net
remaining to SG Beneficiaries

10

WOODEND HOUSE
Banchory AB31 4AY
Mr and Mrs J McHardy

Tucked away in a secluded woodland location. Mature rhododendrons and azaleas with extensive lawns create a stunning backdrop for Woodend House set on the banks of the River Dee. There is a small walled cottage garden and a glorious riverside walk amongst the cowslips and wildflowers giving way to ancient and majestic beech trees.

Directions: Four miles west of Banchory on the A93 (Banchory to Aboyne road).

Disabled Access:
Partial

Opening Times:
Sunday 31 May
1:30pm - 4:30pm

Admission:
£4.00

Charities:
Sandpiper Trust receives
40%, the net remaining to
SG Beneficiaries

KIRKCUDBRIGHTSHIRE

Scotland's Gardens 2015 Guidebook is sponsored by **INVESTEC WEALTH & INVESTMENT**

District Organiser

Dr Janet Brennan	Barholm Castle, Gatehouse of Fleet DG7 2EZ

Area Organisers

Mrs Val Bradbury	Glenisle, Jubilee Path, Kippford DG5 4LW
Mrs W N Dickson	Chipperkyle, Kirkpatrick, Durham DG7 3EY
Mrs C McIver	Loxley, Abercrombie Road, Castle Douglas DG7 1BA
Mrs Lesley Pepper	Anwoth Old Schoolhouse, Gatehouse of Fleet DG7 2EF
Mrs K Ross	Slate Row, Auchencairn, Castle Douglas DG7 1QL
Mrs C V Scott	14 Castle Street, Kirkcudbright DG6 4JA

Treasurer

Mr Duncan Lofts	Balcary Tower, Auchencairn, Castle Douglas DG7 1QZ

Gardens open on a specific date

Danevale Park, Crossmichael	Date to be advised		
Brooklands, Crocketford	Sunday 22 February	12:00pm	-	3:00pm
Netherhall, Castle Douglas	Sunday 10 May	2:00pm	-	5:00pm
Threave Garden, Castle Douglas	Sunday 10 May	10:00am	-	5:00pm
Corsock House, Castle Douglas	Sunday 24 May	2:00pm	-	5:00pm
Cally Gardens, Gatehouse of Fleet	Sunday 31 May	10:00am	-	5:30pm
Brooklands, Crocketford	Sunday 7 June	2:00pm	-	5:00pm
Broughton House Garden, Kirkcudbright	Thursday 11 June	6:00pm	-	9:00pm
Stockarton, Kirkcudbright	Friday 12 June	10:00am	-	4:00pm
Stockarton, Kirkcudbright	Saturday 13 June	10:00am	-	4:00pm
Stockarton with The Waterhouse Gardens	Sunday 14 June	10:00am	-	4:00pm
The Waterhouse Gardens at Stockarton with Stockarton	Sunday 14 June	10:00am	-	4:00pm
Seabank, Rockcliffe	Sunday 21 June	2:00pm	-	5:00pm
Glenlivet with The Limes, Kirkcudbright	Sunday 28 June	1:00pm	-	5:00pm
The Limes with Glenlivet, Kirkcudbright	Sunday 28 June	1:00pm	-	5:00pm
Crofts, Kirkpatrick Durham	Sunday 5 July	2:00pm	-	5:00pm
Southwick House, Southwick	Sunday 5 July	2:00pm	-	5:00pm
Glensone Walled Garden, Southwick	Sunday 26 July	2:00pm	-	5:00pm
Cally Gardens, Gatehouse of Fleet	Sunday 2 August	10:00am	-	5:30pm
Threave Garden, Castle Douglas	Sunday 9 August	10:00am	-	5:00pm

KIRKCUDBRIGHTSHIRE

Gardens open by arrangement

Anwoth Old Schoolhouse, Anwoth, Gatehouse of Fleet	15 February - 15 November	01557 814444
Barholm Castle, Gatehouse of Fleet	1 February - 4 October	01557 840327
Corsock House, Corsock, Castle Douglas	1 April - 30 June	01644 440250
The Mill House at Gelston, Gelston	12 July - 13 September	01556 503955

Danevale, Kirkcudbrighshire © Mary McIlvenna

Key to symbols

 New in 2015   Homemade teas   Accommodation

 Teas   Dogs on a lead allowed   Plant stall

 Cream teas   Wheelchair access   Scottish Snowdrop Festival

Garden locations

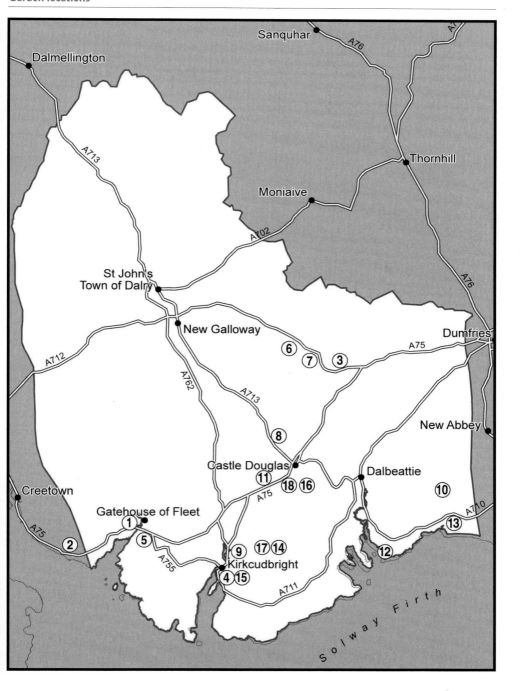

ANWOTH OLD SCHOOLHOUSE
Anwoth, Gatehouse of Fleet DG7 2EF
Mr & Mrs Pepper T: 01557 814444
E: lesley.pepper@btinternet.com

Two acres of delightful cottage-style gardens behind the old schoolhouse and cottage in a picturesque setting opposite Anwoth old church (in ruins) and graveyard. Winding paths alongside burn, informally planted with unusual woodland perennials and shrubs. Wildlife pond, fish pond, rock garden, wildflower area and viewpoint, vegetable garden.

Directions: Driving west on the A75, take the Anwoth turnoff about half a mile after Gatehouse of Fleet. Anwoth Church is about half a mile along the road and Anwoth Old Schoolhouse is a little further along, opposite Anwoth Old Church (in ruins).

Disabled Access:
None

Opening Times:
By arrangement
15 February - 15 November

Admission:
£3.00

Charities:
Dogs for the Disabled receives 40%, the net remaining to SG Beneficiaries

BARHOLM CASTLE
Gatehouse of Fleet DG7 2EZ
Dr John and Dr Janet Brennan T: 01557 840327
E: barholmcastle@gmail.com

Barholm Castle, a 16th century tower, was restored from a ruin in 2006 and the owners moved in permanently in 2011. Since the restoration, the three acre gardens surrounding the tower have been slowly developing from scratch. There is a small walled garden, a wooded ravine, a greenhouse and newly developing shrub borders, ponds, rockeries and herbaceous beds. Good snowdrop display in February. Lots of colour March to October. The views over Wigtown Bay are magnificent.

Directions: Off the A75 at the Cairn Holy turn-off, fork right three times up a steep narrow road for ½ mile.

Disabled Access:
Partial

Opening Times:
By arrangement
1 February - 4 October

Admission:
£4.00

Charities:
Home-Start Wigtownshire receives 40%, the net remaining to SG Beneficiaries

BROOKLANDS
Crocketford DG2 8QH
Mr and Mrs Robert Herries

Large old walled garden, richly planted with a wide variety of perennials, including many unusual species, soft fruit and vegetables. Mature woodland garden full of rhododendrons and carpeted with snowdrops in spring.

Directions: Turn off the A712 Crocketford to New Galloway Road one mile outside Crocketford at the Gothic gatehouse (on the right travelling north).

Disabled Access:
Partial

Opening Times:
Sunday 22 February
12:00pm - 3:00pm
for the Snowdrop Festival
Sunday 7 June
2:00pm - 5:00pm

Admission:
£4.00

Charities:
ReMission receives 40%, the net remaining to SG Beneficiaries

BROUGHTON HOUSE GARDEN
12 High Street, Kirkcudbright DG6 4JX
The National Trust for Scotland T: 01557 330 437
E: broughtonhouse@nts.org.uk www.nts.org.uk

This event will offer visitors an evening of live music, gardens walks and refreshments (included in the entry price). It is a chance to see the garden by a different light! Broughton House Garden is a fascinating town house garden that belonged to E A Hornel - artist, collector and one of the 'Glasgow boys'. Full of colour, mostly herbaceous, old apple trees, greenhouse with old pelargonium varieties, fruit and vegetable garden.

Directions: In Kirkcudbright High Street.

Disabled Access:
Partial

Opening Times:
Thursday 11 June
6:00pm - 9:00pm

Admission:
£4.00 (refreshments included in admission price)

Charities:
All proceeds to
SG Beneficiaries

CALLY GARDENS
Gatehouse of Fleet DG7 2DJ
Mr Michael Wickenden T: 01557 815 029
E: info@callygardens.co.uk www.callygardens.co.uk

A specialist nursery in a densely planted 2.7 acre 18th century walled garden with old vinery and bothy, all surrounded by the Cally Oak Woods. Our collection of 3,500 varieties of plants can be seen and a selection will be available pot-grown. Excellent range of rare herbaceous perennials.

Directions: From Dumfries take the Gatehouse turning off A75 and turn left through the Cally Palace Hotel gateway from where the gardens are well signposted.

Disabled Access:
Full

Opening Times:
Sunday 31 May
10:00am - 5:30pm
Sunday 2 August
10:00am - 5:30pm

Admission:
£2.50

Charities:
ROKPA Tibetan Charity receives 40%, the net remaining to SG Beneficiaries

CORSOCK HOUSE
Corsock, Castle Douglas DG7 3DJ
The Ingall Family T: 01644 440250

Rhododendrons and azaleas throughout wonderful woodland walks with temples, water gardens and loch. One acre formal walled garden under development. David Bryce turreted Scottish Baronial house in background. "The most photogenic woodland garden in Scotland. Corsock is a triumph; anyone looking for woodland garden ideas should come here for inspiration." Kenneth Cox in *Scotland for Gardeners*.

Directions: Off A75 Dumfries fourteen miles, Castle Douglas ten miles, Corsock village ½ mile on A712.

Disabled Access:
Full

Opening Times:
Sunday 24 May
2:00pm - 5:00pm
Also by arrangement
1 April - 30 June

Admission:
£4.00

Charities:
Corsock and Kirkpatrick Durham Church receives 40%, the net remaining to SG Beneficiaries

CROFTS
Kirkpatrick Durham, Castle Douglas DG7 3HX
Mrs Andrew Dalton T: 01556 650235

Victorian country house garden with mature trees, a walled garden with fruit and vegetables and glasshouses, hydrangea garden and a pretty water garden. Delightful woodland walk, colourfully planted with bog plants, with stream running through.

Directions: A75 to Crocketford, then three miles on A712 to Corsock and New Galloway.

Disabled Access:
Partial

Opening Times:
Sunday 5 July
2:00pm - 5:00pm

Admission:
£4.00

Charities:
Kirkpatrick Durham Church receives 40%, the net remaining to SG Beneficiaries

DANEVALE PARK
Crossmichael DG7 2LP
Mrs M R C Gillespie T: 01556 670223
E: danevale@tiscali.co.uk

Mature policies with woodland walk alongside the River Dee. One of the finest displays of snowdrops in Scotland. We also get great praise for our teas.

Directions: On the A713. Crossmichael one mile, Castle Douglas two miles.

Disabled Access:
Partial

Opening Times:
Date and times to be advised
check website
Admission:
£2.50

Charities:
Poppy Scotland receives 40%, the net remaining to SG Beneficiaries

GLENLIVET WITH THE LIMES
Tongland Road, Kirkcudbright DG6 4UR
Alec and Doreen Blackadder T: 01557 332333
E: alec@alecblackadder.wanadoo.co.uk

This new town garden of half an acre on the edge of Kirkcudbright has been developed by the owners from scratch over the past seven years. It has a remarkably mature appearance already and is packed with colour and a huge variety of thriving plants, shrubs and trees, all carefully tended. There are two small ponds connected by a rill, with fountains at each end, herbaceous beds, gravel beds and a variety of statuary and garden structures. The garden is in a lovely position overlooking the River Dee.

Other Details: Parking on main road.

Directions: Coming in to Kirkcudbright via the A711 and Tongland Bridge, on the outskirts of town pass the Arden House hotel on left. Glenlivet is about ½ mile further on the right. It is exactly half a mile from the town centre crossroads on the Tongland Road.

Disabled Access:
Partial

Opening Times:
Sunday 28 June
1:00pm - 5:00pm

Admission:
£5.00 includes both gardens

Charities:
Friends of Kirkcudbright Swimming Pool receives 40%, the net remaining to SG Beneficiaries

GLENSONE WALLED GARDEN
Southwick DG2 8AW
William and Josephine Millar T: 01387 780215
E: millar.josephine@gmail.com

A restored walled garden complete with central water feature. There are borders of perennials and shrubs with beds interspersed through the lawn. A large kitchen garden has a variety of vegetables and fruit occupies a section of the garden. Bee boles, a unique feature, are positioned in two opposite corners of the wall. The garden is set in an idyllic valley with views of the Solway Firth and the Cumbrian hills.

Other Details: Homemade teas are available at £1.50.

Directions: Off the A710 Dumfries to Dalbeattie coast road at Caulkerbush. Take the B793 to Dalbeattie for two miles then turn right and follow the arrows.

Disabled Access:
Full

Opening Times:
Sunday 26 July
2:00pm - 5:00pm

Admission:
£3.50

Charities:
Combat Stress receives 40%, the net remaining to SG Beneficiaries

NETHERHALL
Glenlochar, Castle Douglas DG7 2AA
Sir Malcolm and Lady Ross T: 01556 680208
E: susieross@netherhall.com

Traditional landscaped country house garden with shrub borders, surrounding a charming 19th century house. Wonderful views across the River Dee to Threave Castle and beyond, with riverside walk. Miniature Shetland ponies. Ospreys, red kites and many species of wildfowl are regular visitors.

Directions: Travelling west along the A75, take the turnoff for Glenlochar (opposite the turnoff for Bridge of Dee) shortly after the second Castle Douglas roundabout. Netherhall is about ¾ mile along the Glenochar road on the right.

Disabled Access:
Partial

Opening Times:
Sunday 10 May
2:00pm - 5:00pm

Admission:
£4.00, concessions £3.00

Charities:
RNLI Kirkcudbright receives 40%, the net remaining to SG Beneficiaries

SEABANK
The Merse, Rockcliffe DG5 4QH
Julian and Theodora Stanning T: 01556 630244

The one and a half acre gardens extend to the high water mark with fine views across the Urr Estuary, Rough Island and beyond. Herbaceous borders surround the house and there is a new walled garden for fruit and vegetables. A plantswoman's garden with a range of interesting and unusual plants.

Directions: Park in the public car park at Rockcliffe. Walk down the road about fifty metres towards the sea and turn left along The Merse, a private road. Seabank is the sixth house on the left.

Disabled Access:
Partial

Opening Times:
Sunday 21 June
2:00pm - 5:00pm

Admission:
£3.50

Charities:
Marie Curie (DG5 Fundraising Group) receives 40%, the net remaining to SG Beneficiaries

SOUTHWICK HOUSE
Southwick DG2 8AH
Mr and Mrs R H L Thomas

The extensive gardens at Southwick House comprise three main areas. The first is a traditional formal walled garden with potager and large glasshouse producing a range of fruit, vegetables and cutting flowers. Adjacent to this is a hedged formal garden with herbaceous, shrub and rose beds centred around a lily pond, with roses predominating as an interesting feature. Outwith the formal gardens there is a large water garden with two connected ponds with trees, shrubs and lawns running alongside the Southwick Burn.

Directions: On A710 near Caulkerbush. Dalbeattie seven miles, Dumfries seventeen miles.

Disabled Access:
Partial

Opening Times:
Sunday 5 July
2:00pm - 5:00pm

Admission:
£4.00

Charities:
Friends of Loch Arthur
Community receives
40%, the net remaining to
SG Beneficiaries

STOCKARTON
Kirkcudbright DG6 4XS
Lt. Col. and Mrs Richard Cliff T: 01557 330430

This charming garden was started in 1994. The aim has been to create small informal gardens around a Galloway farmhouse, leading down to a lochan, where there are a number of unusual small trees and shrubs. In 1996 a small arboretum of oak was planted, including some very rare ones, as a shelter belt.

Directions: On B727 Kirkcudbright to Gelston Road. Kirkcudbright three miles, Castle Douglas seven miles.

Disabled Access:
Partial

Opening Times:
Fri & Sat 12 - 13 June
10:00am - 4:00pm
Sunday 14 June 10:00am -
4:00pm (opening with The
Waterhouse Gardens)

Admission:
Friday and Saturday £3.00
Sunday £5.00 (includes entry
to The Waterhouse Gardens)

Charities:
Friends of Loch Arthur
Comm. receives 40%, the net
remaining to SG Beneficiaries

THE LIMES WITH GLENLIVET
Kirkcudbright DG6 4XD
Mr and Mrs McHale

Seven years ago this one and a quarter acre garden was mainly lawn, a few mature trees and some shrubs. There is now a large rock garden, gravel garden, mixed perennial and shrub borders and three woodland areas. The McHales grow most of their own fruit and vegetables. The greenhouse is used for propagating and protecting tender plants in winter, and tomatoes are grown in summer. Many new introductions are grown from seed, obtained from the seed exchanges of specialist plant groups.

Directions: In Kirkcudbright go straight along St Mary Street towards Dundrennan. The Limes is on the right, about ½ mile from the town centre crossroads, on the edge of the town (i.e. ½ mile in the opposite direction from Glenlivet.)

Disabled Access:
Partial

Opening Times:
Sunday 28 June
1:00pm - 5:00pm

Admission:
£5.00 includes entry to both
gardens

Charities:
Friends of Kirkcudbright
Swimming Pool receives
40%, the net remaining to
SG Beneficiaries

16 THE MILL HOUSE AT GELSTON
Gelston DG7 1SH
Malcolm and Sheila McEwan T: 01556 503955
E: sheilamcewan@yahoo.co.uk

Large cottage garden on several levels surrounding former Mill House, with adjacent stream and path along former mill lade. The garden is owned by a retired wildlife ranger who has recently planted swathes of colourful perennials especially to attract wildlife. It is now a haven for insects, butterflies and birds. Some of the conifers, planted by the previous owner, remain; in addition, large numbers of flowering plants, shrubs and trees have been planted during the past five years, giving this garden, which was previously opened by the former owner, a new emphasis and layout.

Directions: Travelling west along the A75, take the turnoff for Castle Douglas at the second Castle Douglas roundabout, then follow signs for Gelston. The Mill House is the last/first house in the village within the 30mph limit.

Disabled Access:
Partial

Opening Times:
By arrangement
12 July - 13 September

Admission:
£3.00

Charities:
World Wide Fund for Nature
(WWF) receives 40%, the net
remaining to SG Beneficiaries

17 THE WATERHOUSE GARDENS AT STOCKARTON WITH STOCKARTON
Kirkcudbright DG6 4XS
Martin Gould & Sharon O'Rourke T: 01557 331266
E: waterhousekbt@aol.com www.waterhousekbt.co.uk

One acre of densely planted terraced cottage style gardens attached to a Galloway cottage. Three ponds surround the oak framed eco-polehouse 'The Waterhouse' available to rent 52 weeks a year. Climbing roses, clematis and honeysuckles are a big feature as well as pond-side walk. Over 50 photos on our website. Featured on BBC Scotland's 'Beechgrove Garden' 2007.

Directions: On B727 Kirkcudbright to Gelston - Dalbeattie road. Kirkcudbright three miles, Castle Douglas seven miles.

Disabled Access:
None

Opening Times:
Sunday 14 June
10:00am - 4:00pm

Admission:
£5.00 includes entry to
Stockarton

Charities:
Friends of Loch Arthur
Community receives
40%, the net remaining to
SG Beneficiaries

18 THREAVE GARDEN
Castle Douglas DG7 1RX
The National Trust for Scotland T: 01556 502 575
E: rapolley@nts.org.uk www.nts.org.uk

Home of the Trust's School of Heritage Gardening. Spectacular daffodils in spring, colourful herbaceous borders in summer, striking autumn trees, interesting water features and a heather garden. There is also a working walled garden. For more information on the Scotland's Gardens event, please contact the property or visit http://www.nts.org.uk/Events/.

Other Details: Champion Trees: Acer platanoides 'Princeton Gold'. Self-catering accommodation available. Cafe open daily. Plants and garden produce for sale.

Directions: Off A75, one mile west of Castle Douglas.

Disabled Access:
Full

Opening Times:
Sunday 10 May
10:00am - 5:00pm
Sunday 9 August
10:00am - 5:00pm

Admission:
£7.50, concessions £6.50
(including NTS members).
N.B. Prices correct at time of
going to print

Charities:
Donation to SG Beneficiaries

LANARKSHIRE

Scotland's Gardens 2015 Guidebook is sponsored by **INVESTEC WEALTH & INVESTMENT**

District Organisers

Mrs V C Rogers   1 Snowberry Field, Thankerton ML12 6RJ

Area Organisers

Mrs M Maxwell Stuart   Baitlaws, Lamington, Biggar ML12 6HR

Treasurer

Mr Gordon Bell   9 Muirkirk Gardens, Strathaven ML10 6FS

Gardens open on a specific date

Cleghorn, Lanark	Sunday 22 February	2:00pm	4:00pm
The Scots Mining Company House, Biggar	Saturday 2 May	2:00pm	4:30pm
The Scots Mining Company House, Biggar	Sunday 3 May	2:00pm	4:30pm
Nemphlar Village Garden Trail, Lanark	Sunday 24 May	1:30pm	5:00pm
Dippoolbank Cottage, Carnwath	Sunday 14 June	2:00pm	6:00pm
Lindsaylands, Biggar	Sunday 12 July	2:00pm	6:00pm
Dippoolbank Cottage, Carnwath	Sunday 19 July	2:00pm	6:00pm
Wellbutts, Elsrickle	Sunday 26 July	1:00pm	5:00pm
Culter Allers, Biggar	Sunday 16 August	2:00pm	5:00pm

Gardens open by arrangement

20 Smithycroft, Hamilton	1 April - 30 September	01698 281838 M: 07980 378716
Carmichael Mill, Lanark	On request	01555 665880
The Scots Mining Company House, Biggar	1 April - 30 September	01659 74235

Key to symbols

 New in 2015   Homemade teas   Accommodation

 Teas   Dogs on a lead allowed   Plant stall

Cream teas   Wheelchair access   Scottish Snowdrop Festival

Garden locations

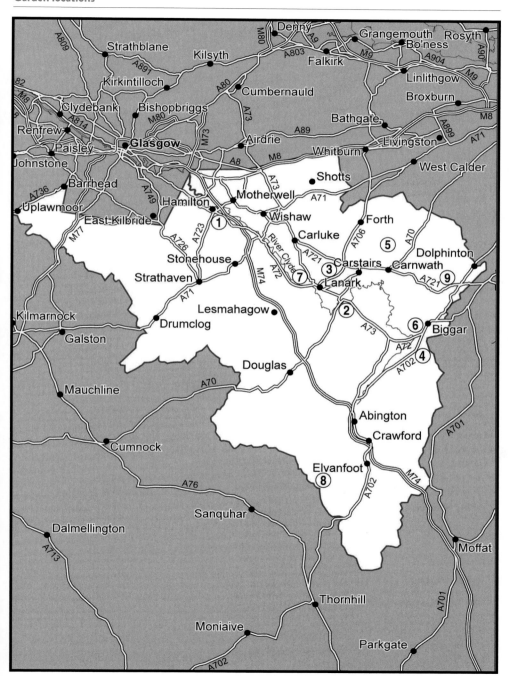

20 SMITHYCROFT
Hamilton ML3 7UL
Mr and Mrs R I Fionda T: 01698 281838 M: 07980 378716
E: idafionda@hotmail.com

A plantswoman's award-winning garden which has developed into a mature oasis. Phormiums and clematis abound and there is a large range of unusual plants which only flourish in sheltered parts of Scotland.

Other Details: Teas available by prior request. Groups welcome.

Directions: Off M74 at Junction 6. One mile on A72. Well signed.

Disabled Access:
Full

Opening Times:
By arrangement
1 April - 30 September

Admission:
£3.50

Charities:
Mary's Meals receives 40%, the net remaining to SG Beneficiaries

CARMICHAEL MILL
Hyndford Bridge, Lanark ML11 8SJ
Chris, Ken and Gemma Fawell T: 01555 665880
E: ken.fawell@btinternet.com

Riverside gardens surrounding the only remaining workable water powered grain mill in Clydesdale. Diverse plant habitats from saturated to bone dry allow a vast range of trees and shrubs, both ornamental and fruit, with a vegetable garden. Herbaceous perennials, annuals and biennials with ornamental/wildlife pond complementing the landscape. Also, archaeological remains of medieval grain mills from circa 1200 and foundry, lint mill and threshing mill activity within the curtilage of the Category B Listed Building.

Other Details: Admission includes entry to the mill which will be turning, river levels permitting.

Directions: Just off A73 Lanark to Biggar road ½ mile east of the Hyndford Bridge.

Disabled Access:
Partial

Opening Times:
By arrangement on request

Admission:
£4.00, children over 12 £2.00

Charities:
Donation to SG Beneficiaries

CLEGHORN
Stable House, Cleghorn Farm, Lanark ML11 7RN
Mr and Mrs R Eliot Lockhart T: 01555 663792
E: info@cleghornestategardens.com www.cleghornestategardens.com

18th century garden which is currently being renovated. Mature trees and shrubs, with masses of snowdrops spread around. Beautiful views to the south of Tinto Hill and the Cleghorn Glen.

Directions: Cleghorn Farm is situated two miles north of Lanark on the A706.

Disabled Access:
None

Opening Times:
Sunday 22 February
2:00pm - 4:00pm
for the Snowdrop Festival

Admission:
By donation

Charities:
Marie Curie Cancer Care receives 40%, the net remaining to SG Beneficiaries

CULTER ALLERS
Coulter, Biggar ML12 6PZ
The McCosh Family

Culter Allers, a late Victorian baronial house, has maintained its traditional one acre walled kitchen garden, half with fruit and vegetables, the other half with mainly cut flowers and herbaceous. The policies of the house are also open and include woodland walks and an avenue of 125 year old lime trees leading to the village church.

Directions: In the village of Coulter, three miles south of Biggar on A702.

Disabled Access:
Partial

Opening Times:
Sunday 16 August
2:00pm - 5:00pm

Admission:
£4.00, children free

Charities:
Coulter Library Trust receives 40%, the net remaining to SG Beneficiaries

DIPPOOLBANK COTTAGE
Carnwath ML11 8LP
Mr Allan Brash

Artist's intriguing cottage garden. Vegetables grown in small beds. Herbs, fruit, flowers, pond in woodland area with tree house and summer house. Fernery completed in 2007. This is an organic garden mainly constructed with recycled materials.

Directions: Off B7016 between Forth and Carnwath near the village of Braehead on the Auchengray road. Approximately eight miles from Lanark. Well signposted.

Disabled Access:
None

Opening Times:
Sunday 14 June
2:00pm - 6:00pm
Sunday 19 July
2:00pm - 6:00pm

Admission:
£4.00

Charities:
The Little Haven receives 40%, the net remaining to SG Beneficiaries

LINDSAYLANDS
Biggar ML12 6NR
Steve and Alison Crichton

Lindsaylands was designed by the well known Scottish architect William Leiper. Although built in 1869 it incorporates a much older building. The garden at Lindsaylands was opened last year for the for the first time in fifty years. The garden features a collection of mature specimen trees set amongst extensive lawns. There are herbaceous borders, a working kitchen garden, greenhouses, and woodland walks.

Directions: On Lindsaylands Road ½ mile south west of Biggar.

Disabled Access:
Full

Opening Times:
Sunday 12 July
2:00pm - 6:00pm

Admission:
£4.00

Charities:
Scottish Autism receives 40%, the net remaining to SG Beneficiaries

NEMPHLAR VILLAGE GARDEN TRAIL
Nemphlar, Lanark ML11 9JG
The Gardeners of Nemphlar Village

A number of interesting small and medium sized gardens in the village of Nemphlar. A pleasant stroll of one mile covers all the gardens with extensive glorious views over the Clyde Valley and Tinto Hill.

Other Details: Homemade cream teas will be served in the village hall.

Directions: Leave A73 at Cartland Bridge (Lanark to Carluke Road) or A72 (Clyde Valley Road) at Crossford. Both routes well signposted.

Disabled Access:
None

Opening Times:
Sunday 24 May
1:30pm - 5:00pm

Admission:
£4.00

Charities:
Tree of Hope receives 40%, the net remaining to SG Beneficiaries

THE SCOTS MINING COMPANY HOUSE
Leadhills, Biggar ML12 6XP
Charlie and Greta Clark T: 01659 74235

The site is c.400 metres above sea level, which is high for a cultivated garden. The surrounding landscape is open moorland with sheep grazing. The garden is largely enclosed by dense planting, but the various walks allow views through the trees into the surrounding countryside. Historic Scotland in its register of "Gardens and designed landscapes" describe the garden as "An outstanding example of a virtually unaltered, small, 18th century garden layout connected with James Stirling, the developer of the profitable Leadhills mining enterprise, and possibly William Adam." Say goodbye to spring walking amongst the last daffodils of the year.

Other Details: Luxurious homemade teas, also available by prior request on the By Arrangement openings.

Directions: On Main Street, Leadhills (B797) six miles from M74 Junction 13 (Abington). Gate in Station Road.

Disabled Access:
Partial

Opening Times:
Saturday 2 May
2:00pm - 4:30pm
Sunday 3 May
2:00pm - 4:30pm
Also by arrangement
1 April - 30 September

Admission:
£3.00

Charities:
Scots Mining Company Trust receives 40%, the net remaining to SG Beneficiaries

WELLBUTTS
Elsrickle, by Biggar ML12 6QZ
Mr and Mrs N Slater

Started in 2000 from a bare brown site around a renovated croft cottage, with additional field ground obtained in 2005, the garden is now approximately two acres. Due to the exposed and elevated (960 foot) position the ongoing priority is hedge and shrub planting to give some protection for the many and varied herbaceous borders, two large ponds and 'boggery'.

Other Details: Strawberry cream teas available.

Directions: Parking on the main road (A721) near to bus stop. Walk to garden (approximately 200 yards).

Disabled Access:
None

Opening Times:
Sunday 26 July
1:00pm - 5:00pm

Admission:
£4.00

Charities:
MS Society receives 40%, the net remaining to SG Beneficiaries

LOCHABER

District Organiser

Norrie and Anna Maclaren	Ard-Daraich, Ardgour, Nr. Fort William PH33 7AB

Area Organisers

Mrs Angela Simpson	The Larch House, Camusdarach, Arisaig PH39 4NT

Treasurer

Norrie Maclaren	Ard-Daraich, Ardgour, Nr. Fort William PH33 7AB

Gardens open on a specific date

Canna House Walled Garden, Isle of Canna	Saturday 2 May	10:00am - 4:30pm
Arisaig House, Beasdale, Arisaig	Saturday 9 May	11:00am - 4:00pm
Aberarder with Ardverikie, Kinlochlaggan	Sunday 24 May	2:00pm - 5:30pm
Ardverikie with Aberarder, Kinlochlaggan	Sunday 24 May	2:00pm - 5:30pm
Roshven House, Lochailort	Sunday 9 August	2:00pm - 4:30pm
Canna House Walled Garden, Isle of Canna	Wednesday 12 August	10:30am - 4:00pm

Gardens open regularly

Ardtornish, By Lochaline, Morvern	1 January - 31 December	10:00am - Dusk

Gardens open by arrangement

Ard-Daraich, Ardgour, by Fort William	On request	01855 841384

Key to symbols

	New in 2015		Homemade teas		Accommodation
	Teas		Dogs on a lead allowed		Plant stall
	Cream teas		Wheelchair access		Scottish Snowdrop Festival

Garden locations

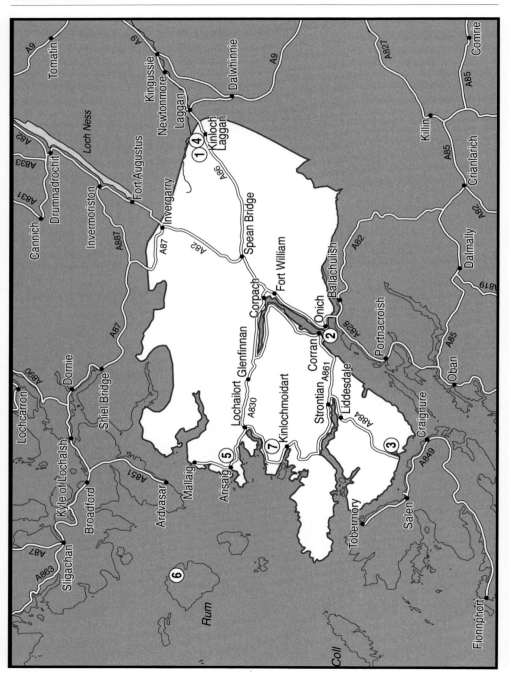

ABERARDER WITH ARDVERIKIE
Kinlochlaggan PH20 1BX
The Feilden Family T: 01528 544300

The garden has been laid out over the last 20 years to create a mixture of spring and autumn plants and trees, including rhododendrons, azaleas and acers. The elevated view down Loch Laggan from the garden is exceptional.

Directions: On A86 between Newtonmore and Spean Bridge at east end of Loch Laggan.

Disabled Access:
Partial

Opening Times:
Sunday 24 May
2:00pm - 5:30pm

Admission:
£5.00 includes entrance to
Ardverikie

Charities:
Highland Hospice receives
20%, Laggan Church receives
20%, the net remaining to
SG Beneficiaries

ARD-DARAICH
Ardgour, by Fort William PH33 7AB
Norrie and Anna Maclaren T: 01855 841384
www.arddaraich.co.uk

Glorious seven acre hill garden, in a spectacular setting, with many fine and uncommon rhododendrons, an interesting selection of trees and shrubs and a large collection of camellias, acers and sorbus.

Directions: West from Fort William, across the Corran Ferry, turn left and a mile on the right further west.

Disabled Access:
None

Opening Times:
By arrangement on request

Admission:
£4.00

Charities:
Donation to SG Beneficiaries

ARDTORNISH
By Lochaline, Morvern PA80 5UZ
Mrs John Raven

Wonderful gardens of interesting mature conifers, rhododendrons, deciduous trees, shrubs and herbaceous, set amid magnificent scenery.

Directions: A884 Lochaline three miles.

Disabled Access:
None

Opening Times:
1 January - 31 December
10:00am - 6:00pm or Dusk

Admission:
£4.00

Charities:
Donation to SG Beneficiaries

ARDVERIKIE WITH ABERARDER
Kinlochlaggan PH20 1BX
Mrs P Laing and Mrs E T Smyth-Osbourne T: 01528 544300

Lovely setting on Loch Laggan with magnificent trees. Walled garden with large collection of acers, shrubs and herbaceous. Architecturally interesting house (not open). Site of the filming of the TV series "Monarch of the Glen".

Other Details: Teas at Aberarder.

Directions: On A86 between Newtonmore and Spean Bridge. Entrance at east end of Loch Laggan by gate lodge over bridge.

Disabled Access:
Partial

Opening Times:
Sunday 24 May
2:00pm - 5:30pm

Admission:
£5.00 includes entrance to Aberarder

Charities:
Highland Hospice receives 20%, Laggan Church receives 20%, the net remaining to SG Beneficiaries

---

ARISAIG HOUSE
Beasdale, Arisaig PH39 4NR
Ms. Emma Weir T: 01687 450730
E: sarahwi@arisaighouse.co.uk www.arisaighouse.co.uk

Arisaig House, designed in 1864 by Philip Webb, is a luxurious guest house offering dinner, bed and breakfast. Wander through twenty acres of well-established and cared for woodlands and gardens. Extensive collection of specimen trees, rhododendrons and shrubs. Exquisite terrace with formal rose and herb beds. Visit the kitchen garden with its orchard, soft fruit cages, productive polytunnel, and vegetable beds. Whatever can be found in the garden that day is on the menu that night! Birds and wildlife abound.

Other Details: Live music on the terrace. Delicious homemade teas in the dining room. Works by local artists on sale in the house.

Directions: Arisaig House is 32 miles from Fort William on the A830 road to Mallaig. Approximately 1.2 miles from Beasdale train station turn left into junction signposted Arisaig House & Cottages.

Disabled Access:
None

Opening Times:
Saturday 9 May
11:00am - 4:00pm

Admission:
£4.00

Charities:
Local Feis receives 40%, the net remaining to SG Beneficiaries

Arisaig House

CANNA HOUSE WALLED GARDEN
Isle of Canna PH44 4RS
National Trust for Scotland T: 01687 462998
E: sconnor@nts.org.uk www.nts.org.uk

Formerly derelict two acre walled garden brought back to life following a five year restoration project. There are soft fruits, top fruits, vegetables, ornamental lawns and flower beds. There is also a stunning 80 foot Escallonia arch. The garden has been replanted to attract bees, butterflies and moths. The woodland walks outside walls are not to be missed along with the spectacular views of neighbouring islands. Don't miss your chance to see this gem.

Directions: Access Isle of Canna via Calmac ferry from Mallaig pier.

Disabled Access:
Partial

Opening Times:
Saturday 2 May
10:00am - 4:30pm
Wednesday 12 August
10:30am - 4:00pm

Admission:
£3.00 (including NTS members). N.B. Prices correct at the time of going to print

Charities:
Donation to SG Beneficiaries

ROSHVEN HOUSE
Lochailort PH38 4NB
Mr and Mrs Angus MacDonald

Roshven House, a recently restored large, historic house spectacularly sited overlooking one of the great romantic views of the west towards a pattern of islands including Eigg, Muck and Rhum. The house is surrounded by nearly 30 acres of grounds. The formal garden is the most recent creation, joining mature trees, box edged shrubbery, azaleas, rhododendrons, and unusual species extending the flowering season from summer into autumn colour. Woodland walks under construction.

Directions: From Fort William, take the A830 to Lochailort. Left at Lochailort Inn onto A861, five miles to Roshven signpost, a further 400 metres turn right at stone pillar entrance.

Disabled Access:
None

Opening Times:
Sunday 9 August
2:00pm - 4:30pm

Admission:
£4.00

Charities:
RNLI receives 40%, the net remaining to SG Beneficiaries

MIDLOTHIAN

Scotland's Gardens 2015 Guidebook is sponsored by **INVESTEC WEALTH & INVESTMENT**

District Organiser

Mrs Sarah Barron DL	Laureldene, Kevock Road, Lasswade EH18 1HT

Area Organisers

Mrs Margaret Drummond	Pomathorn House, Penicuik EH26 8PJ
Mrs R Hill	Law House, 27 Biggar Road, Silverburn EH26 9LJ
Mrs Eilidh Liddle	21 Craigiebield Crescent, Penicuik EH26 9EQ

Treasurer

Mrs Margaret Drummond	Pomathorn House, Penicuik EH26 8PJ

Gardens open on a specific date

Kevock Road Gardens, Lasswade	Sunday 1 March	12:00pm	-	3:00pm
Temple Village Gardens, Temple	Sunday 7 June	2:00pm	-	5:00pm
Kevock Road Gardens, Lasswade	Saturday 13 June	12:00pm	-	5:00pm
Kevock Road Gardens, Lasswade	Sunday 14 June	12:00pm	-	5:00pm
Kirkhill Gardens, Penicuik	Sunday 16 August	2:00pm	-	5:00pm

Gardens open by arrangement

Newhall, Carlops	1 June - 31 July	01968 660206
The Old Sun Inn, Dalkeith	1 June - 31 July	0131 663 2648

Key to symbols

 New in 2015

 Homemade teas

 Accommodation

 Teas

 Dogs on a lead allowed

 Plant stall

 Cream teas

 Wheelchair access

 Scottish Snowdrop Festival

Garden locations

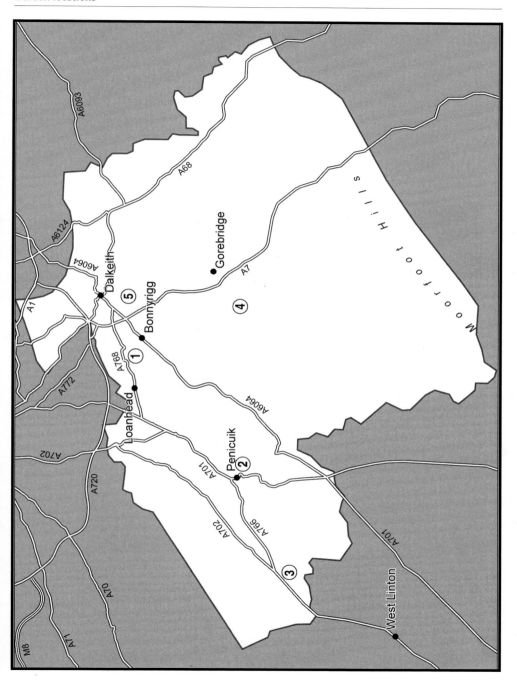

KEVOCK ROAD GARDENS
Lasswade EH18 1HT
The Gardeners of Kevock Road

Several gardens including Kevock Garden and Greenfield Lodge will be open. All very different but complementary to each other with a wonderful range of unusual trees, shrubs, herbaceous and bulbs. March opening for snowdrops and spring flowers. Glorious summer displays in June.

Other Details: Soup and rolls in March, homemade teas in June at Greenfield Lodge. Parking available in Drummond Grange Nursing Home and at the Edinburgh & Lasswade Riding Centre at the foot of Kevock Road. Disabled parking only on Kevock Road and Green Lane please. Greenfield Lodge can be accessed on foot from Kevock Road. All open gardens will be signposted.

Directions: Kevock Road lies to the south of the A678 Loanhead/Lasswade Road. Five minutes from the city by-pass Lasswade Junction and on the 31 Lothian Bus route to Polton/Bonnyrigg.

Disabled Access:
Partial

Opening Times:
Sunday 1 March
12:00pm - 3:00pm
Saturday 13 June
12:00pm - 5:00pm
Sunday 14 June
12:00pm - 5:00pm

Admission:
£6.00

Charities:
WOW Wellbeing of Women eceives 40%, the net remaining to SG Beneficiaries

KIRKHILL GARDENS
Kirkhill, Penicuik EH26 8JE
Kirkhill Gardeners T: 01968 674046
E: med1002@btinternet.com

A group of modern gardens varying in size and style within walking distance of one another, with lovely views, in an elevated situation to the east of Penicuik Town Centre.

Other Details: Disabled access is very limited due to steps.

Directions: From Edinburgh City Bypass, take A701 Penicuik/Peebles route to Sacred Heart Church, 56 John Street, Penicuik EH26 8NE, where you will be given directions and a map of the gardens, which are a short drive away. From Edinburgh City Centre take buses 15, 27 and 47 to Penicuik town centre. For further information and directions contact Margaret Drummond on T: 01968 674046 or E: med1002@btinternet.com (M: 07984 818191 on the day).

Disabled Access:
Partial

Opening Times:
Sunday 16 August
2:00pm - 5:00pm

Admission:
£4.00 includes all gardens, children free

Charities:
Marie Curie Cancer Care receives 40%, the net remaining to SG Beneficiaries

NEWHALL
Carlops EH26 9LY
John and Tricia Kennedy T: 01968 660206
E: tricia.kennedy@newhalls.co.uk

Traditional 18th century walled garden with huge herbaceous border, shrubberies, fruit and vegetables. Many unusual plants for sale. Stunning glen running along the North Esk river in process of restoration (stout shoes recommended). Large pond with evolving planting. Young arboretum and collection of Rosa pimpinellifolia. As in *Good Gardens Guide 2010, Scottish Field, Gardens Monthly, Scotland on Sunday.*

Directions: On A702 Edinburgh/Biggar, ¼ mile after Ninemileburn and a mile before Carlops. Follow signs.

Disabled Access:
Partial

Opening Times:
By arrangement
1 June - 31 July

Admission:
£4.00

Charities:
Stable Life receives 40%, the net remaining to SG Beneficiaries

TEMPLE VILLAGE GARDENS
Temple EH23 4SG
Temple Village Gardeners T: 01875 830253
E: sandydelap@btconnect.com

Temple Village is situated on the east bank of the River South Esk, to the south west of Gorebridge and is one of Midlothian's most attractive and historic conservation villages. Between the 12th and 14th centuries, Temple was the headquarters of the Knights Templar, more recently the village has been home to Sir William Gillies the famous Scottish painter. A number of village gardens will be open, from the charming riverside garden of The Mill House, to the delightful front and rear gardens of one or two of the village houses on the Main Street. Planted in a variety of different styles, they display contrasting designs and plant combinations, reflecting the villager's many distinctive horticultural interests. The early 14th century Parish Church Yard will be open.

Other Details: Homemade teas in the village hall. Route maps will be available of gardens around village which are open.

Directions: On B6372, three miles off the A7 from Gorebridge.

Disabled Access:
Partial

Opening Times:
Sunday 7 June
2:00pm - 5:00pm

Admission:
£5.00, children under 12 free

Charities:
Temple Village Hall receives 40%, the net remaining to SG Beneficiaries

THE OLD SUN INN
Newbattle, Dalkeith EH22 3LH
Mr and Mrs James Lochhead T: 0131 663 2648
E: randjlochhead@uwclub.net

An interesting and beautifully designed half acre garden of island and raised beds, containing a collection of species lilies, rock plants and some unusual bulbs. There are also two small interconnecting ponds and a conservatory.

Directions: Take B703 (Newtongrange) from Eskbank Toll. The garden is immediately opposite Newbattle Abbey College entrance. Buses 95 and 95X. Parking at Newbattle Abbey College.

Disabled Access:
Full

Opening Times:
By arrangement
1 June - 31 July

Admission:
£3.50, children free

Charities:
All proceeds to
SG Beneficiaries

MORAY & NAIRN

Scotland's Gardens 2015 Guidebook is sponsored by INVESTEC WEALTH & INVESTMENT

District Organiser

Mr James Byatt	Lochview Cottage, Scarffbanks, Pitgaveny IV30 5PQ

Area Organisers

Mrs Lorraine Dingwall	10 Pilmuir Road West, Forres IV36 2HL
Mrs Rebecca Russell	12 Duff Avenue, Elgin, Moray IV30 1QS
Mrs Annie Stewart	33 Albert Street, Nairn IV12 4HF

Treasurer

Mr Michael Barnett	Drumdelnies, Nairn IV12 5NT

Gardens open on a specific date

Brodie Castle, Forres	Saturday 11 April	10:30am	- 4:30pm
Brodie Castle, Forres	Sunday 12 April	10:30am	- 4:30pm
Newbold House, Forres	Sunday 24 May	11:00am	- 4:00pm
Carestown Steading, Buckie	Saturday 30 May	10:00am	- 4:00pm
Gordonstoun, Duffus	Sunday 7 June	2:00pm	- 4:30pm
Glenrinnes Lodge, Dufftown	Saturday 13 June	2:00pm	- 5:00pm
Bruntlands Bungalow, Elgin	Thursday 25 June	7:00pm	- 9:00pm
Haugh Garden, College of Roseisle	Saturday 27 June	2:00pm	- 5:00pm
10 Pilmuir Road West , Forres	Sunday 5 July	2:00pm	- 6:00pm
Bruntlands Bungalow, Elgin	Saturday 18 July	11:00am	- 3:00pm
Haugh Garden, College of Roseisle	Saturday 18 July	2:00pm	- 5:00pm
Bruntlands Bungalow, Elgin	Sunday 19 July	11:00am	- 3:00pm
Newbold House, Forres	Sunday 26 July	11:00am	- 4:00pm
Haugh Garden, College of Roseisle	Saturday 15 August	2:00pm	- 5:00pm

MORAY & NAIRN

Gardens open by arrangement

Bruntlands Bungalow, Elgin	1 June - 31 August	07999 817715
Castleview, Dufftown	1 June - 31 August	01340 820941
10 Pilmuir Road West , Forres	1 February - 15 March	01309 674634

Carestown Steading

Key to symbols

	New in 2015		Homemade teas		Accommodation
	Teas		Dogs on a lead allowed		Plant stall
	Cream teas		Wheelchair access		Scottish Snowdrop Festival

Garden locations

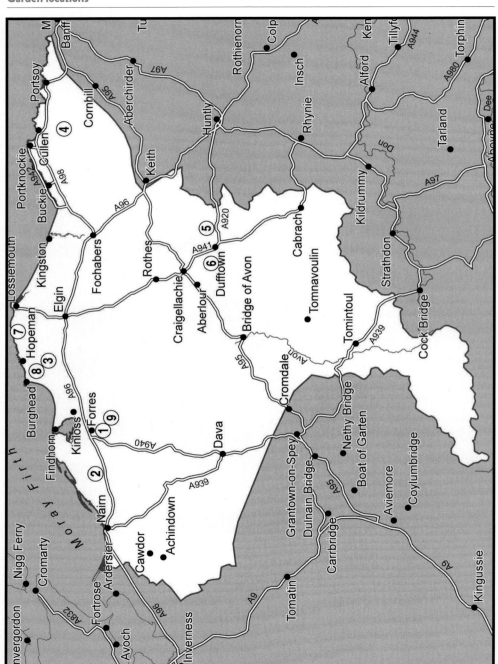

10 PILMUIR ROAD WEST

Forres IV36 2HL
Mrs Lorraine Dingwall T: 01309 674634
E: fixandig@aol.com   www.simplesite.com/hosta

Plantsman's small town garden with over 300 cultivars of hostas, an extensive collection of hardy geraniums together with many other unusual plants. Managed entirely without the use of artificial fertilizers or chemicals, the owner encourages hedgehogs, toads and wild birds to control slugs.
In early spring there are approximately 150 named snowdrops, some of which are very rare, to be seen. Please phone to arrange viewing as parking is limited and weather variable during snowdrop season.

Directions: From Tesco roundabout at Forres continue along Nairn Road. Take first left onto Ramflat Road, then go right at the bottom and first left onto Pilmuir West.

Disabled Access:
None

Opening Times:
Sunday 5 July
2:00pm - 6:00pm
Also by arrangement
1 February - 15 March for the
Snowdrop Festival

Admission:
£3.00

Charities:
Macmillan Cancer Support
receives 40%, the net
remaining to SG Beneficiaries

BRODIE CASTLE

Brodie, Forres IV36 2TE
The National Trust for Scotland T: 0844 493 2156
E: sferguson@nts.org.uk   www.nts.org.uk

In springtime the grounds are carpeted with the daffodils for which the castle is rightly famous. Bred by Ian Brodie, these daffodils are internationally significant. Some are found nowhere else in the world but the castle grounds! There is also a shrubbery garden with rhododendrons and a good tree collection plus wildflowers.

Other Details: National Plant Collection®: Narcissus (Brodie cvs). On these special days the garden team will lead guided walks in support of Scotland's Gardens. There will also be a plant stall selling pots of daffodils. Contact property for further information.

Directions: Off A96 4½ miles west of Forres and 24 miles east of Inverness.

Disabled Access:
Full

Opening Times:
Saturday 11 April
10:30am - 4:30pm
Sunday 12 April
10:30am - 4:30pm

Admission:
Garden tour £3.00 (including
NTS members).
N.B. Price correct at the time
of going to print.

Charities:
Donation to SG Beneficiaries

BRUNTLANDS BUNGALOW

Alves, Elgin IV30 8UZ
Mitch and Colin Buss T: 07999 817715
E: buss.shelter@virgin.net   http://in-the-buss-shelter.webs.com

A circular pergola acts as a centrepiece and gives definition to the raised beds and curving paths, made from recycled materials. Huge collection of Daylilies complement choice plants for seasonal interest, colour and impact.
The owners have transformed a dull, lifeless, uninteresting flat area into an exciting, lively, imaginatively designed space, full of colour, motion and vibrancy.

Other Details: Cold drinks and home baking will be served at the garden openings. There will be a craft stall at the Daylily weekend openings. Parking is limited. Children and dogs will not be admitted.

Directions: A96, Alves, turn into the road next to Crooked Inn, Burghead Road. Follow road for 1½ miles, last bungalow on left. From B9089 Kinloss Road, turn right at Wards Crossroads by Roseisle Maltings, towards Alves, first bungalow on right.

Disabled Access:
None

Opening Times:
Thursday 25 June
7:00pm - 9:00pm
Sat & Sun 18 - 19 July
11:00am - 3:00pm
for Daylily weekend
Also by arrangement
1 June - 31 August

Admission:
£3.00

Charities:
Macmillan Nurses receives
40%, the net remaining to
SG Beneficiaries

CARESTOWN STEADING
Deskford, Buckie AB56 5TR
Tom and Cherie Timney-Gunn T: 01542 841245
E: cherietg@sky.com

The Garden History Society in Scotland paid this garden the best compliment in describing it a 'garden history in the making'. It was started in 1990 and has received press, TV and web accolades ever since. Every year a new addition is made, the latest, the epitome of the modern vegetable plot which is proving very successful, four year rotation, raised beds, seeping irrigation. Trees and shrubs are maturing, the maze is growing, the ducks are reproducing in the three ponds and the atmosphere is as happy as ever. The 'pearl' of the garden, the courtyard with knot beds and topiary is now fully mature.

Other Details: Toilet facilities available. Parking in the field next to the house. Teas will be served in the Garden room.

Directions: East of B9018 Cullen/Keith (Cullen three miles, Keith 9½ miles). Follow SG signs towards Milton and Carestown.

Disabled Access:
Partial

Opening Times:
Saturday 30 May
10:00am - 4:00pm

Admission:
£4.00

Charities:
Scottish Autism receives 40%, the net remaining to SG Beneficiaries

---

CASTLEVIEW
Auchindoun, Dufftown AB55 4DY
Mr and Mrs Ian Sharp T: 01340 820941
E: castleview10@hotmail.com

A small secluded riverside garden, created on three levels from scrub land by two enthusiastic beginners in 2005. The garden consists of two interconnected ponds, one formal, one natural and an abundance of herbaceous plants and shrubs. There are several sitting areas where you can admire the garden from many viewpoints.

Directions: From Dufftown on the A920, travel approximately three miles towards Huntly. Drive until a small cluster of houses is reached; garden on the left is approximately twenty yards off the main road.

Disabled Access:
None

Opening Times:
By arrangement
1 June - 31 August

Admission:
£3.00 (honesty box)

Charities:
All proceeds to
SG Beneficiaries

GLENRINNES LODGE
Dufftown, Keith, Banffshire AB55 4BS
Mrs Kathleen Locke T: 01340 820384
www.glenrinnes.com

The garden and policies surrounding Glenrinnes Lodge are typical of a Victorian Lodge. There is a formal garden which lends itself to quiet reflection and views up the glen. A large walled garden with a large heated greenhouse both of which supply plants, cut flowers and fruit and vegetables. In addition, there is a lovely walk around the pond or along the woodland 'azalea walk'. There are lovely views of the surrounding countryside from all areas. In keeping with the rest of the estate, Glenrinnes Lodge is gardened organically.

Directions: In the centre of Dufftown at the Clock Tower take the B9009 road to Tomintoul for about one mile. After passing Dufftown Golf Club on your right there is a lane to the left which leads to two stone pillars to Glenrinnes Lodge.

Disabled Access:
Partial

Opening Times:
Saturday 13 June
2:00pm - 5:00pm

Admission:
£4.00

Charities:
All proceeds to
SG Beneficiaries

GORDONSTOUN
Duffus, near Elgin IV30 5RF
Gordonstoun School T: 01343 837837
E: richardss@gordonstoun.org.uk   www.gordonstoun.org.uk

The gardens consist of good formal herbaceous borders around lawns, a terrace and an orchard. The school grounds include Gordonstoun House, a Georgian House of 1775/6 incorporating an earlier 17th century house built for 1st Marquis of Huntly, and the school chapel, both of which will be open to visitors. There is also a unique circle of former farm buildings known as the Round Square and a scenic lake.

Directions: Entrance off B9012, four miles from Elgin at Duffus Village.

Disabled Access:
Full

Opening Times:
Sunday 7 June
2:00pm - 4:30pm

Admission:
£4.00, children £2.00

Charities:
All proceeds to
SG Beneficiaries

HAUGH GARDEN
College of Roseisle IV30 5YE
Gwynne and David Hetherington

A new and developing two acre garden with walks through mature woodland extensively planted with shade loving plants and young woodland. Large lawns bordered by extensive herbaceous borders. Ongoing work to develop the garden around the ruins of an 18th century farmhouse. There is a wildlife pond with adjacent bog garden, fruit trees and a soft fruit and vegetable garden. The garden also has a greenhouse and large polytunnel.

Other Details: Car parking at Roseisle Village Hall but drop-off available at the house. There will be a well-stocked plant stall.

Directions: From Elgin take B9015 Burghead Road to the crossroads at the centre of the College of Roseisle. The garden is on the right, enter from Duffus Road. Village Hall car parking is to the left off Kinloss Road.

Disabled Access:
Partial

Opening Times:
Saturday 27 June
2:00pm - 5:00pm
Saturday 18 July
2:00pm - 5:00pm
Saturday 15 August
2:00pm - 5:00pm

Admission:
£4.00

Charities:
CHAS receives 20%,
Alzheimer's Scotland receives
20%, the net remaining to
SG Beneficiaries

NEWBOLD HOUSE
111 St Leonards Road, Forres IV36 2RE
Newbold Trust T: 01309 672659
E: office@newboldhouse.org   www.newboldhouse.org

The garden nestles within the structure of a late 19th century mansion and its now mature conifer plantings and glorious rhododendrons. It features a beautiful walled garden combining vegetables, fruit and flowers together with an original glasshouse. The main part of the garden contains a variety of herbaceous and annual plantings and is being consciously developed as a wildlife friendly space. To this end, a butterfly garden has been planted and parts of the lawns are being managed to increase their wild flower content. Apple trees are a particular feature with nearly a 100 trees of more than 30 varieties. The house is a listed building in recognition of the original conservatory by Mackenzie & Moncur and is planted with a variety of tender plants and fruit.

Other Details: Light lunches are available.

Directions: From Forres High Street turn down Tolbooth Street. Take the second exit on the roundabout onto St Leonard's Road. Continue past Leanchoil Hospital, Newbold House is on the left.

Disabled Access:
None

Opening Times:
Sunday 24 May
11:00am - 4:00pm
Sunday 26 July
11:00am - 4:00pm

Admission:
£3.00

Charities:
The Newbold Trust receives
40%, the net remaining to
SG Beneficiaries

PEEBLESSHIRE

Scotland's Gardens 2015 Guidebook is sponsored by **INVESTEC WEALTH & INVESTMENT**

District Organiser

Mr Graham Buchanan-Dunlop	The Potting Shed, Broughton Pl, Broughton ML12 6HJ

Area Organisers

Mr J Bracken	Gowan Lea, Croft Road, West Linton EH46 7DZ
Mr Matthew Godfrey-Faussett	Tor Hill House, Wester Happrew, Peebles EH45 8PU
Ms R Hume	Llolans, Broughton ML12 6HJ
Lesley McDavid	Braedon, Medwyn Road, West Linton EH46 7HA
Mrs R Parrott	An Sparr, Medwyn Road, West Linton EH46 7HA

Treasurer

Mr J Birchall	The Old Manse, Drumelzier, Biggar ML12 6JD

Gardens open on a specific date

Srongarbh, The Loan, West Linton	Sunday 31 May	2:00pm	-	5:00pm
Stobo Japanese Water Garden, Stobo	Sunday 7 June	1:30pm	-	5:00pm
The Potting Shed, Broughton	Weds 10, 17, 24 June	11:00am	-	5:00pm
Portmore, Eddleston	Weds 1, 8, 15, 22, 29 July	1:00pm	-	4:30pm
The Potting Shed, Broughton	Weds 1, 8, 15 July	11:00am	-	5:00pm
8 Halmyre Mains, West Linton	Sunday 19 July	2:00pm	-	5:00pm
West Linton Village Gardens, West Linton	Sunday 2 August	2:00pm	-	5:00pm
Portmore, Eddleston	Weds 5, 12, 19, 26 August	1:00pm	-	4:30pm
Dawyck Botanic Garden, Stobo	Sunday 4 October	10:00am	-	6:00pm

Gardens open regularly

Dawyck Botanic Garden, Stobo	1 February - 30 November			
	February and November	10:00am	-	4:00pm
	March and October	10:00am	-	5:00pm
	Other dates	10:00am	-	6:00pm
Kailzie Gardens, Peebles	1 January - 31 March	Dawn	-	Dusk
	1 April - 31 October	11:00am	-	5:00pm
	1 November - 31 December	Dawn	-	Dusk

11

042
14.

44141114411

PEEBLESSHIRE

Gardens open by arrangement

Portmore, Eddleston	1 June - 16 September	07825 294388
Stobo Japanese Water Garden, Stobo	1 May - 31 October	01721 760245

Plant sales

Borders Plant and Produce Sale, Melrose	Saturday 16 May	10:30am - 4:00pm
Halmyre Mains Plant Sale, West Linton	Sunday 14 June	10:00am - 12:00pm

Portmore © Ray Cox

Key to symbols

 New in 2015

 Teas

 Cream teas

 Homemade teas

 Dogs on a lead allowed

 Wheelchair access

 Accommodation

 Plant stall

 Scottish Snowdrop Festival

Garden locations

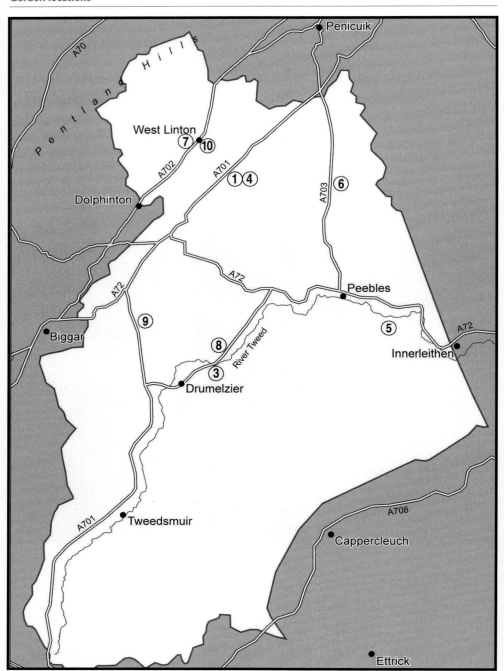

8 HALMYRE MAINS
West Linton EH46 7BX
Joyce Andrews and Mike Madden T: 07774 609 547
E: romanno@btinternet.com

A half acre organic garden with 15 feet deep borders surrounding the lawn. Raised plots, greenhouse, keder house and polytunnel produce large amounts of fruit and vegetables. A pergola leads to a sizable composting area and then down to the main pond with patio area and gazebo. A plant stall will be well stocked with many of the plants growing in the garden.

Other Details: Teas will be provided in the nearby Lamancha Hub.

Directions: Five miles South of Leadburn Junction on the A701 (Moffat).

Disabled Access:
Full

Opening Times:
Sunday 19 July
2:00pm - 5:00pm

Admission:
£4.00, children free

Charities:
Lamancha & District Community Association receives 40%, the net remaining to SG Beneficiaries

BORDERS PLANT AND PRODUCE SALE
Broomhill Steading, Melrose TD6 9DF
Scotland's Gardens

Stock up on all sorts of goodies for your garden, larder or freezer at our mega charity plant sale. Vegetable plants, herbaceous, annuals, shrubs, trees, etc. Produce, second hand potting shed tools and **much more**. If you would like to "bring" as well as "buy" we would be grateful for **ANY** contributions, please bring goods labelled and priced or drop off at one of the collection points prior to day of the sale.
For your nearest collection point or further information contact
Victoria Kostoris E: vakost@aol.com, T: 01896 822151 / 07778 343842
Georgina Seymour E: georgina.stobo@gmail.com, T: 01721 760245 / 07977 464504
Arabella Lewis E: arabella.lewis@btinternet.com, T: 01835 870357 / 07980 073274

Other Details: Refreshments available all day. Cash or cheque sales only.

Directions: Off Melrose bypass, close to A68.

Disabled Access:
Full

Opening Times:
Saturday 16 May
10:30am - 4:00pm

Admission:
Free

Charities:
Scotland's Gardens, Marie Curie (Borders) and Samaritans (Borders) each receives a third of proceeds

DAWYCK BOTANIC GARDEN
Stobo EH45 9JU
A Regional Garden of the Royal Botanic Garden Edinburgh T: 01721 760254
www.rbge.org.uk/dawyck

Stunning collection of rare trees and shrubs. With over 300 years of tree planting, Dawyck is a world famous arboretum with mature specimens of Chinese conifers, Japanese maples, Brewer's spruce, the unique Dawyck beech and Sequoiadendrons from North America which are over 45 metres tall. Bold herbaceous plantings run along the burn. Range of trails and walks. Fabulous autumn colours.

Other Details: National Plant Collection®: Larix and Tsuga. Open for the Snowdrop Festival 1 February - 15 March. Autumn magic guided walk on 4 October at 2:00pm, £3.50 plus admission charge. Please book with Dawyck Botanic Garden. Lunches and teas using local produce are available in the cafe overlooking scenic woodland. Sorry no dogs are allowed.

Directions: Eight miles south west of Peebles on B712.

Disabled Access:
Partial

Opening Times:
Sunday 4 October
10:00am - 6:00pm
for Scotland's Gardens
Open all year 10am-6pm,
closes Feb & Nov 4pm,
Mar & Oct, 5pm

Admission:
£6.00, conc. £5.00, children u16 free (garden donation included). For prices without donation check rbge.org.uk

Charities:
Donation to SG Beneficiaries

HALMYRE MAINS PLANT SALE
8 Halmyre Mains, West Linton EH46 7BX
Joyce Andrews and Mike Madden T: 07774 609 547
E: romanno@btinternet.com

Early season plant sale with a large selection of locally grown specimens. There is also an opportunity to preview the garden five weeks ahead of the main opening.

Other Details: Teas will be provided in the nearby Lamancha Hub.

Directions: Five miles South of Leadburn Junction on the A701 (Moffat).

Disabled Access:
Full

Opening Times:
Sunday 14 June 10:00am - 12:00pm

Admission:
£2.00, children free

Charities:
Lamancha & District Community Association receives 40%, the net remaining to SG Beneficiaries

KAILZIE GARDENS
Peebles EH45 9HT
Lady Buchan-Hepburn T: 01721 720007
E: angela.buchanhepburn@btinternet.com   www.kailzie.com

Semi-formal walled garden with shrubs and herbaceous borders, rose garden and excellent display of plants in large Victorian greenhouses. Woodland and burnside walks among spring bulbs, snowdrops, bluebells, rhododendrons and azaleas. The garden is set among fine old trees including a larch planted in 1725. Osprey watch with live CCTV recordings of Ospreys nesting in the recently extended nature centre. Kailzie has been featured on Landward and the Beechgrove Garden.

Other Details: Walled garden open 1 April - 31 Oct only. Wild garden and woodland walks open throughout the year, including for Snowdrop Festival. Children's play area. Restaurant and tearoom open daily during the summer months. See website for spring and winter restaurant hours. Admission shows adult prices only. For concessions, children and groups see website.

Directions: Two and a half miles east of Peebles on B7062.

Disabled Access:
Partial

Opening Times:
1 Jan - 31 March Dawn - Dusk
(open for the Snowdrop
Festival 1 Feb - 15 Mar)
1 April - 31 October
11:00am - 5:00pm
1 Nov - 31 Dec Dawn - Dusk

Admission:
Apr-May £3.50, Jun-Oct
£4.50, other dates £2.50

Charities:
Donation of which Erskine
Hospital receives 40%, the net
remaining to SG Beneficiaries

PORTMORE
Eddleston EH45 8QU
Mr and Mrs David Reid T: 07825 294388
www.portmoregardens.co.uk

Lovingly created by current owners over the past 20 years the gardens surrounding the David Bryce mansion house contain mature trees and offer fine views of the surrounding countryside. Large walled garden with box-edged herbaceous borders planted in stunning colour harmonies, potager, rose garden, pleached lime walk and ornamental fruit cages. The Victorian glasshouses contain fruit trees, roses, geraniums, pelargoniums and a wide variety of tender plants. Italianate grotto. Water garden with shrubs and meconopsis and woodland walks lined with rhododendrons, azaleas and shrub roses. Starred in "Good Gardens Guide".

Other Details: Homemade cream teas for groups by prior arrangement. Self service refreshments on Wednesday openings.

Directions: Off A703 one mile north of Eddleston. Bus no.62.

Disabled Access:
Partial

Opening Times:
Wednesdays 1, 8, 15, 22, 29
July and 5, 12, 19, 26 August
1:00pm - 4:30pm
Also by arrangement 1 June -
16 September for groups

Admission:
£5.00

Charities:
Nomad Beat Community
Music School (Peebles)
receives 40%, the net
remaining to SG Beneficiaries

SRONGARBH
The Loan, West Linton EH46 7HE
Mr and Mrs O Arnesen

The property consists of an Arts and Crafts house (not open) with a large well established garden dating from the 1930s surrounded by woodland, with many trees and shrubs within the garden. This garden is approximately 1,000 feet above sea level, with acidic soil, high rainfall and low winter temperatures. In spring the azaleas and rhododendrons provide a beautiful array of colours and the wide herbaceous borders continue flowering throughout the year. There is a formal rose garden with hybrid teas and old varieties of climbing, rambling and shrub roses. Below the formal terracing there is an original swimming pool as well as an ornamental pool under Japanese acers. The new owners are opening up areas of the garden with naturalistic paths.

Other Details: Teas served in the village hall. Owing to access problems a continuous minibus service will ferry visitors from West Linton.

Directions: A701 or A702 and follow the signs.

Disabled Access:
None

Opening Times:
Sunday 31 May
2:00pm - 5:00pm

Admission:
£4.00

Charities:
The Ben Walton Trust receives
40%, the net remaining to
SG Beneficiaries

STOBO JAPANESE WATER GARDEN
Home Farm, Stobo EH45 8NX
Hugh and Charles Seymour T: 01721 760245
E: hugh.seymour@btinternet.com

June and October are the prime months to visit this secluded woodland garden. While water is probably the main feature of the garden now, the layout echoes facets of a more conventional Japanese garden - stepping stones, humpback bridges, azaleas, acers, rhododrendrons, and other specialist trees and shrubs. Several Japanese lanterns and a tea house still remain from the original design, which was completed in the early years of the last century.

Other Details: Sensible footwear for uneven surfaces recommended. Teas available on 7 June. Teas, coffee, lunches available on request for groups of 12 or more. Bed and breakfast available at Home Farm.

Directions: Off B712. Follow signs for Stobo Castle then yellow signs on drive.

Disabled Access:
Partial

Opening Times:
Sunday 7 June
1:30pm - 5:00pm
By arrangement 1 May - 31 October - Guided tours for groups of 12 minimum

Admission:
£5.00, children free

Charities:
Marie Curie Cancer Care receives 20%, Margaret Kerr Unit, Borders General Hospital receives 20%, the net remaining to SG Beneficiaries

THE POTTING SHED
Broughton Place, Broughton, Biggar ML12 6HJ
Jane and Graham Buchanan-Dunlop T: 01899 830574
E: buchanandunlop@btinternet.com

A one acre garden, begun from scratch in 2008, on an exposed hillside at 900 feet. It contains herbaceous plants, climbers, shrubs and trees, all selected for wind resistance and ability to cope with the poor, stony soil. There are (usually) fine views to the Southern Uplands.

Other Details: Lunch and tea available at Laurel Bank in Broughton Village. T: 01899 830462.

Directions: Signed from the main A701 Edinburgh - Moffat road, immediately North of Broughton Village.

Disabled Access:
Partial

Opening Times:
Wednesdays 10, 17, 24 June, and 1, 8, 15 July
11:00am - 5:00pm

Admission:
£4.00, children free.

Charities:
Borders Forest Trust receives 40%, the net remaining to SG Beneficiaries

WEST LINTON VILLAGE GARDENS
West Linton EH46 7EL
West Linton Village Gardeners

At least three gardens will be opening this year, all situated in the heart of the village and within close proximity to each other. All medium/large gardens with contrasting styles and some very interesting features, including large herbaceous borders, specimen trees and shrubs and garden ornaments.

Directions: A701 or A702 and follow signs.

Disabled Access:
Partial

Opening Times:
Sunday 2 August
2:00pm - 5:00pm

Admission:
£4.00

Charities:
The Ben Walton Trust receives 40%, the net remaining to SG Beneficiaries

PERTH & KINROSS

Scotland's Gardens 2015 Guidebook is sponsored by **INVESTEC WEALTH & INVESTMENT**

District Organisers

Mrs Margaret Gimblett	Croftcat Lodge, Grandtully PH15 2QS
Mrs Miranda Landale	Clathic House, By Crieff PH7 4JY

Area Organisers

Mrs Sonia Dunphie	Wester Cloquhat, Bridge of Cally, Perthshire PH10 7JP
Miss Henrietta Harland	Easter Carmichael Cottage, Forgandenny Road, Bridge of Earn PH2 9EZ
Mrs Elizabeth Mitchell	Woodlee, 28 St Mary's Drive, Perth PH2 7BY
Mrs Lizzie Montgomery	Burleigh House, Milnathort, Kinross KY13 9SR
Mrs Judy Nichol	Rossie House, Forgandenny PH2 9EH
Miss Judy Norwell	Dura Den, 20 Pitcullen Terrace, Perth PH2 7EQ
Miss Bumble Ogilvy Wedderburn	Garden Cottage, Lude, Blair Atholl PH18 5TR

Treasurer

Mr Michael Tinson	Parkhead House, Parkhead Gardens, Burghmuir Road PH1 1JF

Gardens open on a specific date

Fingask Castle, Rait	Sunday 8 February	Dawn	-	Dusk
Kilgraston School, Bridge of Earn	Saturday 28 February	1:30pm	-	4:00pm
Megginch Castle, Errol	Sunday 12 April	2:00pm	-	5:00pm
Branklyn Garden, Perth	Sunday 3 May	10:00am	-	4:00pm
Fingask Castle, Rait	Sunday 3 May	2:00pm	-	5:30pm
Machany House, Auchterarder	Sunday 17 May	2:00pm	-	5:00pm
Wester House of Ross, Comrie	Saturday 23 May	1:30pm	-	4:30pm
Dowhill, Cleish	Sunday 24 May	10:00am	-	4:00pm
Wester House of Ross, Comrie	Sunday 24 May	1:30pm	-	4:30pm
Bradystone House, Murthly	Thursday 4 June	11:00am	-	4:00pm
Delvine, Murthly	Sunday 7 June	2:00pm	-	5:00pm
Explorers Garden, Pitlochry	Sunday 7 June	10:00am	-	5:00pm
Bradystone House, Murthly	Thursday 11 June	11:00am	-	4:00pm
Blair Castle Gardens, Blair Atholl	Saturday 13 June	9:30am	-	5:30pm
Bonhard House, Perth	Sunday 14 June	10:00am	-	4:00pm
Mill of Forneth, Blairgowrie	Sunday 14 June	2:00pm	-	5:00pm
Bradystone House, Murthly	Thursday 18 June	11:00am	-	4:00pm

PERTH & KINROSS

Bradystone House, Murthly	Thursday 25 June	11:00am	- 4:00pm
The Bield at Blackruthven, Tibbermore	Saturday 27 June	2:00pm	- 5:00pm
Bradystone House, Murthly	Thursday 2 July	11:00am	- 4:00pm
Bradystone House, Murthly	Thursday 9 July	11:00am	- 4:00pm
Hollytree Lodge, Muckhart, Dollar	Sunday 12 July	11:00am	- 5:00pm
Bradystone House, Murthly	Thursday 16 July	11:00am	- 4:00pm
Bradystone House, Murthly	Thursday 23 July	11:00am	- 4:00pm
Drummond Castle Gardens, Crieff	Sunday 2 August	1:00pm	- 5:00pm
Wester House of Ross, Comrie	Saturday 19 September	1:30pm	- 4:30pm
Wester House of Ross, Comrie	Sunday 20 September	1:30pm	- 4:30pm

Gardens open regularly

Ardvorlich, Lochearnhead	1 May - 1 June	9:00am	- Dusk
Blair Castle Gardens, Blair Atholl	1 April - 31 October	9:30am	- 5:30pm
Bolfracks, Aberfeldy	1 January - 31 December	10:00am	- 6:00pm
Braco Castle, Braco	1 February - 31 October	10:00am	- 5:00pm
Cluny House, Aberfeldy	1 January - 15 March	10:00am	- 4:00pm
	16 March - 31 October	10:00am	- 6:00pm
	1 November - 31 December	10:00am	- 4:00pm
Dowhill, Cleish	18 May - 31 May	10:00am	- 4:00pm
Drummond Castle Gardens, Crieff	1 May - 31 October	1:00pm	- 6:00pm
Glendoick, by Perth	1 April - 31 May weekends	2:00pm	- 5:00pm
	1 April - 31 May weekdays	10:00am	- 4:00pm
Glenericht House, Blairgowrie	1 January - 31 December	9:00am	- Dusk

Gardens open by arrangement

Bradystone House, Murthly	5 June - 22 July	01738 710308
Carig Dhubh, Bonskeid	1 May - 30 September	01796 473469
Croftcat Lodge, Grandtully	15 May - 15 October	01887 840288
Delvine, Murthly	15 April - 15 October	01738 710485
Easter Meikle Fardle, Meikleour	31 March - 1 September	01738 710330
Hollytree Lodge, Muckhart	1 April - 30 October	0797 337 4687
Little Tombuie, Aberfeldy	15 May - 15 June and	
	15 September - 15 October	sallycrystal@gmail.com
Mill of Forneth, Blairgowrie	30 April - 30 September	gaw@gwpc.demon.co.uk
Parkhead House, Perth	1 June - 31 August	01738 625983
The Steading, Blairgowrie	25 April - 17 May	
	6 June - 21 June	01250 884263

PERTH & KINROSS

Carig Dhubh

Key to symbols

 New in 2015

 Teas

 Cream teas

 Homemade teas

 Dogs on a lead allowed

 Wheelchair access

 Accommodation

 Plant stall

 Scottish Snowdrop Festival

Garden locations

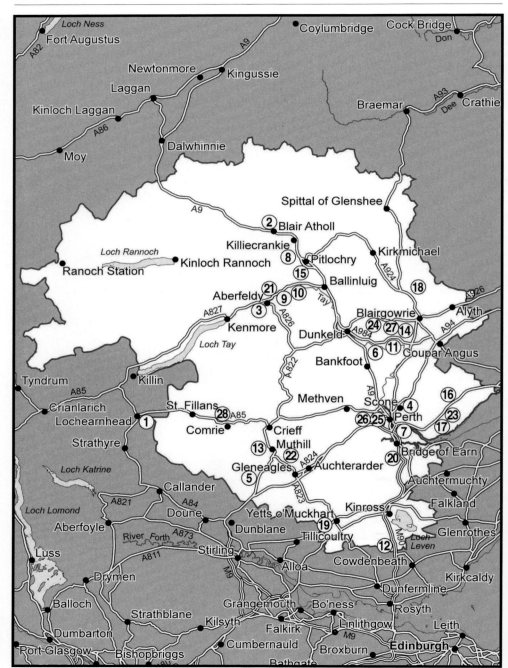

ARDVORLICH
Lochearnhead FK19 8QE
Mr and Mrs Sandy Stewart

Beautiful hill garden featuring over 300 different species and hybrid rhododendrons, grown in a glorious setting of oaks and birches on either side of the Ardvorlich Burn. The ground is quite steep in places and boots are advised.

Directions: On South Loch Earn Road three miles from Lochearnhead, five miles from St Fillans.

Disabled Access:
None

Opening Times:
1 May - 1 June
9:00am - Dusk

Admission:
£4.00

Charities:
The Gurkha Welfare Trust receives 40%, the net remaining to SG Beneficiaries

BLAIR CASTLE GARDENS
Blair Atholl PH18 5TL
Blair Charitable Trust T: 01796 481207
E: office@blair-castle.co.uk www.blair-castle.co.uk

Blair Castle stands as the focal point in a designed landscape of some 2,500 acres within a large and traditional estate. Hercules Garden is a walled enclosure of about nine acres recently restored to its original 18th century form with landscaped ponds, a Chinese bridge, plantings, vegetables and an orchard of more than one hundred fruit trees. The glory of this garden in summer is the herbaceous borders which run along the 275 metre south facing wall. A delightful sculpture trail incorporates contemporary and 18th century sculpture as well as eight new works, letter-carving on stone from the Memorial Arts Charity's Art and Memory Collection. Diana's Grove is a magnificent stand of tall trees including Grand Fir, Douglas Fir, Larch and Wellingtonia in just two acres.

Directions: Off A9, follow signs to Blair Castle, Blair Atholl.

Disabled Access:
Partial

Opening Times:
Saturday 13 June
9:30am - 5:30pm
1 April - 31 October
9:30am - 5:30pm

Admission:
£5.80, children £2.50 and families £14.50

Charities:
Donation to SG Beneficiaries

BOLFRACKS
Aberfeldy PH15 2EX
The Douglas Hutchison Trust T: 01887 820344
E: athel@bolfracks.com www.bolfracks.com

Special three acre garden with wonderful views overlooking the Tay Valley. Burn garden with rhododendrons, azaleas, primulas and meconopsis in a woodland garden setting. Walled garden with shrubs, herbaceous borders and rose rooms with old fashioned roses. There is also a beautiful rose and clematis walk. Peony beds are underplanted with tulips and Japanese anemone. The garden has a great selection of bulbs in spring and good autumn colour.

Other Details: Refreshments available for groups by prior arrangement. Slippery paths in wet weather.

Directions: Two miles west of Aberfeldy on A827. White gates and Lodge are on the left. Look out for the brown tourist signs.

Disabled Access:
None

Opening Times:
1 January - 31 December
10:00am - 6:00pm

Admission:
£4.50, children under 16 free

Charities:
Donation to SG Beneficiaries

BONHARD HOUSE
Perth PH2 7PQ
Stephen and Charlotte Hay T: 01738 552471

A marvellous traditional 19th century garden of five acres with mature trees, lawns, rhododendrons, azaleas, hollies, herbaceous borders, ponds and an oak drive lined with primulas and daffodils. There is also a kitchen garden, Pinetum and wooded area.

Other Details: Sensible shoes should be worn.

Directions: From Perth take A94 north to Scone. Before you reach Scone turn right at sign to Murrayshall Hotel. Continue about one mile. House drive on right where road turns sharp left. From Balbeggie take A94. Turn left signposted for Bonhard one mile north of Scone and in ½ mile turn right. House drive on left where the road turns sharp right shortly after Bonhard Nursery.

Disabled Access:
Partial

Opening Times:
Sunday 14 June
10:00am - 4:00pm

Admission:
£3.50

Charities:
Freedom From Fistula
Foundation receives 40%,
the net remaining to
SG Beneficiaries

BRACO CASTLE
Braco FK15 9LA
Mr and Mrs M van Ballegooijen T: 01786 880437

A 19th century landscaped garden with a plethora of wonderful and interesting trees, shrubs, bulbs and plants. It is an old garden for all seasons that has been extensively expanded over the last 26 years. The partly walled garden is approached on a rhododendron and tree lined path and features an ornamental pond with endless paths taking you to yet another special corner of this garden. Spectacular spring bulbs, exuberant shrub and herbaceous borders, and many ornamental trees are all enhanced by the spectacular views across the park to the Ochils.
The magical mystery tour starts early as you might think the driveway is never going to end but you are in for a treat! From snowdrops through to vibrant autumn colour this garden is a gem. Look out for the Embothrium in June, Hoheria in August, Eucryphia in September and an interesting collection of rhododrons and azaleas with long flowering season.

Other Details: Catering facilities are not available.

Directions: One to one and a half mile drive from gates at north end of Braco Village, just west of bridge on A822.

Disabled Access:
Partial

Opening Times:
1 February - 31 October
10:00am - 5:00pm
Open for the Snowdrop
Festival 1 February - 15 March

Admission:
£3.50

Charities:
The Woodland Trust receives
40%, the net remaining to
SG Beneficiaries

6 BRADYSTONE HOUSE
Murthly PH1 4EW
Mrs James Lumsden T: 01738 710308

True cottage courtyard garden converted 16 years ago from derelict farm steadings. Beautifully planted to produce an ever changing picture. Unusual plants complementing others in wonderful combinations. Ponds, free roaming ducks and hens and many interesting shrubs and ornamental trees.

Other Details: Refreshments available by prior arrangement.

Directions: From south/north follow A9 to Bankfoot, then sign to Murthly. At crossroads in Murthly take private road to Bradystone.

Disabled Access:
Full

Opening Times:
Thursdays 4, 11, 18, 25 June
and 2, 9, 16, 23 July
11:00am - 4:00pm
Also by arrangement
5 June - 22 July

Admission:
£4.50

Charities:
Scottish Air Ambulance
receives 40%, the net
remaining to SG Beneficiaries

7 BRANKLYN GARDEN
116 Dundee Road, Perth PH2 7BB
The National Trust for Scotland T: 0844 493 2193
E: smcnamara@nts.org.uk www.nts.org.uk

This attractive garden in Perth was once described as 'the finest two acres of private garden in the country'. It contains an outstanding collection of plants particularly rhododendrons, alpine, herbaceous and peat-loving plants, which attract gardeners and botanists from all over the world. This is the perfect time to see the Meconopsis in their glory!

Other Details: National Plant Collection®: Cassiope, Meconopsis (Himalayan poppy) and Rhododendron. Champion Trees: Pinus sylvestris 'Globosa.' Head Gardener's walk at 2:00pm. Weather permitting homemade scones will be served on the patio.

Directions: On A85 Perth/Dundee road.

Disabled Access:
Partial

Opening Times:
Sunday 3 May
10:00am - 4:00pm

Admission:
£6.50, concessions £5.00,
family £16.50, one parent
£11.20 (including NTS
members). N.B. Prices
correct at time of going to
print.

Charities:
Donation to SG Beneficiaries

8 CARIG DHUBH
Bonskeid PH16 5NP
Jane and Niall Graham-Campbell T: 01796 473469
E: niallgc@btinternet.com

The garden is comprised of mixed shrubs and herbaceous plants with meconopsis and primulas. It extends to about one acre on the side of a hill with some steep paths and uneven ground. The soil is sand overlying rock - some of which projects through the surface. There are beautiful surrounding country and hill views.

Directions: Take old A9 between Pitlochry and Killiecrankie, midway turn west on the Tummel Bridge Road B8019, ¾ mile on north side of the road.

Disabled Access:
None

Opening Times:
By arrangement
1 May - 30 September

Admission:
£4.00, children free

Charities:
Help for Heroes receives
40%, the net remaining to
SG Beneficiaries

CLUNY HOUSE
Aberfeldy PH15 2JT
Mr J and Mrs W Mattingley T: 01887 820795
E: wmattingley@btinternet.com www.clunyhousegardens.com

A wonderful, wild woodland garden overlooking the scenic Strathtay valley. Experience the grandeur of one of Britain's widest trees, the complex leaf variation of the Japanese maple, the beauty of the American trillium or the diversity of Asiatic primulas. There is a good display of snowdrops. Cluny's red squirrels are usually very easily seen. A treasure not to be missed.

Other Details: Open for the Snowdrop Festival 1 February - 15 March. Plant seeds available for sale.

Directions: Three and a half miles from Aberfeldy on Weem to Strathtay Road.

Disabled Access:
Partial

Opening Times:
1 January - 31 December
16 March - 31 October
10:00am - 6:00pm.
Other dates 10:00am -
4:00pm

Admission:
2 Feb-15 Mar £4.00, children £1.00; 16 Mar-31 Oct £5.00, children £1.00; other dates free, but donations towards squirrel food are welcome

Charities:
Donation to SG Beneficiaries

CROFTCAT LODGE
Grandtully PH15 2QS
Margaret and Iain Gimblett T: 01887 840288
E: iain@gimblettsmill.plus.com

This garden is a garden for all seasons with colour or interest in almost every month of the year. It is welcoming, inspiring and unusual. It was featured on the "Beechgrove Garden" in 2013 and will be appearing on Sky television in 2015. Although it extends to over one acre now it was largely created and is cared for only by its owners, both now retired. The garden, a series of smaller gardens all linked together, is set on a stony, windy hillside but has panoramic views which have been incorporated into the garden wherever possible. There are lawns, spring and autumn gardens, a small gravel garden, rose terraces, clipped beehive laurels, a collection of clematis, and most lovely of all, a small Japanese water garden with stepping stones and tea pavilion. In 2014 the garden was extended to include a small wildlife pond with marginal plants, shrub roses and other specimen shrubs and trees, all framing the remains of an old ruined mill and mature ash trees. In 2015 Margaret and Iain will be making a garden around an adjoining small farmhouse, inspired by the countryside and gardens seen in Scandinavia and travels in Wyoming in 2014. Come and see what is happening!
There will be no open day this year but the Garden Owners welcome visitors and groups by arrangement and will endeavour to provide tea and home baking whenever possible for all visitors, and, given notice, can provide special afternoon teas for up to six people or a light lunch for up to fourteen people.

Other Details: Wheelchair access is possible to most of the garden with assistance. Light lunch or old fashioned afternoon tea with all the trimmings are negotiable.

Directions: From A9 take A827 signposted Aberfeldy. Through Grandtully village and one mile from traffic lights on bridge turn left by cream house set back from road. Croftcat is on left 300 yards up lane.

Disabled Access:
Partial

Opening Times:
By arrangement
15 May - 15 October

Admission:
£5.00 includes tea or coffee.

Charities:
Scotland's Charity Air Ambulance receives 40%, the net remaining to SG Beneficiaries

DELVINE
Murthly PH1 4LD
Mr and Mrs David Gemmell T: 01738 710485

The gardens at Delvine are situated on Inchtuthill (the island that floods), an old Roman legionary fortress abandoned 85AD. A new arboretum and water project is taking shape in a wild and secluded setting below the existing gardens with wonderful views. The area is surrounded by particularly fine and very old trees.

Directions: On A984, seven miles east of Dunkeld, four miles south west of Blairgowrie.

Disabled Access:
Partial

Opening Times:
Sunday 7 June
2:00pm - 5:00pm
By arrangement
15 April - 15 October

Admission:
£5.00, children £0.50

Charities:
ABF Soldiers' Charity receives 40%, the net remaining to SG Beneficiaries

DOWHILL
Cleish KY4 0HZ
Mr and Mrs Colin Maitland Dougall

A garden set off by the background of Benarty Hill and magnificent old trees. Lovely woodland walks to the ruins of Dowhill Castle.

There are nine linked ponds. Blue poppies and primulas together with temptingly placed seats make the garden a wonderful place for a picnic in fine weather.

Other Details: There will be teas and a plant stall on Sunday 24 May opening only.

Directions: Three quarters of a mile off M90, exit 5, towards Crook of Devon on the B9097 in the trees.

Disabled Access:
None

Opening Times:
Sunday 24 May
10:00am - 4:00pm
18 May - 31 May
10:00am - 4:00pm

Admission:
£4.00

Charities:
Motor Neurone Disease Association receives 40%, the net remaining to SG Beneficiaries

DRUMMOND CASTLE GARDENS
Crieff PH7 4HZ
Grimsthorpe & Drummond Castle Trust Ltd
www.drummondcastlegardens.co.uk

The Gardens of Drummond Castle were originally laid out in 1630 by John Drummond, second Earl of Perth. In 1830 the parterre was changed to an Italian style. One of the most interesting features is the multi-faceted sundial designed by John Mylne, Master Mason to Charles I. The formal garden is said to be one of the finest in Europe and is the largest of its type in Scotland.

Other Details: Admission charges outwith Sunday 2 August £5.00, OAPs £4.00, children £2.00, family £12.00.

Directions: Entrance two miles south of Crieff on Muthill road (A822).

Disabled Access:
Partial

Opening Times:
Sunday 2 August
1:00pm - 5:00pm
1 May - 31 Oct 1pm - 6pm

Admission:
Sun 2 Aug: £4.00, OAPs
£3.00, children £2.00, family
£10.00 (For admission on
other dates see Other Details)

Charities:
British Limbless Ex-
Servicemen's Assoc receives
40% on 2 Aug, the net
remaining to SG Beneficiaries

EASTER MEIKLE FARDLE
Meikleour PH2 6EF
Rear Admiral and Mrs John Mackenzie T: 01738 710330

A delightful old-fashioned two acre garden. Herbaceous borders backed by soft sandstone walls or beech hedges. Small enclosed garden with raised beds. There is also a maturing water garden and walks through mature woodland.

Directions: Take A984 - Dunkeld to Coupar Angus - one and a half miles from Spittalfield towards Meikleour, third house on left after turning to Lethendy.

Disabled Access:
Partial

Opening Times:
By arrangement
31 March - 1 September

Admission:
£4.00

Charities:
National Rheumatoid
Arthritis Society receives
40%, the net remaining to
SG Beneficiaries

EXPLORERS GARDEN
Pitlochry PH16 5DR
Pitlochry Festival Theatre
www.explorersgarden.com

This six acre woodland garden, now thirteen years old, is maturing nicely. More and more visitors are coming to see the wonders this four star VisitScotland attraction reveals: art and architecture, wildlife and birds, exotic plants, peat and rock gardens, extraordinary landscaping and magnificent views. Try the guided tours that reveal the stories of the Scottish Plant Hunters who risked their lives travelling the globe in search of new plants and trees. In this garden, which is divided into different parts of the world, you will see the plants they collected for cultivation, commerce and conservation.

Directions: A9 to Pitlochry town, follow signs to Pitlochry Festival Theatre.

Disabled Access:
Partial

Opening Times:
Sunday 7 June
10:00am - 5:00pm

Admission:
£4.00 or £5.00 with guided
tour

Charities:
Acting for Others receives
40%, the net remaining to
SG Beneficiaries

16

FINGASK CASTLE
Rait PH2 7SA
Mr and Mrs Andrew Murray Threipland T: 01821 670777
E: andrew@fingaskcastle.com www.fingaskcastle.com

Explore the large landscaped policies of the castle including (but not confined to) Belvederes, medieval wishing well, statues, topiary, Chinese bridge and much more.

Other Details: Champion Trees: Bhutan Pine. Cream teas 3 May opening only. The Fingask Follies 20th season will take place in April and May. Details can be found on the website.

Directions: Halfway between Perth and Dundee. From A90 follow signs to Rait until small crossroad, turn right and follow signs to Fingask.

Disabled Access:
Partial

Opening Times:
Sunday 8 Feb Dawn - Dusk
for the Snowdrop Festival
Sunday 3 May
2:00pm - 5:30pm

Admission:
£4.00, children free, there
will be an honesty box for the
Snowdrop Opening.

Charities:
All Saints Church, Glencarse
and Fingask Follies receives
40%, the net remaining to
SG Beneficiaries

17

GLENDOICK
by Perth PH2 7NS
Peter, Patricia, Kenneth and Jane Cox T: 01738 860205
E: orders@glendoick.com www.glendoick.com

Glendoick was included in the *Independent on Sunday* survey of Europe's top 50 Gardens and boasts a unique collection of plants from three generations of Cox plant-hunting expeditions in China and the Himalaya.
You can see one of the finest collections of rhododendrons and azaleas, primulas, meconopsis and other acid-loving plants in the woodland garden, peat garden and nursery. Many of the Rhododendron and Azalea species and hybrids have been introduced from the wild or bred by the Cox family and the gardens boast a huge range of plants from as far afield as Chile, Tasmania and Tibet. Three new waterfall viewing platforms have been built in the woodland gardens. In the walled garden where you'll find new as yet unnamed hybrids from the Glendoick breeding programme trial beds.
The award winning Glendoick Garden Centre and Cafe has one of Scotland's best selections of plants including their world famous rhododendrons and azaleas.

Other Details: National Plant Collection®: Rhododendron two collections - Rhododendron (Cox hybrids) and Rhododendron sect. Pogonanthum, subsect. Uniflora, subsect. Campylogyna and subsect. Glauca. Mail Order rhododendrons and azaleas in winter months only. For group bookings contact Jane Cox by post at the above address or E: jane@glendoick.com. Refreshments for groups should be pre-booked. The woodland garden is not easily accessible to wheelchairs but some of the gardens by the house are. Disabled toilets at the garden centre only.
Peter and Kenneth Cox have written numerous books on rhododendrons and gardens. Kenneth Cox's book "*Scotland for Gardeners*" describes 500 of Scotland's finest gardens.

Directions: Follow brown signs to Glendoick Garden Centre off A90 Perth - Dundee road. Gardens are ½ mile behind Garden Centre. After buying tickets at the garden centre please drive up and park at gardens (free parking).

Disabled Access:
None

Opening Times:
1 April - 31 May
2:00pm - 5:00pm weekends
10:00am - 4:00pm weekdays

Admission:
£5.00, school age children
free.
Tickets available from the
garden centre.

Charities:
Donation to SG Beneficiaries

GLENERICHT HOUSE
Blairgowrie PH10 7JD
Mr William McCosh T: 01250 872092

Spectacular collection of Victorian planted trees and shrubs which are centred around a Grade 'A' listed suspension bridge (1846). Ninety-two tree varieties, mostly conifers including a Top Douglas Fir which is 171 feet and still growing, also a collection of younger trees.
In May you will be able to view the wonderful daffodils and the rhododendrons in flower.

Directions: Off A93, the Lodge House is five miles north of Blairgowrie on right hand side A93 from Blairgowrie. Follow avenue to house.

Disabled Access:
Partial

Opening Times:
1 January - 31 December
9:00am - 7:00pm or Dusk

Admission:
£4.00

Charities:
Seafarers UK receives 40%, the net remaining to SG Beneficiaries

HOLLYTREE LODGE
Muckhart, Dollar FK14 7JW
Liz and Peter Wyatt T: 0797 337 4687
E: elizwyatt @aol.com

We have a mature one acre garden which is made up of various focused areas, providing interest throughout the year. Spring bulbs, a collection of rhododendrons, azaleas and number of other unusual trees and shrubs, some of which colour beautifully in autumn. Herbaceous borders, a small Japanese garden, and at the other end of the spectrum, some more natural areas and a wildlife pond. Recent developments include a mini wildflower meadow and cordoned apples and pears.

Directions: Hollytree lodge is off the A91 down the small lane directly opposite the Inn at Muckhart entrance. Parking available for disabled only, otherwise please park in the village.

Disabled Access:
Full

Opening Times:
Sunday 12 July
11:00am - 5:00pm
Also by arrangement
1 April - 30 October Small groups (up to ten) welcome.

Admission:
£4.00

Charities:
The Coronation Hall, Muckhart. receives 20%, The Prince's Trust, Scotland receives 20%, the net remaining to SG Beneficiaries

KILGRASTON SCHOOL
Bridge of Earn PH2 9BQ
Kilgraston School T: 01738 815517
E: marketing@kilgraston.com www.kilgraston.com

Set within the grounds of Kilgraston School, this is a wonderful opportunity to see the snowdrops whilst exploring the woodlands and surroundings of this very unique garden. Statues and sculptures (including work by Hew Lorimer) intermingle with ancient trees, snowdrops and even the resident red squirrels. Spend a Sunday afternoon wandering along wild woodland pathways and through the extensive grounds, and explore the chapel, main hall and artworks within the school.

Other Details: Teas from the school's award-winning catering team are available (indoors, if the weather is against us), alongside a wide range of activities for children.

Directions: Bridge of Earn is three miles south of Perth on the A912. Kilgraston School is well signposted from the main road. Maps are available from the website.

Disabled Access:
Partial

Opening Times:
Saturday 28 February
1:30pm - 4:00pm
for the Snowdrop Festival

Admission:
£4.00

Charities:
Mary's Meals receives 40%, the net remaining to SG Beneficiaries

21 LITTLE TOMBUIE
Killiechassie, Aberfeldy PH15 2JS
Mrs Sally Crystal
E: sallycrystal@gmail.com

Perched high up, facing south on the hill overlooking Aberfeldy and the Tay, this is not a garden where everything is finished and perfect. But if you want to meet a gardener who is diffidently very knowledgeable but warm and welcoming and see a garden which has huge potential, then this is the garden for you. The views alone are worth the journey. Mrs Crystal is not only a compost queen, but a builder of dry stone walls, plantswoman and tree planter. Her raised bed vegetable garden would put most of us to shame. The older part of the garden is immaculate with emerald lawns, a wide selection of trees and shrubs and an interesting collection of old stone cheese presses. In the newer part a garden has been carved out from the hill for roses and shrubs with single flowers. In early summer, azaleas and meconopsis are flowering but the autumn colours are wonderful, and you may hear the red deer roaring in the neighbouring fields.

Directions: From the A9 take the A827 to Aberfeldy. At traffic lights turn right and take the B846. Take the first right to Strathtay. Tombuie is approximately two miles along this road opposite a graveyard and beside a large copper beech tree.

Disabled Access:
Partial

Opening Times:
By arrangement
15 May - 15 June
By arrangement 15
September - 15 October

Admission:
£4.00

Charities:
Prostate Cancer UK receives 40%, the net remaining to SG Beneficiaries

22 MACHANY HOUSE
Auchterarder PH3 1NW
Mr and Mrs John Robertson

An informal garden within an arboriculturalist's heaven. The open lawns allow visual space to appreciate the splendour of mature trees, in particular, giants of the American Pacific coast, majestic specimens of Wellingtonia and Douglas Fir and many hardwoods. A magnificent array of rhododendrons, azaleas, bamboos and much more. A developing collection of herbaceous and a comprehensive display of bulbs feature throughout the garden. Wander through a variety of settings, ranging from the informal woodland dell leading to a tranquil burn to the more formal around the house.

Other Details: Machany last opened in the Autumn of 2008, so this is a rare opportunity to see the garden. No dogs please.

Directions: Machany is five miles from Crieff (turn left in Muthill), four miles from Auchterarder (Castleton Road via Tullibardine towards Strathallan Airfield), three miles from Gleneagles Hotel. From the north and south: A9 to Gleneagles, signposted to Crieff A823. Follow road approx two miles and look for SG signs.

Disabled Access:
Partial

Opening Times:
Sunday 17 May
2:00pm - 5:00pm

Admission:
£4.00, children under 16 free

Charities:
St Kessogs Episcopal Church, Auchterarder receives 40%, the net remaining to SG

23 MEGGINCH CASTLE
Errol PH2 7SW
Mr Giles Herdman and The Hon. Mrs Drummond-Herdman of Megginch

Fifteenth century turreted castle (not open) with Gothic stable yard and pagoda dovecote. Nineteenth century formal front garden, topiary and ancient yews. There is a splendid array of daffodils and rhododendrons. There is also a double walled kitchen garden and heritage orchard with extensive replanting of old Scottish fruit trees, as featured in "The Beechgrove Garden".

Other Details: Homebaking stalls.

Directions: Approach from Dundee only, directly off A90, on south side of carriageway half a mile on left after Errol flyover, between lodge gatehouses. Seven miles from Perth, eight from Dundee.

Disabled Access:
Full

Opening Times:
Sunday 12 April
2:00pm - 5:00pm

Admission:
£4.00, children free

Charities:
Maggie's Cancer Care Centre receives 20%, Dundee and Glencarse Church receives 20%, the net remaining to SG Beneficiaries

MILL OF FORNETH
Forneth, Blairgowrie PH10 6SP
Mr and Mrs Graham Wood
E: gaw@gwpc.demon.co.uk

Formerly a watermill, originally laid out in the 1970s by James Aitken, the Scottish landscape designer and naturalist. The sheltered four acre garden has a range of mature trees, including a Himalyan Blue Cedar, large rhododendrons, azaleas and a wide range of shrubs. A 75 metre long mill lade feeds rocky waterfalls and a lily pond. Planting includes established perennials with seasonal colours, many bulbs, primulas and heathers.

Other Details: This garden is an old watermill with deep and fast flowing water. It is not safe for children under 12. Grassy parking and picnic area available. Take care if weather has been wet and ground is soft!

Directions: Take the A923 Dunkeld to Blairgowrie road. Six miles east of Dunkeld turn south onto a minor road signposted Snaigow and Clunie. Mill of Forneth is the first gate on the left hand side.

Disabled Access:
Partial

Opening Times:
Sunday 14 June
2:00pm - 5:00pm
By arrangement
30 April - 30 September

Admission:
£4.00

Charities:
Perth & Kinross District Nurses receives 20%, Blairgowrie Black Watch Army Cadet Force receives 20%, the net remaining to SG Beneficiaries

PARKHEAD HOUSE
Parkhead Gardens, Burghmuir Road, Perth PH1 1JF
Mr & Mrs M.S. Tinson T: 01738 625983
E: maddy.tinson@gmail.com

Parkhead is an old farmhouse sited within an acre of beautiful gardens. Mature trees include an outstanding 300 year old Spanish chestnut. This hidden gem is a garden for all seasons. Gentle terracing and meandering paths lead you past a large variety of unusual and interesting plants and shrubs. Holder of the National Collection of 'Mylnefield Lilies' originally developed by Dr Christopher North at the Scottish Horticultural Research Institute, Dundee.

Other Details: National Plant Collection®: Mylnefield Lilies, in flower July. Homemade teas by request. Plant stall when available.

Directions: Parkhead Gardens is a small lane off the west end of Burghmuir Road in Perth. More detailed directions on request.

Disabled Access:
Partial

Opening Times:
By arrangement
1 June - 31 August

Admission:
£4.00

Charities:
Plant Heritage receives 40%, the net remaining to SG Beneficiaries

26 THE BIELD AT BLACKRUTHVEN

Blackruthven House, Tibbermore PH1 1PY
The Bield Christian Co Ltd T: 01738 583238
E: info@bieldatblackruthven.org.uk www.bieldatblackruthven.org.uk

The Bield is set in extensive grounds comprising well maintained lawns and clipped hedges, a flower meadow and a large collection of specimen trees. Visitors are encouraged to stroll around the grounds and explore the labyrinth cut into the grass of the old orchard. The main garden is a traditional walled garden containing extensive herbaceous borders, manicured lawns and an organic vegetable plot. The walled garden also contains a wide variety of trained fruit trees, a fruit cage, glasshouse and a healing garden.

Directions: From Dundee or Edinburgh, follow signs for Glasgow, Stirling Crianlarich which lead onto the Perth bypass. Head west on the A85 signed to Crieff/Crianlarich to West Huntingtower. Turn left at the crossroads to Madderty / Tibbermore. The entrance is on your left after ½ mile and is marked by stone pillars and iron gates. Take a left up the tarmac road passing the gate lodge. Turn right to park at the Steading.

Disabled Access:
Full

Opening Times:
Saturday 27 June
2:00pm - 5:00pm

Admission:
£5.00 includes tea/coffee and home baking

Charities:
Southton Smallholding receives 40%, the net remaining to SG Beneficiaries

27 THE STEADING

Newmill of Kinloch, Clunie, Blairgowrie PH10 6SG
Jean and Dave Trudgill T: 01250 884263

Newmill is at its best in spring and early summer. Its main attractions centre around water and include both garden and 'wild' ponds, the Lunan Burn and a mill lade, once converted to trap eels. There is a small 'cottage' garden and a wooded walk along the Lunan Burn, with bridges and some narrow paths, with bluebells and primroses in spring. There is also a wild flower meadow carpeted with cowslips in spring and with several species of wild orchids, including both species of butterfly orchid that usually flower in early to mid-June. Although rarely seen the Lunan Burn is home to otters and beavers and occasional kingfishers and in early June large numbers of roach are sometimes seen spawning.

Directions: Track on sharp left-hand bend to the south side of the A923 just past a breeze-block wall 800 metres west of The Kinloch House Hotel and three miles west of Blairgowrie.

Disabled Access:
None

Opening Times:
By arrangement 25 April - 17 May and 6 June - 21 June

Admission:
£5.00, includes tea/coffee

Charities:
Save the Children receives 40%, the net remaining to SG Beneficiaries

28 WESTER HOUSE OF ROSS

Comrie PH6 2JS
Mrs Sue Young

A secret waiting to be discovered this year, in May and September. Come and join us and see the four acre garden developed over the last 13 years. It is partly herbaceous with meconopsis, peonies, hostas and woodland walks to enjoy and then in September asters, crocosmias, hydrangeas, verbenas and geraniums.

Other Details: A large and interesting plant stall. A great tea tent with cakes galore!

Directions: On A85 drive westwards through Comrie, past the White Church and at the end of the village take a left turn over a small bridge, signposted Ross. Then take first right, signposted Dalchonzie. After ¼ mile turn left at the three large dustbins and follow signs to parking and the garden.

Disabled Access:
None

Opening Times:
Sat & Sun 23 - 24 May
1:30pm - 4:30pm
Sat & Sun 19/20 September
1:30pm - 4:30pm

Admission:
£4.00, children free

Charities:
Maggie's Centres receives 40%, the net remaining to SG Beneficiaries

RENFREWSHIRE

Scotland's Gardens 2015 Guidebook is sponsored by **INVESTEC WEALTH & INVESTMENT**

District Organisers

Mrs Rosemary Leslie	High Mathernock Farm, Auchentiber Road, Kilmacolm PA13 4SP T: 01505 874032
Mrs Alexandra MacMillan	Langside Farm, Kilmacolm, Inverclyde PA13 4SA T: 01475 540423

Area Organisers

Mrs Helen Hunter	2 Bay Street, Fairlie, North Ayrshire KA29 0AL
Mrs B McLean	49 Middlepenny Road, Langbank, Inverclyde PA14 6XE
Mr J A Wardrop OBE DL	St Kevins, Victoria Road, Paisley PA2 9PT

Treasurer

Mrs Jean Gillan	Bogriggs Cottage, Carlung, West Kilbride KA23 9PS

Gardens open on a specific date

Ardgowan, Inverkip	Sunday 8 February	2:00pm	- 5:00pm
Carruth, Bridge of Weir	Sunday 31 May	2:00pm	- 5:00pm
Quarriers Village Gardens, Bridge of Weir	Sunday 7 June	2:00pm	- 5:00pm
Duchal, Kilmacolm	Sunday 14 June	2:00pm	- 5:00pm
Gardening Leave, Bishopton	Sunday 23 August	12:00pm	- 4:00pm

Plant sales

Kilmacolm Plant Sale, Kilmacolm	Saturday 18 April	10:00am	- 12:00pm
Kilmacolm Plant Sale, Kilmacolm	Saturday 12 September	10:00am	- 12:00pm

Key to symbols

	New in 2015		Homemade teas		Accommodation
	Teas		Dogs on a lead allowed		Plant stall
	Cream teas		Wheelchair access		Scottish Snowdrop Festival

Garden locations

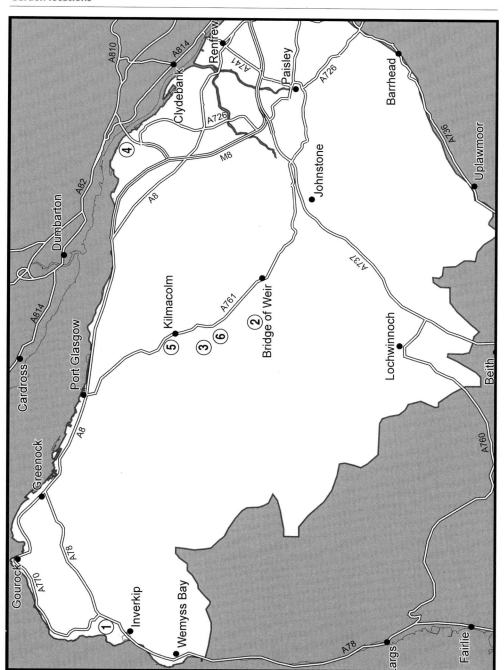

ARDGOWAN
Inverkip PA16 0DW
Sir Ludovic Shaw Stewart T: 01475 521656/226
E: info@ardgowan.co.uk

Woodland walks carpeted with masses of snowdrops in a lovely setting overlooking the River Clyde.

Other Details: Snowdrops, both bunches and plants for sale. If the weather is wet, the paths can be very muddy - sturdy waterproof footwear and clothing should be worn and wheelchair access in garden not possible.

Directions: Inverkip 1½ miles. Glasgow/Largs buses to and from Inverkip Village. Please use main entrance at roundabout to come in and leave by the Marina entrance to avoid congestion.

Disabled Access:
Partial

Opening Times:
Sunday 8 February
2:00pm - 5:00pm

Admission:
£2.00

Charities:
Ardgowan Hospice receives 40%, the net remaining to SG Beneficiaries

CARRUTH
Bridge of Weir PA11 3SG
Mr and Mrs Charles Maclean

Over 20 acres of long established rhododendrons, woodland with good bluebells and lawn gardens in lovely landscaped setting. Young arboretum.

Directions: Access from B786 Kilmacolm/Lochwinnoch road. From Bridge of Weir take Torr Road until you get to the B786. Turn right and after approximately 100 yards, garden entrance is on the right.

Disabled Access:
Partial

Opening Times:
Sunday 31 May
2:00pm - 5:00pm

Admission:
£4.00

Charities:
Marie Curie Cancer Care receives 40%, the net remaining to SG Beneficiaries

DUCHAL
Kilmacolm PA13 4RS
Lord Maclay

Eighteenth century walled garden particularly well planted and maintained, entered by footbridge over the Greenwater. Specie trees, hollies, old fashioned roses, shrubs and herbaceous borders with fruit orchards and vegetable garden. Also in the garden are azaleas and a lily pond.

Directions: On B788 one mile from Kilmacolm (this road links B786 Lochwinnoch Road and A761 Bridge of Weir Road) Greenock/Glasgow bus via Bridge of Weir. Knapps Loch stop is ¼ mile from garden.

Disabled Access:
Partial

Opening Times:
Sunday 14 June
2:00pm - 5:00pm

Admission:
£4.00

Charities:
Ardgowan Hospice receives 40%, the net remaining to SG Beneficiaries

GARDENING LEAVE
Old Garden Centre, Erskine Hospital, Bishopton PA7 5PU
Gardening Leave
www.gardeningleave.org

Large enclosed tarmac garden located on site of old garden centre at Erskine Hospital. Run by charity Gardening Leave providing sessions of horticultural therapy to serving and ex-members of the Armed Forces. A productive garden, housing quirky assortment of raised planters, imaginatively created lawn area, shady wildlife/quiet garden, covered growing areas and other features embracing the upcycling ethos. Still being developed and evolving. An inspirational and worthwhile charity.

Other Details: There will be a stall with gardening goods for sale made on the premises.

Directions: From M8, take exit for Erskine Bridge and turn off to Bishopton. From the north, go over Erskine Bridge, take turning to Bishopton. Located on the south side of the Erskine Bridge, enter the Erskine Home Estate and follow signs for Gardening Leave.

Disabled Access:
Full

Opening Times:
Sunday 23 August
12:00pm - 4:00pm

Admission:
£4.00, children under 16 free

Charities:
Gardening Leave receives 40%, the net remaining to SG Beneficiaries

KILMACOLM PLANT SALE
Outside Kilmacolm Library, Lochwinnoch Road, Kilmacolm PA13 4EL
Scotland's Gardens - Renfrewshire

Spring and end of season plant sales in the centre of Kilmacolm.

Directions: The plant sale will be held at the Cross outside the Library and Cargill Centre.

Disabled Access:
Full

Opening Times:
Saturday 18 April
10:00am - 12:00pm
Saturday 12 September
10:00am - 12:00pm

Admission:
Free, donations welcome

Charities:
Parklea "Branching Out" receives 40%, the net remaining to SG Beneficiaries

QUARRIERS VILLAGE GARDENS
Craigends Avenue, Bridge of Weir PA11 3SQ
The Gardeners of Quarriers Village
www.petersrailway.com

Adjacent gardens in Craigends Avenue all different in character ranging from a cottage style with raised borders of herbaceous plants and vegetable plot to a well stocked informal family garden also with a vegetable plot and miniature steam railway to a Japanese style garden with architectural planting and specimen trees. Something for everyone!

Other Details: Train rides, weather permitting.

Directions: Access to Quarriers Village from Bridge of Weir via Torr Road or from A761 Bridge of Weir-Kilmacolm Road. Craigends Avenue is off Torr Road and will be signposted on the day. Access also from B786 Lochwinnoch to Kilmacolm, follow signs to Quarriers Village.

Disabled Access:
Full

Opening Times:
Sunday 7 June
2:00pm - 5:00pm

Admission:
£4.00

Charities:
Gardening Leave receives 40%, the net remaining to SG Beneficiaries

ROSS, CROMARTY, SKYE & INVERNESS

District Organiser

Lady Lister-Kaye	House of Aigas, Beauly IV4 7AD

Area Organiser

Emma MacKenzie	Glenkyllachy, Tomatin IV13 7YA

Treasurer

Mrs Sheila Kerr	Lilac Cottage, Struy, By Beauly IV4 7JU

Gardens open on a specific date

Dundonnell House, Little Loch Broom	Thursday 16 April	2:00pm	-	5:00pm
Old Allangrange, Munlochy	Saturday 2 May	11:00am	-	5:30pm
Inverewe Garden and Estate, Poolewe	Wednesday 20 May	10:00am	-	4:00pm
Oldtown of Leys Garden, Inverness	Saturday 23 May	2:00pm	-	5:00pm
Aultgowrie Mill, Muir of Ord	Sunday 24 May	1:00pm	-	5:00pm
House of Gruinard, by Achnasheen	Wednesday 27 May	2:00pm	-	5:00pm
Dundonnell House, Little Loch Broom	Thursday 28 May	2:00pm	-	5:00pm
Duirinish Lodge, Kyle of Lochalsh	Saturday 30 May	2:00pm	-	6:00pm
Duirinish Lodge, Kyle of Lochalsh	Sunday 31 May	2:00pm	-	6:00pm
Duirinish Lodge, Kyle of Lochalsh	Mon - Sat 1 to 6 June	2:00pm	-	6:00pm
Inverewe Garden and Estate, Poolewe	Wednesday 3 June	10:00am	-	4:00pm
The New House, Dingwall	Saturday 6 June	12:00pm	-	4:00pm
Field House, Beauly	Sunday 7 June	2:00pm	-	5:00pm
Gorthleck, Stratherrick	Wednesday 10 June	10:00am	-	9:00pm
Brackla Wood, Dingwall	Wednesday 17 June	1:30pm	-	5:00pm
House of Aigas and Field Centre, By Beauly	Sunday 28 June	2:00pm	-	5:00pm
The New House, Dingwall	Saturday 11 July	12:00pm	-	4:00pm
Aultgowrie Mill, Muir of Ord	Sunday 12 July	1:00pm	-	5:00pm
House of Gruinard, by Achnasheen	Wednesday 22 July	2:00pm	-	5:00pm
House of Aigas and Field Centre, By Beauly	Sunday 26 July	2:00pm	-	5:00pm
2 Durnamuck, Little Loch Broom	Friday 7 August	11:00am	-	5:00pm
2 Durnamuck, Little Loch Broom	Saturday 8 August	11:00am	-	5:00pm
Hugh Miller's Birthplace Cottage & Museum, Cromarty	Saturday 8 August	12:00pm	-	5:00pm
2 Durnamuck, Little Loch Broom	Sunday 9 August	11:00am	-	5:00pm
Dundonnell House, Little Loch Broom	Thursday 13 August	2:00pm	-	5:00pm
Rubha Phoil Forest Gardens, Isle of Skye	Saturday 22 August	10:30am	-	5:00pm

ROSS, CROMARTY, SKYE & INVERNESS

Highland Liliums, Kiltarlity	Sunday 30 August	12:00pm	4:00pm
Old Allangrange, Munlochy	Saturday 12 September	11:00am	5:30pm
Dundonnell House, Little Loch Broom	Thursday 17 September	2:00pm	5:00pm

Gardens open regularly

Abriachan Garden Nursery, Loch Ness Side	1 February - 30 November	9:00am	7:00pm
Applecross Walled Garden, Strathcarron	15 March - 31 October	11:00am	9:00pm
Attadale, Strathcarron	1 April - 31 Oct (Not Suns)	10:00am	5:30pm
Balmeanach House, Isle of Skye	5 May - 31 Oct (Mons & Thurs)	10:30am	3:30pm
Clan Donald Skye, Isle of Skye	1 January - 31 March	Dawn	Dusk
	1 April - 31 October	9:30am	5:30pm
	1 November - 31 December	Dawn	Dusk
Coiltie Garden, Drumnadrochit	22 June - 12 July	12:00pm	6:00pm
Dunvegan Castle and Gardens, Isle of Skye	1 April - 15 October	10:00am	5:30pm
Highland Liliums, Kiltarlity	1 January - 31 December	9:00am	5:00pm
Leathad Ard, Isle of Lewis	1 June - 31 Aug (Not Fris & Suns) and Wednesday 5th August	10:00am	6:00pm
Oldtown of Leys Garden, Inverness	1 January - 31 December	Dawn	Dusk
The Lookout, Kilmuir, North Kessock	1 May - 31 Aug (Sats & Suns)	12:00pm	4:00pm

Gardens open by arrangement

Brackla Wood, Dingwall	6 April - 27 September	01349 877765
Cardon, Farr	1 March - 30 September	01808 521389
Dundonnell House, Little Loch Broom	1 April - 30 November	07789 390028
Glenkyllachy Lodge, Tomatin	1 May - 31 July and 1 Sept - 31 Oct	emmaglenkyllachy@gmail.com
House of Aigas and Field Centre, By Beauly	1 March - 25 October	01463 782443
Leathad Ard, Isle of Lewis	1 May - 31 May and 1 September - 30 September	01851 643204 01851 643204
The Lookout, Kilmuir	1 January - 31 December	01463 731489

Key to symbols

	New in 2015		Homemade teas		Accommodation
	Teas		Dogs on a lead allowed		Plant stall
	Cream teas		Wheelchair access		Scottish Snowdrop Festival

Garden locations

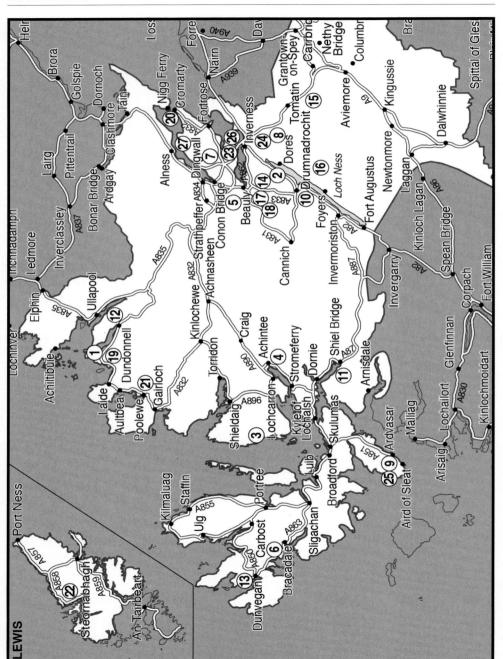

2 DURNAMUCK

Little Loch Broom, Wester Ross IV23 2QZ
Will Soos and Susan Pomeroy T: 01854 633761
E: sueandwill@icloud.com

Our garden is situated on the edge of Little Loch Broom and is south east facing. It is a coastal plantsman's garden with a rich mix of herbaceous borders, trees and shrubs, vegetables, drystone wall planting, South African plants, Mediterranean plants, wild meadow and stunning views. Many of the plants have been collected from all over the world and growing them in Durnamuck has provided the obvious challenges but with an overall pleasing outcome. The ground in places is a bit stony, including the drive. There is parking down by the house if needed.

Other Details: 7 and 8 August, teas at Maggie's Tearoom, three miles towards Little Loch Broom. 9 August, teas served in the garden.

Directions: On the west coast take the A832, then take the turning along single track road signed Badcaul, continue to yellow salt bin, turn right, go to bottom of hill, house with red roof.

Disabled Access:
None

Opening Times:
Friday 7 August
11:00am - 5:00pm
Saturday 8 August
11:00am - 5:00pm
Sunday 9 August
11:00am - 5:00pm

Admission:
£3.00

Charities:
Cancer Research receives 40%, the net remaining to SG Beneficiaries

ABRIACHAN GARDEN NURSERY

Loch Ness Side IV3 8LA
Mr and Mrs Davidson T: 01463 861232
E: info@lochnessgarden.com   www.lochnessgarden.com

An outstanding garden. Over four acres of exciting plantings with winding paths through native woodlands. Seasonal highlights - snowdrops, hellebores, primulas, meconopsis, hardy geraniums and colour-themed summer beds. Views over Loch Ness. New path to pond through the Bluebell Wood.

Other Details: Working retail nursery. Drinks machine in nursery.

Directions: On A82 Inverness/Drumnadrochit road, approximately eight miles south of Inverness.

Disabled Access:
Partial

Opening Times:
1 February - 30 November
9:00am - 7:00pm
(opening for the Snowdrop Festival 1 February - 16 March)

Admission:
£3.00

Charities:
Highland Hospice receives 40%, the net remaining to SG Beneficiaries

APPLECROSS WALLED GARDEN

Strathcarron IV54 8ND
Applecross Organics T: 01520 744440

Walled garden of 1¼ acres in spectacular surroundings. Derelict for 50 years but lovingly restored since 2001. Lots of herbaceous borders, fruit trees and raised vegetable beds. We try to have an interesting plant table in this wonderful peaceful setting. Award winning cafe/restaurant within the garden. Open every day from March to October.

Other Details: Restaurant open from 11:00am till late, last orders 8:30pm.

Directions: Take the spectacular Bealach na Ba hill road after Kishorn. At the T-junction in Applecross, turn right for half a mile. Entrance to Applecross House is immediately in front of you.

Disabled Access:
Full

Opening Times:
15 March - 31 October
11:00am - 9:00pm

Admission:
By donation

Charities:
Smile Train receives 40%, the net remaining to SG Beneficiaries

ATTADALE
Strathcarron IV54 8YX
Mr and Mrs Ewen Macpherson T: 01520 722603
E: info@attadalegardens.com www.attadalegardens.com

The Gulf Stream, surrounding hills and rocky cliffs, create a microclimate for 20 acres of outstanding water gardens, old rhododendrons, unusual trees and a fern collection in a geodesic dome. There is also a sunken fern garden developed on the site of an early 19th century drain, a waterfall into a pool with dwarf rhododendrons, a sunken garden and kitchen garden. Other features include a conservatory, Japanese garden, sculpture collection and giant sundial.

Other Details: Car parking for disabled by the house.

Directions: On A890 between Strathcarron and South Strome.

Disabled Access:
Partial

Opening Times:
1 April - 31 October
10:00am - 5:30pm
Closed Sundays

Admission:
£6.00, OAPs £4.00, children
£1.00

Charities:
Howard Doris Centre receives
40%, the net remaining to
SG Beneficiaries

AULTGOWRIE MILL
Aultgowrie, Urray, Muir of Ord IV6 7XA
Mr and Mrs John Clegg T: 01997 433699
E: john@johnclegg.com

Aultgowrie Mill is an 18th century converted water mill set in gardens and woodland river walks of 13 acres. Features include a wooded island, a half acre wildflower meadow and a wildlife pond, all with outstanding views of the surrounding hills. The gardens are being developed with much new landscaping and planting, including terraces, lawns, two mixed orchards and raised vegetable beds with glasshouse. *BBC Beechgrove Garden* featured this garden in July 2014

Other Details: Homemade teas are served on the balcony and millpond lawn. Plans and photographs of the gardens, island and river walks will be on display and there is ample field parking. Well behaved dogs on leads are very welcome.

Directions: From the south, turn left at Muir of Ord Distillery, Aultgowrie Mill is 3.2 miles. From the north and west, after Marybank Primary School, Aultgowrie Mill is 1.7 miles up the hill.

Disabled Access:
Partial

Opening Times:
Sunday 24 May
1:00pm - 5:00pm
Sunday 12 July
1:00pm - 5:00pm

Admission:
£4.50, children under 12 free.

Charities:
R.N.L.I. receives 40% of
all monies raised, the net
remaining to SG Beneficiaries

BALMEANACH HOUSE
Struan, Isle of Skye IV56 8FH
Mrs Arlene Macphie T: 01470 572320
E: info@skye-holiday.com www.skye-holiday.com

During the late 1980s, a ⅓ acre of croft land was fenced in to create a garden. Now there is a glorious herbaceous border, bedding plants area and a small azalea/rhododendron walk. In addition, there is a woodland dell with fairies, three ponds and a small shrubbery.

Other Details: Plant stall at Plants 'n Stuff, Atholl Service Station. Teas at Waterside Cafe, Atholl Service Station.

Directions: A87 to Sligachan, turn left, Balmeanach is five miles north of Struan and five miles south of Dunvegan.

Disabled Access:
None

Opening Times:
5 May - 31 October
10:30am - 3:30pm
Mondays and Thursdays

Admission:
£3.00

Charities:
SSPCA receives 40%,
the net remaining to
SG Beneficiaries

BRACKLA WOOD
Culbokie, Dingwall IV7 8GY
Susan and Ian Dudgeon T: 01349 877765
E: smdbrackla@aol.com

Mature one acre plot consisting of woodland, wildlife features, ponds, mixed borders, a kitchen garden, rockery and mini-orchard. Spring bulbs and hellebores, rhododendrons, wisteria and roses followed by crocosmia, clematis and deciduous trees provide continuous colour and interest throughout the seasons. There is always the chance of seeing red squirrels. New borders for 2015.

Other Details: Strictly no dogs except guide dogs.

Directions: From the north: Take the A9 and turn off to Culbokie. At the far end of the village, turn right after the playing fields signposted Munlochy. A mile up the road, turn right into 'No Through Road' signposted Upper Braefindon. From the south: Take the A9 and turn off to Munlochy. At the far end of the village, turn right and then sharp left up road signposted Culbokie and Killen. After about 4½ miles turn left onto road signposted Upper Braefindon. Brackla Wood is first house on left.

Disabled Access:
Partial

Opening Times:
Wednesday 17 June
1:30pm - 5:00pm
Also by arrangement 6 April - 27 September

Admission:
£3.00, children free

Charities:
Black Isle MacMillan Cancer Care receives 40%, the net remaining to SG Beneficiaries

CARDON
Balnafoich, Farr IV2 6XG
Caroline Smith T: 01808 521389
E: csmith@kitchens01.fsnet.co.uk

The garden is set in approximately five acres of woodlands with a feature pond and lawn area. There are also rockeries, wild woodland areas and cottage style plantings.

Other Details: Self-catering accommodation available at Cardon House. See www.holidaylettings.co.uk. Cardon will also be open on a date to be confirmed, for details check our website.

Directions: From Inverness: head south, turn right to Daviot (seven miles) and head to Balnafoich. Cardon three and a half miles. From Inverness Academy: take B861. Four and a half miles take left to Daviot and garden is 400 yards on the left.

Disabled Access:
Full

Opening Times:
Date to be confirmed, check our website.
Also by arrangement
1 March - 30 September

Admission:
£3.00, children free

Charities:
Local charities will receives 40%, the net remaining to SG Beneficiaries

CLAN DONALD SKYE
Armadale, Isle of Skye IV45 8RS
Clan Donald Lands Trust T: 01471 844305
E: office@clandonald.com www.clandonald.com

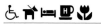

Exotic trees, shrubs and flowers, expansive lawns and stunning scenery combine to make this a real treat for garden lovers. When the Clan Donald Lands Trust took over, the gardens were overgrown and neglected. Years of hard pruning, rebuilding and planting around the centrepiece of historic Armadale Castle has resulted in 40 acres of stunning woodland gardens and lawns that provide a tranquil place to sit or walk. Specimen trees, some planted in the early 1800s, tower above the gardens. Beyond the formal gardens visitors can enjoy woodland walks and nature trails, with beautiful views to the Sound of Sleat, the mountains of Knoydart forming a spectacular backdrop. Children's adventure playground. A new garden interpretation began in 2013.

Other Details: Times of opening may be subject to change, please check our website.

Directions: From Skye Bridge: Head north on A87 and turn left just before Broadford onto A851 signposted Armadale 15 miles.
From Armadale Pier: ¼ mile north on A851 to car park.

Disabled Access:
Full

Opening Times:
1 Jan - 31 March Dawn - Dusk
1 April - 31 October
9:30am - 5:30pm
1 Nov - 31 Dec Dawn - Dusk

Admission:
Adults £8.50, conc/children £6.95, under 5 free, families £25.00
Free admission Jan - March and Nov - Dec.

Charities:
Donation to SG Beneficiaries

COILTIE GARDEN
Divach, Drumnadrochit IV63 6XW
Gillian and David Nelson T: 01456 450219

A garden made over the past 35 years from a long neglected Victorian garden, now being somewhat reorganised to suit ageing gardeners. Many unusual trees, shrubs, herbaceous borders, roses, all set in beautiful hill scenery with a fine view of the 100 feet Divach Falls. Trees planted 30 years ago are showing well now.

Directions: Take turning to Divach off A82 in Drumnadrochit village. Proceed two miles uphill, passing Falls. 150 metres beyond Divach Lodge.

Disabled Access:
Partial

Opening Times:
22 June - 12 July
12:00pm - 6:00pm

Admission:
£3.00, children free

Charities:
Amnesty International receives 40%, the net remaining to SG Beneficiaries

---

DUIRINISH LODGE
Kyle of Lochalsh IV40 8BE
Willy Roe & Bill Taylor
E: willyroe@gmail.com

The development of our 18 acre woodland garden continues apace. Rare rhododendrons and azaleas grow amongst ancient oaks and pines, and the newly planted Duirinish Jubilee Wood, reintroducing broadleaf native trees to this part of the west coast. New water features, including a glorious fountain add considerable interest to this wonderful garden. Enjoy tea and home baking on the terrace with fabulous views over the Inner Sound to Raasay, Skye, Applecross and Torridon.

Directions: Off the minor road between Reraig/Balmacara and Plockton.

Disabled Access:
Partial

Opening Times:
Sat & Sun 30 - 31 May
2:00pm - 6:00pm
Mon to Sat 1 - 6 June
2:00pm - 6:00pm

Admission:
£5.00, under 18s and disabled people free

Charities:
Local charities receives 40%, the net remaining to SG Beneficiaries

---

DUNDONNELL HOUSE
Little Loch Broom, Wester Ross IV23 2QW
Dundonnell Estates T: 07789 390028

Camellias, magnolias and bulbs in spring, rhododendrons and laburnum walk in this ancient walled garden. Exciting planting in new borders gives all year colour centred around one of the oldest yew trees in Scotland. A new water sculpture, midsummer roses, restored Edwardian glasshouse, riverside walk, arboretum - all in the valley below the peaks of An Teallach.

Other Details: On 28 May homemade teas are available in the house. On other dates teas are available at Maggie's Tearoom three miles towards Little Loch Broom.

Directions: Off A835 at Braemore on to A832. After 11 miles take Badralloch turn for ½ mile.

Disabled Access:
Partial

Opening Times:
Thursdays 16 April, 28 May, 13 August and 17 September
2:00pm - 5:00pm
Also by arrangement
1 April - 30 November

Admission:
£3.50, children free

Charities:
Edinburgh Botanical Gardens and Born Free Foundation receives 40%, the net remaining to SG Beneficiaries

DUNVEGAN CASTLE AND GARDENS
Isle of Skye   IV55 8WF
Hugh Macleod of Macleod   T: 01470 521206
E: info@dunvegancastle.com   www.dunvegancastle.com

Dunvegan Castle's five acres of formal gardens began life in the 18th century. In stark contrast to the barren moorland that dominates Skye's landscape, the gardens are a hidden oasis featuring an eclectic mix of plants, woodland glades, shimmering pools fed by waterfalls and streams flowing down to the sea. After experiencing the Water Garden with its ornate bridges and islands replete with a rich and colourful plant variety, wander through the elegant surroundings of the formal Round Garden. The Walled Garden is well worth a visit to see its colourful herbaceous borders and recently added Victorian style glasshouse. In what was formerly the castle's vegetable garden, there is a garden museum and a diverse range of plants and flowers which complement the attractive features including a waterlily pond, a neoclassical urn and a Larch pergola. A considerable amount of replanting and landscaping has taken place over the last thirty years to restore and develop the gardens at Dunvegan.

Directions: One mile from Dunvegan Village, 23 miles west of Portree.

Disabled Access:
Partial

Opening Times:
1 April - 15 October
10:00am - 5:30pm

Admission:
Gardens only: £9.00, child £6.00, concessions £8.00. **Castle & Gardens:** £11.00, child 5-15 years £8.00, family ticket £29.00, concessions £9.00.

Charities:
Donation to SG Beneficiaries

FIELD HOUSE
Belladrum, Beauly IV4 7BA
Mr & Mrs D Paterson
www.dougthegarden.co.uk

An informal country garden in a one acre site with mixed borders and some unusual plants - a plantsman's garden. Featured in The Beechgrove Garden.

Directions: Four miles from Beauly on A833 Beauly to Drumnadrochit road, then follow signs to Belladrum.

Disabled Access:
None

Opening Times:
Sunday 7 June
2:00pm - 5:00pm

Admission:
£4.00

Charities:
Macmillan Cancer Care receives 40%, the net remaining to SG Beneficiaries

GLENKYLLACHY LODGE
Tomatin IV13 7YA
Mr and Mrs Philip Mackenzie
E: emmaglenkyllachy@gmail.com

In a remote highland glen and at an altitude of 1150 feet this is a glorious garden of shrubs, herbaceous, rhododendrons and trees planted round a pond with a backdrop of a juniper and birch covered hillside. There is also a vegetable garden, a polytunnel and a short wooded walk with stunning views down the Findhorn. A wild flower meadow and amazing stone wall folly are new this year. Various original sculptures are situated around the garden. Second pond with oriental bridges and ornamental ducks.

Other Details: Teas are available by prior arrangement.

Directions: Turn off the A9 at Tomatin and take the Coignafearn and Garbole single track road down north side of River Findhorn, cattle grid and gate on right 500 metres after sign to Farr.

Disabled Access:
Partial

Opening Times:
By appointment
1 May - 31 July and
1 September - 31 October

Admission:
£5.00, children free

Charities:
Marie Curie Cancer Care receives 40%, the net remaining to SG Beneficiaries

16 GORTHLECK
Stratherrick IV2 6UJ
Steve & Katie Smith T: 07710325903
E: visit@gorthleckgarden.co.uk

Gorthleck is an unusual 20 acre woodland garden built in an unlikely place, on and around an exposed rocky ridge. The layout of the garden works with the natural features of the landscape rather than against them, with numerous paths, hedges and shelter belts creating clearly defined spaces that enable a large collection of plants and trees to thrive. It has extensive collections of both rhododendrons and bamboos. The challenges presented by the site become a bonus with the ridge offering long views of the surrounding countryside in the 'borrowed landscape' tradition of Japanese gardens. It didn't exist ten years ago and Gorthleck is very much a work-in-progress that is well-maintained by plantsman Graham Chattington and groundsman Lindsay MacDonald.

Directions: From the A9, join the B862. Go through of Errogie. About one mile after the sharp left-hand bend there is a small church on the left. The Gorthleck drive is opposite the church and the house can be seen on the hill to the left as you follow the drive (follow it to the left of the new house). Park outside the house on the gravel.

Disabled Access:
None

Opening Times:
Wednesday 10 June
10:00am - 9:00pm

Admission:
£5.00

Charities:
All proceeds to
SG Beneficiaries

---

17 HIGHLAND LILIUMS
10 Loaneckheim, Kiltarlity IV4 7JQ
Neil and Frances Macritchie T: 01463 741365
E: neil.macritchie@btconnect.com www.highlandliliums.co.uk

A working retail nursery with spectacular views over the Beauly valley and Strathfarrar hills. A wide selection of home grown plants available including Alpines, Ferns, Grasses, Herbaceous, Herbs, Liliums, Primulas and Shrubs.

Other Details: Teas on 30 August only.

Directions: Signposted from Kiltarlity village, which is just off the Beauly to Drumnadrochit road (A833), approximately 12 miles from Inverness.

Disabled Access:
Full

Opening Times:
Sunday 30 August
12:00pm - 4:00pm
1 January - 31 December
9:00am - 5:00pm

Admission:
Free but donations welcome

Charities:
Highland Hospice receives
40%, the net remaining to
SG Beneficiaries

---

18 HOUSE OF AIGAS AND FIELD CENTRE
By Beauly IV4 7AD
Sir John and Lady Lister-Kaye T: 01463 782443
E: sheila@aigas.co.uk www.aigas.co.uk

The House of Aigas has a small arboretum of named Victorian specimen trees and modern additions. The garden consists of extensive rockeries, herbaceous borders, ponds and shrubs. Aigas Field Centre rangers lead regular guided walks on nature trails through woodland, moorland and around a loch.

Other Details: Champion Trees: Douglas Fir, Atlas Cedar and Sequoiadendron Homemade teas in the house on both 28 June and 26 July. Lunches/teas are available on request on other dates. Check out Aigas website for details of other events.

Directions: Four and a half miles from Beauly on A831 Cannich/Glen Affric road.

Disabled Access:
Partial

Opening Times:
Sunday 28 June
2:00pm - 5:00pm
Sunday 26 July
2:00pm - 5:00pm
By arrangement
1 March - 25 October

Admission:
£3.00, children free

Charities:
Highland Hospice (Aird
branch) receives 40%, the net
remaining to SG Beneficiaries

HOUSE OF GRUINARD
Laide, by Achnasheen IV22 2NQ
The Hon Mrs A G Maclay T: 01445 731235
E: office@houseofgruinard.com

Superb hidden and unexpected garden developed in sympathy with stunning west coast estuary location. Wide variety of interesting herbaceous and shrub borders with water garden and extended wild planting.

Other Details: Homemade teas available on 27 May. No teas on 22 July.

Directions: On A832 twelve miles north of Inverewe and nine miles south of Dundonnell.

Disabled Access:
None

Opening Times:
Wednesday 27 May
2:00pm - 5:00pm
Wednesday 22 July
2:00pm - 5:00pm

Admission:
£3.50, children under 16 free

Charities:
Highland Hospice receives 40%, the net remaining to SG Beneficiaries

---

HUGH MILLER'S BIRTHPLACE COTTAGE & MUSEUM
Church Street, Cromarty IV11 8XA
The National Trust for Scotland T: 0844 493 2158
E: millersmuseum@nts.org.uk www.nts.org.uk

The Garden of Wonders, created in 2008, with its theme of natural history, features fossils, exotic ferns, ornamental letter-cutting and a 'mystery' stone. The sculptural centrepiece of this award-winning small but beautiful area is a scrap metal ammonite created by Helen Denerley. Named after Hugh's wife, Lydia, the garden was completed in 2010. Walk around the crescent-shaped, sandstone path of fragrant climbing roses, herbs and wild plant areas which reflect Miller's own love of nature and curiosity in the natural landscape.

Directions: By road via Kessock Bridge and A832 to Cromarty. Twenty-two miles north east of Inverness.

Disabled Access:
None

Opening Times:
Saturday 8 August
12:00pm - 5:00pm (last entry 4:30pm).

Admission:
£6.50, concession £5.00, family £16.50. N.B.Prices correct at time of going to print.

Charities:
Donation to SG Beneficiaries

INVEREWE GARDEN AND ESTATE
Poolewe, Achnasheen, Ross-shire IV22 2LG
The National Trust for Scotland T: 0844 493 2225
E: inverewe@nts.org.uk www.nts.org.uk

Magnificent 54 acre Highland garden, surrounded by mountains, moorland and sea loch. Created by Osgood Mackenzie in the late 19th century, it now includes a wealth of exotic plants from Australian tree ferns to Chinese rhododendrons to South African bulbs. Recent plantings include a grove of Wollemi pines and other 'fossil' trees.

Other Details: National Plant Collection®: Olearia, Rhododendron (subsect. Barbata, subsect. Glischra, subsect. Maculifera). Champion Trees: over twenty.
20 May: The Head Gardener's walk will focus on Woodland Gardening.
3 June: The First Gardener's walk will take in the National Collection plantings. Meet at Visitor Centre at 2:00pm for all walks.
A shop and self-service restaurant are available.

Directions: Signposted on A832 by Poolewe, six miles northeast of Gairloch.

Disabled Access:
Partial

Opening Times:
Wednesday 20 May
10:00am - 4:00pm
Wednesday 3 June
10:00am - 4:00pm

Admission:
Adult £10.50, concessions £7.50.
NT/NTS members free.

Charities:
Donation to SG Beneficiaries

LEATHAD ARD
Upper Carloway, Isle of Lewis HS2 9AQ
Rowena and Stuart Oakley T: 01851 643204
E: oakley1a@clara.co.uk www.whereveriam.org/leathadard

Three quarters of an acre sloping garden with stunning views over East Loch Roag. It has evolved along with the shelter hedges that divide the garden into a number of areas. With shelter and raised beds, the different conditions created permit a wide variety of plants to be grown. Beds include herbaceous borders, cutting borders, bog gardens, grass garden, exposed beds, patio, a new pond and vegetable and fruit patches, some of which are grown to show.

Other Details: Rowena and Stuart are happy to show visitors around in the afternoons, although this could take a couple of hours.

Directions: A858 Shawbost - Carloway. First right after Carloway football pitch. First house on right. The Westside circular bus ex Stornoway to road end and ask for the Carloway football pitch.

Disabled Access:
None

Opening Times:
1 Jun - 31 Aug 10:00am - 6:00pm except Fris & Suns and Wed 5 August
Also by arrangement 1 - 31 May & 1 - 30 Sep except Fris & Suns

Admission:
Recommended minimum donation is £4.00 per head, children free.

Charities:
Red Cross receives 40%, the net remaining to SG Beneficiaries

OLD ALLANGRANGE
Munlochy IV8 8NZ
J J Gladwin T: 01463 811304
E: jayjaygladwin@gmail.com

A 17th century lime washed house is the backdrop to a formal(ish) garden. There is an ice house, horse path, vegetable garden, a mound and an orchard. The garden uses sculpted hedges to play with perspective and to block or expose views. Because the garden is planted for wildlife, particularly bees, wildflowers and beneficial weeds are encouraged. There is a grove of ancient yew trees which are particularly fine, linking the formal garden with the rest of the garden.

Other Details: Champion Trees: Yew. The farm and garden are gardened organically and we work closely with the BBCT to develop habitat for bees. We have our own charitable society which puts in bee gardens for private people.

Directions: From Inverness head four miles north on the A9, and follow the directions for Black Isle Brewery. Park in the brewery car park and you will be given directions in the shop.

Disabled Access:
Partial

Opening Times:
Saturday 2 May 11:00am - 5:30pm
Saturday 12 September 11:00am - 5:30pm

Admission:
£6.00 including organic teas

Charities:
Highland Gardens for Bees receives 40%, the net remaining to SG Beneficiaries

OLDTOWN OF LEYS GARDEN
Inverness IV2 6AE
David and Anne Sutherland T: 01463 238238
E: ams@oldtownofleys.com

Large garden established ten years ago on the outskirts of Inverness and overlooking the town. Herbaceous beds with lovely rhododendron and azalea displays in spring. There are specimen trees, three ponds surrounded by waterside planting and a small woodland area.

Directions: Turn off Southern distributor road (B8082) at Leys roundabout towards Inverarnie (B861). At T-junction turn right. After fifty metres turn right into Oldtown of Leys.

Disabled Access:
Partial

Opening Times:
Saturday 23 May 2:00pm - 5:00pm
1 January - 31 December 8:00am - 8:00pm
or Dawn - Dusk

Admission:
23rd May: £3.00.
Other days: By donation

Charities:
Local Charities receives 40%, the net remaining to SG Beneficiaries

RUBHA PHOIL FOREST GARDENS
Armadale Pier Road, Ardvasar, Sleat, Isle of Skye IV45 8RS
Sandy Masson T: 01471 844700
E: rubhaphoil@yahoo.co.uk   www.skyeforestgarden.com

A wild natural forest garden managed on permaculture principles with a woodland walk to seal and bird islands. Look out for otters and other wildlife! There is an interesting Alchemy Centre with a composting display.

Other Details: Accommodation is available in tent/bothy retreat.
Follow us on Facebook at **http:www.facebook.com/RubhaPhoil** and
Skye Permaculture at **http://www.facebook.com/skyepermaculture**

Directions: Turn right at the car park on Armadale Pier.

Disabled Access:
Partial

Opening Times:
Saturday 22 August
10:30am - 5:00pm

Admission:
£4.00, children free

Charities:
Donation to SG Beneficiaries

THE LOOKOUT
Kilmuir, North Kessock IV1 3ZG
David and Penny Veitch T: 01463 731489
E: david@veitch.biz

A ¾ acre elevated coastal garden with incredible views over the Moray Firth which is only for the sure-footed. This award winning garden is created out of a rock base with shallow pockets of ground, planted to its advantage to encourage all aspects of wildlife. There is a small sheltered courtyard, raised bed vegetable area, pretty cottage garden, scree and rock garden, rose arbour, rhododendrons, flowering shrubs, bamboos, trees and lily pond with waterside plants.

Other Details: Coffee, tea and home baking outside if weather permits. Studio with exhibition of landscape pictures for sale. Dogs on lead allowed.

Directions: From Inverness, take North Kessock left turn from A9, and third left at roundabout to go on underpass then sharp left onto Kilmuir road. From Tore, take slip road for North Kessock and immediately right for Kilmuir. Follow signs for Kilmuir (three miles) until you reach the shore. The Lookout is near the far end of village with a large palm tree on the grass in front.

Disabled Access:
None

Opening Times:
1 May - 31 August
12:00pm - 4:00pm
Saturdays and Sundays
Also by arrangement on request

Admission:
£3.00, children under 16 free

Charities:
Alzeimers Scotland receives 40%, the net remaining to SG Beneficiaries

---

THE NEW HOUSE
Wester Alness Ferry, by Balblair, Dingwall IV7 8LJ
Mrs Adele Farrar T: 01381 610755
E: Adelefarrar@outlook.com

A woodland garden with lots of interesting plants. Raised beds, herbaceous borders and alpine plants. Overlooking the the Cromarty Firth, lots of birds.

Other Details: Small seating areas in the garden

Directions: Turn off the A9, head through Culbokie on to Resolis. When you reach the school, across the road is a war memorial - go down to the bottom of the lane.

Disabled Access:
Partial

Opening Times:
Saturday 6 June
12:00pm - 4:00pm
Saturday 11 July
12:00pm - 4:00pm

Admission:
£3.00, children free

Charities:
M S Centre (Therapy Centre) receives 40%, the net remaining to SG Beneficiaries

ROXBURGHSHIRE

Scotland's Gardens 2015 Guidebook is sponsored by **INVESTEC WEALTH & INVESTMENT**

District Organiser

Mrs Sally Yonge	Newtonlees House, Kelso TD5 7SZ

Area Organisers

Mrs Clare Leeming	Loanend, Earlston, Berwickshire TD4 6BD
Mrs Marion Livingston	Bewlie House, Lilliesleaf, Melrose TD6 9ER

Treasurer

Mr Peter Jeary	Kalemouth House, Eckford, Kelso TD5 8LE

Gardens open on a specific date

Floors Castle, Kelso	Fri - Mon 3 to 6 April	10:30am - 4:00pm
Yetholm Village Gardens, Town Yetholm	Sunday 12 July	2:00pm - 5:30pm
West Leas, Bonchester Bridge	Sunday 19 July	2:00pm - 5:00pm

Gardens open regularly

Floors Castle, Kelso	1 May - 25 October	10:30am - 4:00pm
Monteviot, Jedburgh	1 April - 31 October	12:00pm - 5:00pm

Gardens open by arrangement

Lanton Tower, Jedburgh	On request	01835 863443
West Leas, Bonchester Bridge	On request	01450 860711

BORDERS PLANT AND PRODUCE SALE
MELROSE SATURDAY 16 MAY 10:30AM - 4:00PM

Stock up on all sorts of goodies for your garden
at our mega charity plant sale.

See pages 174 or 238 for more details.

PLANT DONATIONS WELCOME

Key to symbols

	New in 2015		Homemade teas		Accommodation
	Teas		Dogs on a lead allowed		Plant stall
	Cream teas		Wheelchair access		Scottish Snowdrop Festival

Garden locations

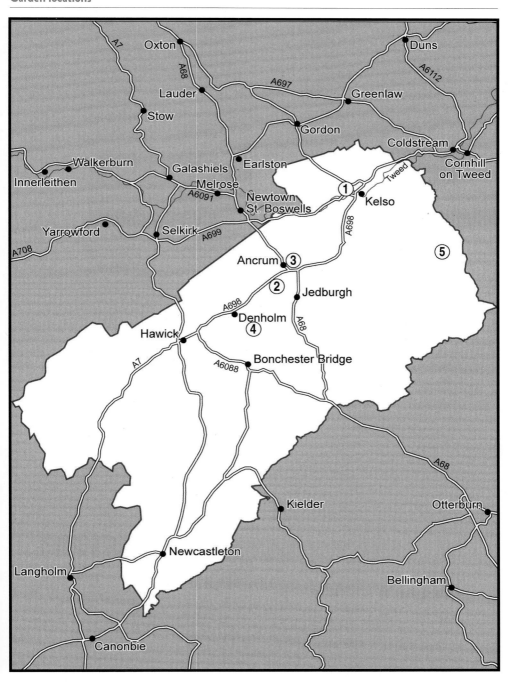

FLOORS CASTLE
Kelso TD5 7SF
The Duke of Roxburghe T: 01573 223333
www.floorscastle.com

The largest inhabited house in Scotland enjoys glorious views across parkland, the River Tweed and the Cheviot Hills. Delightful woodland garden, riverside and woodland walks, formal French style Millennium Parterre and the traditional walled garden. The walled garden contains colourful herbaceous borders, vinery and peach house, and in keeping with tradition, the kitchen garden still supplies vegetables and soft fruit for the Castle.

Other Details: Floors Castle Plant Centre and Walled Gardens open all year round from 10:30am to 4:30pm. Free admission.

Directions: Floors Castle can be reached by following the A6089 from Edinburgh; the B6397 from Earlston or the A698 from Coldstream. Go through Kelso, up Roxburgh Street to the Golden Gates.

Disabled Access:
Partial

Opening Times:
Friday - Monday
3, 4, 5, 6 April
10:30am - 4:00pm
1 May - 25 October
10:30am - 4:00pm
Please check our website for any special closing dates

Admission:
Castle, Grounds & Gardens
£8.50
Grounds & Gardens £4.50

Charities:
Donation to SG Beneficiaries

LANTON TOWER
Jedburgh TD8 6SU
Lady Reid T: 01835 863443

The garden, divided into 'rooms' by beech, holly and yew hedges and stone walls, is architectural rather than botanical, with an emphasis on shrubs, bulbs and fruit trees. A parterre near the tower, with steps leading to a croquet lawn, is surrounded by shrub borders, with orchards on each side of a beech hedge and wall. An azalea and mixed shrub border is next to a pond surrounded by bog garden. Nearby, lies a border of low-growing herbaceous plants with a york stone path leading to a large curved bench, the space contained by hedges of Charles de Mills roses. There is a vegetable garden, and a herb garden near the house. A walk between a holly and Rosa spinosissima hedge towards a large mirror framed in ivy leads to a paddock well-furnished with trees and a fine view towards the Eildon Hills.

Directions: Two and a half miles west of Jedburgh.

Disabled Access:
Full

Opening Times:
By arrangement on request

Admission:
£4.00

Charities:
Maggie's Cancer Caring
Centres receives 40%,
the net remaining to
SG Beneficiaries

MONTEVIOT
Jedburgh TD8 6UQ
Marquis & Marchioness of Lothian T: 01835 830380
www.monteviot.com

A series of differing gardens including a herb garden, rose garden, water garden linked by bridges, and river garden with herbaceous shrub borders. There is also the Dene garden featuring ponds and bridges and planted with a variety of foliage plants.

Directions: Turn off A68, three miles north of Jedburgh B6400.

Disabled Access:
Partial

Opening Times:
1 April - 31 October
12:00pm - 5:00pm

Admission:
£5.00, children under 16 free. RHS members free with membership card

Charities:
Donation to SG Beneficiaries

WEST LEAS
Bonchester Bridge TD9 8TD
Mr and Mrs Robert Laidlaw T: 01450 860711
E: ann.laidlaw@btconnect.com

The visitor to West Leas can share in the exciting and dramatic project on a grand scale still in the making. At its core is a passion for plants allied to a love and understanding of the land in which they are set. Collections of perennials and shrubs, many in temporary holding quarters, lighten up the landscape to magical effect. New landscaped water features, bog garden and extensive new shrub and herbaceous planting.

Directions: Signposted off the Jedburgh/Bonchester Bridge Road.

Disabled Access:
Partial

Opening Times:
Sunday 19 July
2:00pm - 5:00pm
Also by arrangement on request

Admission:
£4.00

Charities:
Macmillan Cancer Support,
Borders Appeal receives 40%,
the net remaining to
SG Beneficiaries

YETHOLM VILLAGE GARDENS
Town Yetholm TD5 8RL
The Gardeners of Yetholm Village

The village of Town Yetholm is situated at the north end of the Pennine Way and lies close to the Bowmont Water in the dramatic setting of the foothills of the Cheviots. A variety of gardens with their own unique features have joined the Yetholm Village Gardens Open Day this year. In addition The Yew Tree Allotments running along the High Street will open again providing an ever popular feature. The day offers visitors the chance to walk through several delightful gardens planted in a variety of styles and reflecting many distinctive horticultural interests. From newly established, developing and secret gardens to old and established gardens there is something here to interest everyone. The short walking distance between the majority of the gardens provides the added advantage of being able to enjoy the magnificence of the surrounding landscape to include Staerough and The Curr which straddle both the Bowmont and Halterburn Valleys where evidence of ancient settlements remains.

Other Details: Champion Trees: The Old Yew Tree in Yew Tree Lane. Attractions include the ever popular poetry reading and music, local wood turning at Almond Cottage, a bric-a-brac stall, home baking and produce, an excellent plant stall supported by Woodside and a propagation workshop is also planned for during the afternoon. Tickets are available in the local village hall. Dogs on leads allowed. Cream teas £2.00.

Directions: Equidistant between Edinburgh and Newcastle. South of Kelso in the Scottish Borders take the B6352 to Yetholm Village. Ample parking available along the High Street.

Disabled Access:
Partial

Opening Times:
Sunday 12 July
2:00pm - 5:30pm

Admission:
£4.00, children under 10 free

Charities:
Riding for the Disabled
Association - Borders Group
receives 40%, the net
remaining to SG Beneficiaries

STIRLINGSHIRE

Scotland's Gardens 2015 Guidebook is sponsored by **INVESTEC WEALTH & INVESTMENT**

District Organiser

Mandy Readman	Hutchison Farm, Auchinlay Road, Dunblane FK15 9JS

Area Organisers

Gillie Drapper	Kilewnan Cottage, Fintry, By Glasgow G63 0YH
Maurie Jessett	The Walled Garden, Doune FK16 6HJ
Rosemary Leckie	Auchengarroch, 16 Chalton Road, Bridge of Allan FK9 4DX
Pippa Maclean	Quarter, Denny FK6 6QZ
Iain Morrison	Clifford House, Balkerach Street, Doune FK16 6DE
Rachel Nunn	The Byre, Newton, Port of Menteith FK8 3LF
Douglas Ramsay	The Tors, 2 Slamannan Road, Falkirk FK1 5LG
Fiona Wallace	Netherspittalton, Coldoch, Blair Drummond FK8 4XD
Gillie Welstead	Ballingrew, Thornhill FK8 3QD

Treasurer

To be confirmed

Gardens open on a specific date

West Plean House, by Stirling	Sunday 22 February	1:00pm	-	4:00pm
West Plean House, by Stirling	Sunday 19 April	2:00pm	-	5:00pm
The Pass House, Callander	Sunday 26 April	2:00pm	-	5:00pm
Broich, Kippen	Sunday 3 May	2:00pm	-	5:00pm
Bridge of Allan Gardens, Bridge of Allan	Sunday 10 May	1:00pm	-	5:00pm
Dunblane Community Gardens, Perthshire	Sunday 17 May	12:00pm	-	5:00pm
Gargunnock House, Gargunnock	Sunday 17 May	2:00pm	-	5:00pm
Dun Dubh, Aberfoyle	Sunday 24 May	2:00pm	-	5:00pm
Touch, Stirling	Sunday 24 May	2:00pm	-	5:00pm
Fintry Village Gardens, By Glasgow	Sunday 31 May	1:30pm	-	5:30pm
Thornhill Village, Stirling	Sunday 7 June	1:30pm	-	5:00pm
Lanrick, Doune	Sunday 14 June	2:00pm	-	5:00pm
Doune Village Gardens	Sunday 21 June	2:00pm	-	5:30pm
Thorntree, Arnprior	Sunday 28 June	2:00pm	-	5:00pm
Woodstone House, Kippen	Sunday 28 June	2:00pm	-	5:00pm
Moon Cottage, Dunblane	Sunday 12 July	2:00pm	-	5:00pm
The Tors, Falkirk	Sunday 19 July	2:00pm	-	5:30pm

STIRLINGSHIRE

Gean House , Alloa	Tuesday 28 July	2:00pm	- 5:00pm
The Steading, By Dollar	Sunday 16 August	2:00pm	- 5:00pm
The Pineapple, Falkirk	Sunday 30 August	10:30am	- 5:00pm
Little Broich, Kippen	Sunday 4 October	2:00pm	- 5:00pm

Gardens open regularly

Duntreath Castle, Blanefield	1 March - 8 March	11:00am	- 4:00pm
Gargunnock House, Gargunnock	1 February - 16 March	11:00am	- 3:30pm
	13 Apr - 30 Sep (weekdays)	11:00am	- 3:30pm

Gardens open by arrangement

Arndean, by Dollar	15 May - 15 June	01259 743525
Duntreath Castle, Blanefield	1 February - 30 November	01360 770215
Milseybank, Bridge of Allan	1 April - 31 May	01786 833866
Rowberrow, Dollar	1 February - 31 December	01259 742584
The Linns, Sheriffmuir	15 February - 30 September	01786 822295
The Steading, By Dollar	1 April - 15 October	01259 781559
The Tors, Falkirk	1 May - 30 September	01324 620877
Thorntree , Arnprior	1 April - 15 October	01786 870710

Plant sales

Gargunnock House Plant Sale, Gargunnock	Sunday 17 May	2:00pm	- 5:00pm

Key to symbols

	New in 2015		Homemade teas		Accommodation
	Teas		Dogs on a lead allowed		Plant stall
	Cream teas		Wheelchair access		Scottish Snowdrop Festival

Garden locations

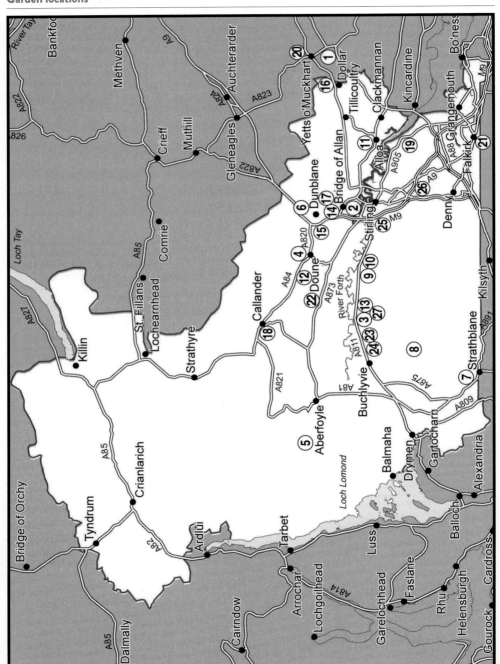

ARNDEAN
by Dollar FK14 7NH
Johnny and Katie Stewart T: 01259 743525
E: johnny@arndean.co.uk

This is a beautiful mature garden extending to 15 acres including the woodland walk. There is a formal herbaceous part, a small vegetable garden and orchard. In addition, there are flowering shrubs, abundant and striking rhododendrons and azaleas as well as many fine specimen trees. There is a tree house for children.

Other Details: Groups welcome.

Directions: Arndean is well sign posted off the A977

Disabled Access:
Full

Opening Times:
By arrangement
15 May - 15 June

Admission:
£5.00 children free

Charities:
Marie Curie Cancer
Care receives 40%,
the net remaining to
SG Beneficiaries.

BRIDGE OF ALLAN GARDENS
Bridge of Allan FK9
The Bridge of Allan Gardeners
E: r.leckie44@btinternet.com

A variety of gardens with a wide range of spring blossoms including rhododendrons, azaleas and camellias. Wonderful selection of specimen trees and shrubs, herbaceous borders, water features, ponds and many unusual plants. There is also a stumpery, rockeries, some sculptures and vegetable gardens. Full details of all the gardens will be on the website and posters nearer the time.

Other Details: Tickets and maps available from all gardens. Teas will be served in St. Saviour's Church Hall, Keir Street.

Directions: Signposted from village.

Disabled Access:
Partial

Opening Times:
Sunday 10 May
1:00pm - 5:00pm

Admission:
£5.00, children free

Charities:
St Saviour's Church receives
20%, Artlink Central receives
20%, the net remaining to
SG Beneficiaries

BROICH
Kippen FK8 3EN
Sir Peter and Lady Hutchison
01786 870317

Ten acres of woodland garden with many unusual plants, including rhododendrons collected on the owner's travels. Spectacular trees including a Handkerchief Tree and a yew, which in 1839 was described as "one of Scotland's finest" and is still expanding! A Victorian walk along the burn with a small waterfall and attractive bridges leads to the recently restored walled garden. Some lovely ornamental items to be found throughout the garden.

Other Details: Informal garden tours may take place on the day. Some paths may be slippery when wet.

Directions: Loop Road to Kippen off A811 one mile west of Kippen Cross.

Disabled Access:
Partial

Opening Times:
Sunday 3 May
2:00pm - 5:00pm

Admission:
£5.00, children free

Charities:
SPANA receives 40%, the
net remaining to
SG Beneficiaries

DOUNE VILLAGE GARDENS
FK16 6DE
The Gardeners of Doune Village T: 01786 841 007
E: Mor990@aol.com

A variety of creative gardens in Doune Village and Wood of Doune, most of which have never opened before. An opportunity to see behind the hedges and be inspired!

Other Details: All gardens will be clearly signposted. Maps and tickets available at all the gardens. Teas at St. Modoc's Church. Further details about the gardens will be available on the website nearer the time.

Directions: Doune is situated at junction of A820 from Dunblane and A84 Stirling to Callander main road.

Disabled Access:
Partial

Opening Times:
Sunday 21 June
2:00pm - 5:30pm

Admission:
£5.00, children free

Charities:
St Modoc's Church Fund receives 40%, the net remaining to SG Beneficiaries

---

DUN DUBH
Kinlochard Road, Aberfoyle FK8 3TJ
Callum Pirnie, Head Gardener T: 01877 382698
E: callumpirnie@gmail.com

A late Victorian garden of 6 acres undergoing restoration and development. It is set on a series of terraces and slopes which run down to the shores of Loch Ard with superb views west to Ben Lomond framed by stands of mature conifers. There is an enclosed, colour themed formal garden laid out on three terraces and a new Victorian style glasshouse overlooking a terraced kitchen and fruit garden. The formal paved terrace at the front of the house overlooks a newly developed rock garden and crag while the lower walk running from the boat house to the main lawn gives views across the Loch. A developing woodland garden leads on to a formal late summer herbaceous border and terraced heather garden. Featured on *The Beechgrove Garden* in May 2014 and the Scottish Field in November 2014.

Other Details: Car parking is limited to disabled badge holders and helpers, but there will be free transport to and from Aberfoyle car park throughout the afternoon. Parking on the road outside Dun Dubh is dangerous and will be stopped. Guide Dogs only.

Directions: Follow the signs to the car park in the centre of Aberfoyle, look for the Garden Open signs. The minibus will leave from the bus stop beside the Tourist Office. Turn around time about 15 minutes.

Disabled Access:
Partial

Opening Times:
Sunday 24 May
2:00pm - 5:00pm

Admission:
£4.00, children free

Charities:
Help for Heroes receives 40%, the net remaining to SG Beneficiaries

DUNBLANE COMMUNITY GARDENS
Dunblane, Perthshire FK15 9JS
The Gardeners of Dunblane Community Gardens

A delightful walk along the banks of the Allan Water, the gardens show what can be done by an enthusiastic band of volunteers in a short space of time. In just five years the Rock Garden has been created with retaining walls and colourful planting. The Memorial Garden was started in 2011 and the hosta border is in the process of being verified as "the longest hosta border in the world". All areas have followed organic principles and the planting is designed to encourage wildlife. The garden at Dunblane Musuem will also be open, a lovely hidden public garden and specific herbal planting. Designed and maintained by volunteers.

Other Details: Hosta 'Andy Murray' will be on display. Lunches, teas and snacks available in the many restaurants and cafes that are open in Dunblane.

Directions: Several car parks in Dunblane. Follow the signs towards the Memorial Garden on the south bank of the river and the Rock Garden, at the Haugh on the north side.

Disabled Access:
Partial

Opening Times:
Sunday 17 May
12:00pm - 5:00pm

Admission:
By donation

Charities:
Dunblane in Bloom receives 17.5%, Dunblane Development Trust Environment Group receives 17.5%, Dunblane Museum receives 5%, the net remaining to SG Beneficiaries

DUNTREATH CASTLE
Blanefield G63 9AJ
Sir Archibald & Lady Edmonstone T: 01360 770215
E: juliet@edmonstone.com   www.duntreathcastle.co.uk

Extensive gardens with mature and new plantings. Ornamental landscaped lake and bog garden. Sweeping lawns below formal fountain and rose parterre with herbaceous border leading up to an attractive waterfall garden with shrubs and spring plantings. Stunning display of snowdrops along the side of former drive. A woodland walk and a 15th century keep and chapel.

Other Details: Open for the Snowdrop Festival via an Honesty Box under a Garden Open sign at the side door, maps available here too. Groups welcome.

Directions: A81 north of Glasgow between Blanefield and Killearn.

Disabled Access:
Full

Opening Times:
1 March - 8 March
11:00am - 4:00pm for the Snowdrop Festival
Also by arrangement
1 February - 30 November

Admission:
Snowdrop openings £3.00, children free
Other dates £4.00, children free

Charities:
All proceeds to SG Beneficiaries

Gargunnock House

FINTRY VILLAGE GARDENS
By Glasgow G63
The Gardeners of Fintry T: 01360 860243
E: drapper@kilewnan.org.uk

Several village gardens including:

1. Camallt (William Acton and Rebecca East)
Old and interesting daffodil collection, bluebells, rhododendrons, azaleas,
herbaceous terrace and several water features including a waterfall and burn.

2. Dun Ard (Niall Manning and Alastair Morton)
This is a three acre garden started 25 years ago. Set within a formal structure are
areas of perennial planting, meadows and vegetables.

3. Knockraich Farm (Katy and Robert Rodgers)
Sheltered courtyard planting with a wonderful herb garden, fruit and vegetables and
a large apple orchard.

4. Fintry Community Garden
Opened August 2012 to provide opportunities for the production of sustainable,
low carbon food sources providing an opportunity for community involvement via
individual growing spaces, community growing or to relax and enjoy the garden
environment.

5. Bridge End (Margaret and Bob Rowan)
An informal country garden with spring flowering bulbs,mature rhododendrons and
azaleas. Year round interest with witch hazel, heathers, meconopsis, primulas, roses
and a small herbaceous border.

6. Kilewnan Cottage (Chris and Gillie Drapper)
Informal garden set in 1½ acres with burns dividing the garden. Planting includes
herbaceous borders, vegetable garden, small orchard and a woodland walk.

Other Details: Parking at the Fintry Community Garden at the Sports Club and
a Shuttle Bus, with easy access, will run between all gardens. Details of the bus
route will be announced on the website nearer the time. Teas at Knockraich Farm
with refreshments also available at the Sports Club. Plant stall at the Community
Garden.

Directions: Fintry village is at the junction of the B822 and the B818. Follow the
yellow garden signs in Fintry Village.

Disabled Access:
Partial

Opening Times:
Sunday 31 May
1:30pm - 5:30pm

Admission:
£5.00, children free

Charities:
Crossroads Caring Scotland
(West Stirling Branch)
receives 40%, the net
remaining to SG Beneficiaries

GARGUNNOCK HOUSE
Gargunnock FK8 3AZ
The Gargunnock Trustees T: 01786 860392
E: william.campbellwj@btinternet.com

Five acres of mature gardens, woodland walks, walled garden and 18th century
doocot. Snowdrops in February/March, daffodils in April/May. Glorious display
of azaleas and rhododendrons in May/June. Wonderful trees and shrubs, glorious
autumn colours. Walled garden now restored with new perennial borders, cut
flowers, kitchen garden and newly planted orchard with picnic areas. See the
gardeners propagation tunnels and the rhododendron nursery. Guided tours can be
arranged for parties throughout the year, contact the Head Gardener.

Other Details: Plant stall always available at the rear of Gargunnock House.

Directions: Five miles west of Stirling on A811.

Disabled Access:
Full

Opening Times:
1 Feb - 16 Mar 11:00am -
3:30pm for Snowdrop Festival
13 April - 30 Sept. 11:00am -
3:30pm weekdays only

Admission:
£3.00, children free, by
Honesty Box at the car park.

Charities:
Children's Hospice
Association receives 20%,
Gargunnock Community
Centre receives 20%, the net
remaining to SG Beneficiaries

GARGUNNOCK HOUSE PLANT SALE
Gargunnock FK8 3AZ
The Gargunnock Trustees T: 01786 860392
E: william.campbellwj@btinternet.com

Major Plant Sale with a wonderful selection of Azaleas, Rhododendrons, many other shrubs, bulbs and herbaceous plants. The garden will also be open.

Other Details: Homemade Teas served in Gargunnock House.

Directions: Five miles west of Stirling on A811.

Disabled Access:
Full

Opening Times:
Sunday 17 May
2:00pm - 5:00pm

Admission:
£5.00, children free

Charities:
Children's Hospice Association receives 20%, Gargunnock Community Centre receives 20%, the net remaining to SG Beneficiaries

---

GEAN HOUSE
Tullibody Road, Alloa FK10 2EL
Ceteris (Scotland)
E: ebowie@geanhouse.co.uk www.geanhouse.co.uk

Gean House is an early 20th century Arts & Crafts style mansion. On arrival, the sweeping driveway from the main road takes you through beautiful parkland lined with trees to the mansion set on top of the hill facing north east. The gardens surrounding the house were originally 40 acres and included a Japanese garden in the woods. All that remains now are seven acres on the southern and eastern aspects of the house.

Other Details: Cream Teas in Gean House. No dogs, except guide dogs.

Directions: Gean House is located on the Tullibody Road, Alloa.

Disabled Access:
None

Opening Times:
Tuesday 28 July
2:00pm - 5:00pm

Admission:
£4.00, children free

Charities:
Scottish Society for Autism receives 40%, the net remaining to SG Beneficiaries

---

LANRICK
Doune FK16 6HJ
Alistair & Penny Dickson & Maurie Jessett T: 01786 841684/842280
E: maurie.jessett@hotmail.co.uk www.lanrick.co.uk

Mature policies with lovely woodland walks along the River Teith; a rural oasis where you can enjoy the peace and tranquillity of Scotland. Magnificent rhododendrons. Many interesting sights and features in the grounds. The Walled Garden (two acres) is the original walled garden of Lanrick Castle (now demolished) but now a substantial work in progress. Planting began seven years ago with ornamental shrubs, climbing roses, and many varieties of espalier fruit trees. There are many interesting sights and features.

Other Details: Teas in Indian tent on the site of the original castle.

Directions: Turn off the A84 at Doune onto the B8032 and after about a mile the entrance is on the right.

Disabled Access:
Full

Opening Times:
Sunday 14 June
2:00pm - 5:00pm

Admission:
£4.00, children free

Charities:
The Sandpiper Trust receives 40%, the net remaining to SG Beneficiaries.

LITTLE BROICH
Kippen FK8 3DT
John Smith T: 01786 870275

A tree lover's heaven! A hidden arboretum of about eight acres, planted over the last twenty years, with an extensive collection of native and non-native conifers and broad-leaf specimens. Fern leaf oaks, Hungarian oaks, Cercidiphyllum and Glyptostrobus amongst many others around wide, slightly sloping grass paths (can be slippery when wet). Stunning views across the Carse of Stirling and the autumn colours should be outstanding. The garden featured in the October 2014 issue of *Scotland on Sunday*.

Other Details: No dogs except guide dogs.

Directions: Will be signposted off the B8037. Parking on the road, disabled badge holders can park at the bottom of the lane.

Disabled Access:
Partial

Opening Times:
Sunday 4 October
2:00pm - 5:00pm

Admission:
£4.00, children free

Charities:
Strathcarron Hospice receives 40%, the net remaining to SG Beneficiaries

---

MILSEYBANK
Bridge of Allan FK9 4NB
Murray and Sheila Airth T: 01786 833866
E: smairth@hotmail.com

Wonderful and interesting sloping garden with outstanding views, terraced for ease of access. Woodland with bluebells, rhododendrons, magnolias and camellias, and many other unusual plants, a true plantsman's garden.

Directions: Situated on A9, one mile from junction 11, M9 and a quarter mile from Bridge of Allan. Milseybank is at top of lane at Lecropt Nursery, two hundred and fifty yards from Bridge of Allan train station.

Disabled Access:
Full

Opening Times:
By arrangement
1 April - 31 May

Admission:
£4.00, children free

Charities:
Strathcarron Hospice receives 40%, the net remaining to SG Beneficiaries

---

MOON COTTAGE
Greenyards, Dunblane FK15 9NX
Jeanie and David Ashton
E: macashton@btinternet.com

Moon Cottage has a fairly young garden. It has grown up over the past ten to fifteen years on the edge of farm land adjacent to a wood plantation. There are flower beds, a variety of shrubs and trees, a vegetable patch, fruit trees and a pond. There is also a folly!

Other Details: Grass may be soft if it has been wet. Some paths are a bit rough.

Directions: One and a half miles on B824 - at stone walled entrance to farm track on the right - from Keir roundabout to Doune. (Do not go down to white cottages, Biggins, as per GPS. Take next track on right after half a mile).

Disabled Access:
Partial

Opening Times:
Sunday 12 July
2:00pm - 5:00pm

Admission:
£4.00 Children free

Charities:
Camphill, Blair Drummond receives 40%, the net remaining to SG Beneficiaries

ROWBERROW
18 Castle Road, Dollar FK14 7BE
Bill and Rosemary Jarvis T: 01259 742584
E: rjarvis1000@hotmail.com

On the way up to Castle Campbell overlooking Dollar Glen, this colourful garden has several mixed shrub and herbaceous borders, a wildlife pond, two rockeries, alpine troughs, fruit and vegetable gardens, and a mini-orchard. The owner is a plantaholic and likes to collect unusual specimens. Rowberrow was featured on the *Beechgrove Garden* in summer 2011.

Directions: Pass along the burn side in Dollar, turn right at T junction, follow signs for Castle Campbell and Dollar Glen. Park at the bottom of Castle Road or in the Quarry car park just up from the house.

Disabled Access:
Partial

Opening Times:
By arrangement
1 February - 31 December

Admission:
£4.00, children free

Charities:
Hillfoot Harmony Barbershop Singers receives 40%, the net remaining to SG Beneficiaries.

 THE LINNS
Sheriffmuir, Dunblane FK15 0LP
Drs Evelyn and Lewis Stevens T: 01786 822295
E: evelyn@thelinns.org.uk

A plantsman's garden of 3½ acres of mature woodland created from scratch since 1984 at the west end of the Ochils. The site demonstrates what is possible, with time and dedication, in what would otherwise be a windswept and bleak location. The layout of trees including beautiful species such as Cercidophyllum japonicum, Acer griseum and Betula albo-sinensis to mention just 3, rhododendrons, hedges and walls, has created a wide variety of interesting and attractive garden spaces, giving a real sense of exploration and surprise. The garden display from early Jan onwards delights with drifts of near 100 forms of "special" snowdrops, a variety of large hellebores and dainty winter aconites. Then come corydalis, trilliums, erythroniums, daffodils etc. In summer superb collection of Meconopsis and a woodland meander through many other well-loved perennials.

Other Details: No dogs except guide dogs. There may be plants for sale. Groups welcome. Phone or email for appointment.

Directions: Sheriffmuir by Dunblane.

Disabled Access:
Partial

Opening Times:
By arrangement
15 February - 30 September

Admission:
£4.00, children free

Charities:
Sophie North Charitable Trust receives 40%, the net remaining to SG Beneficiaries.

 THE PASS HOUSE
Kilmahog, Callander FK17 8HD
Dr and Mrs D Carfrae

Well planted, medium-sized garden with steep banks down to a swift river. The garden paths are not steep. There are lovely displays of camellias, magnolias, rhododendrons, azaleas, alpines and shrubs. The Scotland's Gardens plaque awarded for 25 years of opening is on display.

Other Details: Tea/coffee and a biscuit for a donation if the weather is fine.

Directions: Two miles from Callander on A84 to Lochearnhead.

Disabled Access:
None

Opening Times:
Sunday 26 April
2:00pm - 5:00pm

Admission:
£4.00, children free

Charities:
Crossroads Caring Scotland(West Stirling Branch) receives 40%, the net remaining to SG Beneficiaries

THE PINEAPPLE

Near Airth, Falkirk FK2 8LU
The National Trust for Scotland T: 08444 932189
E: mjeffery@nts.org.uk www.nts.org.uk

The Pineapple is named after the bizarre structure built around 1761 in the shape of a pineapple! This folly once held extensive glasshouses and pineapple pits where a variety of exotic fruits and vegetables were grown. It is now an oasis for wildlife including the rare great crested newt - with a dipping pool, an apple orchard and picnic grounds.

Other Details: Join the Pineapple team for a harvest produce and plant sale in this unique setting.

Directions: Seven miles east of Stirling, off A905, then off B9124. One mile west of Airth.

Disabled Access:
Partial

Opening Times:
Sunday 30 August
10:30am - 5:00pm

Admission:
By donation

Charities:
All proceeds to
SG Beneficiaries

THE STEADING

Yetts O'Muckhart, By Dollar FK14 7JT
Fiona and David Chapman T: 01259 781559
E: david.fiona.chapman@gmail.com

Now 20 years old, this south-facing rural garden, situated at the foot of the Ochil Hills, continues to develop and rejuvenate. Curvaceous paths meander through a variety of terraced beds and ponds planted with a wide range of seasonal plants and species trees to give all year colour and interest.

Other Details: No dogs except guide dogs.

Directions: Situated at the Yetts o' Muckhart junction on the A823/A91 Dunfermline/Crieff road.

Disabled Access:
None

Opening Times:
Sunday 16 August
2:00pm - 5:00pm
Also by arrangement
1 April - 15 October

Admission:
£4.00, children free

Charities:
Muckhart Parish Amenity
receives 20%, Alzheimers
Friendship Club receives
20%, the net remaining to
SG Beneficiaries

THE TORS

2 Slamannan Road, Falkirk FK1 5LG
Dr and Mrs D M Ramsay T: 01324 620877
E: dmramsay@yahoo.co.uk

The Tors is an award winning Victorian garden of just over one acre with a secret woodland garden to the side and a small orchard and wild area to the rear. Many unusual maple trees and rhododendrons are the main interest of this garden and there are several wildlife ponds and water features. The Tors was featured on the 'Beechgrove Garden' for autumn colour in September 2010, but the best time to see this garden is at the end of July or the beginning of August.

Other Details: No dogs - except guide dogs.

Directions: The B803 to the south of Falkirk leads to Glenbrae Road. Turn right at the traffic lights into Slamannan Road and The Tors is a Victorian building immediately on the left.

Disabled Access:
Partial

Opening Times:
Sunday 19 July
2:00pm - 5:30pm
Also by arrangement
1 May - 30 September

Admission:
£3.50

Charities:
Strathcarron Hospice receives
40%, the net remaining to
SG Beneficiaries

22 THORNHILL VILLAGE
Thornhill, Stirling FK8 3QD
The Gardeners of Thornhill   T: 01786 850671
E: gillie.welstead@gmail.com

Thornhill village rests on a raised beach with outstanding views in all directions. Charming, small village gardens packed with interest and variety contrast well with the open, natural gardens outside the village. Full details of the gardens will be on Scotland's Gardens website nearer the time.

Other Details: Tickets and maps available from all the gardens. Homemade teas to be served in the church hall.

Directions: On A873, ten miles west of Stirling.

Disabled Access:
Partial

Opening Times:
Sunday 7 June
1:30pm - 5:00pm

Admission:
£5.00, children free

Charities:
SSAFA receives 10%,
MacMillan Cancer Support receives 10%, Norrieston Parish Church receives 10%, British Heart Foundation, Scottish Branch receives 10%, the net remaining to SG Beneficiaries

---

23 THORNTREE
Arnprior FK8 3EY
Mark and Carol Seymour   T: 01786 870710
E: info@thorntreebarn.co.uk   www.thorntreebarn.co.uk

Charming country garden with flower beds around courtyard. Apple walk, Saltire garden and new Meconopsis bed. Lovely views from Ben Lomond to Ben Ledi. A bank of primroses greets you as you drive up to the courtyard at the end of April and the beginning of May.

Directions: A811. In Arnprior take Fintry Road, Thorntree is second on the right.

Disabled Access:
Full

Opening Times:
By arrangement
1 April - 15 October

Admission:
£4.00, children free

Charities:
Stirling RDA Carriage Driving Group receives 40%, the net remaining to SG Beneficiaries

---

24 THORNTREE WITH WOODSTONE HOUSE
Arnprior FK8 3EY
Mark and Carol Seymour   T: 01786 870710
E: info@thorntreebarn.co.uk   www.thorntreebarn.co.uk

Charming country garden with flower beds around courtyard. Apple walk, Saltire garden and new Meconopsis bed. Lovely views from Ben Lomond to Ben Ledi.

Other Details: Teas are at Woodstone House and plant sales at Thorntree.

Directions: A811. In Arnprior take Fintry Road, Thorntree is second on the right.

Disabled Access:
Partial

Opening Times:
Sunday 28 June
2:00pm - 5:00pm

Admission:
£6.00 (includes both gardens) or £4.00 for one, children free

Charities:
Stirling RDA Carriage Driving Group receives 40%, the net remaining to SG Beneficiaries

TOUCH
Stirling FK8 3AQ
Angus Watson T: 01786 448899
E: angus@touchestate.co.uk

Exceptionally fine Georgian House. Walled garden with herbaceous and shrub borders, specie and dwarf rhododendrons, azaleas magnolias and other interesting shrubs. There is a woodland walk.

Other Details: The house will **not** be open. No dogs except guide dogs.

Directions: West from Stirling on A811 then take Cambusbarron Road.

Disabled Access:
Partial

Opening Times:
Sunday 24 May
2:00pm - 5:00pm

Admission:
£5.00, children free

Charities:
Strathcarron Hospice receives 40%, the net remaining to SG Beneficiaries

---

WEST PLEAN HOUSE
Denny Road, by Stirling FK7 8HA
Tony and Moira Stewart T: 01786 812208
E: moira@westpleanhouse.com   www.westpleanhouse.com

Woodland walks with snowdrops in February and March, glorious daffodils in April. Well established garden including site of iron age homestead and panoramic views over seven counties. Woodlands with mature rhododendrons, specimen trees, extensive lawns, shrubs and walled garden with variety of vegetables. Includes woodland walk with planting of azaleas and rhododendrons.

Other Details: 22 February tea or coffee available by donation.
19 April will be a family day with events for children. Cream teas will be served. Please see the website for details nearer the time.

Directions: Leave all routes at Junction 9 roundabout where M9/M80 converge. Take the A872 for Denny, go less than a mile, turn left at the house sign and immediately after lodge cottage. Carry on up the drive.

Disabled Access:
Full

Opening Times:
Sunday 22 February
1:00pm - 4:00pm for the Snowdrop Festival
Sunday 19 April
2:00pm - 5:00pm

Admission:
£4.00, children free

Charities:
Scottish Motor Neurone Disease Association receives 40%, the net remaining to SG Beneficiaries.

WOODSTONE HOUSE WITH THORNTREE
Cauldhame, Kippen FK8 3JB
Roddy and Mary Lawson T: 01786 870202
E: r.lawson@btinternet.com

Bounded to the south by the old Kippen Vinery wall, this is a relatively new garden of around one acre, with some species trees (including a Mulberry), shrubs, rockeries and vegetables. Wonderful views to the Trossachs.

Other Details: Teas at Woodstone House, plant sales at Thorntree.

Directions: Woodstone House is at the top end of Kippen off the Fintry Road.

Disabled Access:
Partial

Opening Times:
Sunday 28 June
2:00pm - 5:00pm

Admission:
£6.00 (includes both gardens) or £4.00 for one, children free

Charities:
Stirling RDA Carriage Driving Group receives 40%, the net remaining to SG Beneficiaries

WIGTOWNSHIRE

Scotland's Gardens 2015 Guidebook is sponsored by **INVESTEC WEALTH & INVESTMENT**

District Organiser

Mrs Ann Watson	Doonholm, Cairnryan Road, Stranraer DG9 8AT

Area Organisers

Mrs Terry Brewis	Ardwell House, Stranraer DG9 9LY
Mr Giles Davies	Elmlea Plants, Minnigaff, Newton Stewart DG8 6PX
Mrs Andrew Gladstone	Craichlaw, Kirkcowan, Newton Stewart DG8 0DQ
Mrs Janet Hannay	Cuddyfield, Carsluith DG8 7DS
Mrs Vicky Roberts	Logan House Gardens, Port Logan, By Stranraer DG9 9ND

Treasurer

Mr George Fleming	Ardgour, Stoneykirk, Stranraer DG9 9DL

Gardens open on a specific date

Logan Botanic Garden, Port Logan	Sunday 1 February	11:00am	-	4:00pm
Logan Botanic Garden, Port Logan	Sunday 8 February	11:00am	-	4:00pm
Dunskey Gardens and Maze, Portpatrick	Saturday 14 February	10:00am	-	4:00pm
Dunskey Gardens and Maze, Portpatrick	Sunday 15 February	10:00am	-	4:00pm
Logan Botanic Garden, Port Logan	Sunday 15 February	11:00am	-	4:00pm
Dunskey Gardens and Maze, Portpatrick	Saturday 21 February	10:00am	-	4:00pm
Dunskey Gardens and Maze, Portpatrick	Sunday 22 February	10:00am	-	4:00pm
Logan Botanic Garden, Port Logan	Sunday 22 February	11:00am	-	4:00pm
Logan House Gardens, Port Logan	Sunday 17 May	2:00pm	-	5:00pm
Logan Botanic Garden, Port Logan	Sunday 24 May	10:00am	-	5:00pm
Burbainie, Stranraer	Sunday 31 May	12:00pm	-	4:00pm
Claymoddie Garden, Newton Stewart	Sunday 31 May	2:00pm	-	5:00pm
Whitehills House, Newton Stewart	Saturday 6 June	11:00am	-	4:00pm
Castle Kennedy and Gardens, Stranraer	Sunday 14 June	10:00am	-	5:00pm
Damnaglaur House, Stranraer	Sunday 21 June	1:00pm	-	5:00pm
The Homestead, Stranraer	Sunday 21 June	1:00pm	-	5:00pm
Woodfall Gardens, Glasserton	Sunday 21 June	10:30am	-	4:30pm
Woodfall Gardens, Glasserton	Sunday 12 July	10:30am	-	4:30pm
Balker Farmhouse, Stranraer	Sunday 26 July	2:00pm	-	5:00pm
Lochnaw Castle, Stranraer	Sunday 16 August	2:00pm	-	5:00pm

WIGTOWNSHIRE

Gardens open regularly

Ardwell House Gardens, Ardwell, Stranraer	1 April - 30 September	10:00am - 5:00pm
Castle Kennedy and Gardens, Stranraer	1 Feb - 29 March (weekends)	
	30 March - 1 November	10:00am - 5:00pm
Claymoddie Garden, Newton Stewart	1 April - 30 Sep (Fri - Sun)	2:00pm - 5:00pm
Glenwhan Gardens, by Stranraer	1 April - 31 October	10:00am - 5:00pm
Logan Botanic Garden, by Stranraer	15 March - 31 October	10:00am - 5:00pm
Logan House Gardens, By Stranraer	1 March - 30 September	10:00am - 5:00pm

Gardens open by arrangement

Balker Farmhouse, Stranraer	1 May - 30 September	01776 702110
Castle Kennedy and Gardens, Stranraer	2 November - 31 December	01581 400225
Claymoddie Garden, Whithorn, Newton Stewart	1 April - 30 September	01988 500422
Craichlaw, Kirkcowan, Newton Stewart	On request	01671 830208
Woodfall Gardens, Glasserton	On request	woodfallgardens@btinternet.com

Glenwhan Garden

Key to symbols

 New in 2015

 Teas

 Cream teas

 Homemade teas

 Dogs on a lead allowed

 Wheelchair access

 Accommodation

 Plant stall

 Scottish Snowdrop Festival

Garden locations

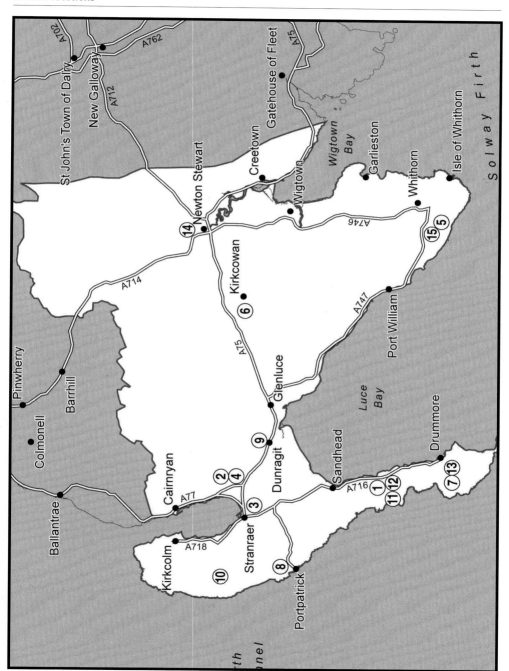

1 ARDWELL HOUSE GARDENS
Ardwell, Stranraer DG9 9LY
Mrs Francis Brewis

Daffodils, spring flowers, rhododendrons, flowering shrubs, coloured foliage and rock plants. Moist garden at smaller pond and a walk around larger ponds with views over Luce Bay.

Other Details: Collection Box. House not open.

Directions: A716 towards Mull of Galloway. Stranraer 10 miles.

Disabled Access:
None

Opening Times:
1 April - 30 September
10:00am - 5:00pm

Admission:
£3.00, concessions £2.00, children under 14 free

Charities:
Donation to SG Beneficiaries

2 BALKER FARMHOUSE
Stranraer DG9 8RS
Davina, Countess of Stair T: 01776 702110

The house was restored and the garden, formerly a ploughed field, was started in 2003-4 . It is now full of wonderful shrubs and plants for all seasons.

Other Details: There are gravel paths on the slope so it is not suitable for wheelchairs. There is a tearoom nearby at Castle Kennedy Gardens.

Directions: One and a half miles off A75, three miles from Stranraer - go through farmyard to blue gate.

Disabled Access:
None

Opening Times:
Sunday 26 July
2:00pm - 5:00pm
also by arrangement
1 May - 30 September

Admission:
£4.00

Charities:
World Horse Welfare receives 20%, Canine Partners receives 20%, the net remaining to SG Beneficiaries

3 BURBAINIE
Westwood Avenue, Stranraer DG9 8BT
Mrs Shona Greenhorn

A wide range of settings, both shady and sunny, which are all helped by the Gulf Stream. The garden has an alpine bed, beautiful rhododendron, a pond and a lovely display of spring flowers. There is also a vegetable garden and a large woodland area to enjoy walking round.

Other Details: Homemade teas served on outside patio (weather permitting).

Directions: From Ayr (A77), Cairnryan Road, take second left onto Ladies Walk. Then go straight over at crossroad onto Westwood Avenue. Burbainie is the house fifth on the right. From Dumfries (A75), London Road, turn left onto Westwood Avenue.

Disabled Access:
Partial

Opening Times:
Sunday 31 May
12:00pm - 4:00pm

Admission:
£3.00

Charities:
Arthritis Research UK receives 40%, the net remaining to SG Beneficiaries

CASTLE KENNEDY AND GARDENS
Stranraer DG9 8RT
The Earl and Countess of Stair T: 01581 400225
castlekennedygardens.com

Romantically situated, these famous 75 acres of landscaped gardens are located on an isthmus surrounded by two large natural lochs. At one end the ruined Castle Kennedy overlooks a beautiful herbaceous walled garden with Lochinch Castle at the other. With over 300 years of planting there is an impressive collection of rare trees, rhododendrons and exotic shrubs, featuring many spectacular Champion Trees (tallest or largest of their type). The stunning snowdrop walks, daffodils, spring flowers, rhododendron and magnolia displays, and herbaceous borders make this a 'must visit' garden through-out the year.

Other Details: Champion Trees: 6 British, 11 Scottish and 25 for Dumfries and Galloway. Wildlife ranger, head gardener guided walks, tree and family trails, charming tea room serving homemade teas and light lunches, plant centre and gift shop. Open weekends 1 February - 15 March for the Snowdrop Festival.

Directions: On A75 five miles east of Stranraer.

Disabled Access:
Partial

Opening Times:
Sunday 14 June
10:00am - 5:00pm for SG
1 Feb - 29 Mar (weekends) &
30 Mar-1 Nov 10am-5pm
By arrangement 2 Nov-31 Dec

Admission:
£5.50, conc £4.50, children £2.00, disabled free, families £12.00 (2 adults & 2 children)

Charities:
Homestart Wigtownshire receives 40%, the net remaining to SG Beneficiaries

CLAYMODDIE GARDEN
Whithorn, Newton Stewart DG8 8LX
Mr and Mrs Robin Nicholson T: 01988 500422
E: gallowayplants@aol.com www.gallowayplants.co.uk

This romantic garden, developed over the last 40 years, with its backdrop of mature trees was designed by the owner, an enthusiastic plantsman. Imaginative hard and soft landscaping provide a wide range of settings, both shady and sunny, for a mass of meticulously placed plants, both old favourites and exotic species, all helped by the proximity of the Gulf Stream. Running through the lower part of the garden is the burn which feeds the pond, all newly planted. There are changes in levels, but most of the garden is accessible to wheelchairs.

Other Details: Very good nursery with a large collection of rare and interesting plants propagated from the Claymoddie garden. Teas on 31 May only.

Directions: Claymoddie is off the A746, two miles south of Whithorn.

Disabled Access:
Partial

Opening Times:
Sunday 31 May
2:00pm - 5:00pm
1 April - 30 September
2:00pm - 5:00pm Friday -
Sunday and by arrangement
Monday - Thursday

Admission:
31 May: £6.00 - includes tea
Other times: £4.00

Charities:
Macmillan Cancer Support receives 40%, the net remaining to SG Beneficiaries

CRAICHLAW
Kirkcowan, Newton Stewart DG8 0DQ
Mr and Mrs A Gladstone T: 01671 830208

Formal garden with herbaceous borders around the house. Set in extensive grounds with lawns, lochs and woodland. A path around the main loch leads to a water garden returning past a recently planted arboretum in the old walled garden. The best times to visit the garden are early February for snowdrops, May to mid-June for the water garden and rhododendrons and mid-June to August for herbaceous borders.

Directions: Take the B733 for Kirkcowan off the A75 at the Halfway House eight miles west of Newton Stewart. Craichlaw House is the first turning on the right.

Disabled Access:
Partial

Opening Times:
By arrangement on request

Admission:
£4.00, concessions £3.00, children under 14 free

Charities:
Donation to SG Beneficiaries

7 DAMNAGLAUR HOUSE WITH THE HOMESTEAD
Damnaglaur, Drummore, Stranraer DG9 9QN
Frances Collins T: 01776 840636
E: chunky.collins@btinternet.com

This is a well established garden, landscaping and planting having been started in 1991, but is constantly a work in progress, around a stone house of 200 years. Full of trees, shrubs and herbaceous plants, it gives colour throughout the year and with its gravel paths, gives access around it even on wet days. Wind-defeating shrubs have helped to form a micro-climate in which tender and unusual plants thrive, while making a series of interlinked areas and providing interesting glimpses through one area to the next. Its surroundings are stunning with views over farmland and down to Luce Bay, with the Machars of Galloway and the Galloway Hills in the distance.

Directions: 100 yards north of Junction of B7041/B7065.

Disabled Access:
Partial

Opening Times:
Sunday 21 June
1:00pm - 5:00pm

Admission:
£4.00 (includes both gardens)

Charities:
Kirkmaiden Parish Church receives 40%, the net remaining to SG Beneficiaries

8 DUNSKEY GARDENS AND MAZE

Portpatrick, Stranraer DG9 8TJ
Mr and Mrs Edward Orr Ewing T: 01776 810211
E: garden@dunskey.com   www.dunskey.com

Come and enjoy welcoming walled and woodland gardens and woodland snowdrop walks. There are forty-three named varieties of snowdrops including: Galanthus 'Dunskey Talia', Galanthus 'Fred's Giant', Galanthus 'Robin Hood', Galanthus 'Sickle'. Featured in The Beechgrove Garden in 2013.

Other Details: Gardener led strolls at 2:00pm each Sunday. Dogs are allowed on snowdrop walks but not in the gardens. Designated dog walk, picnic tables and shaded parking for dog owners. Disabled loos and mobility scooter. Children's games and tree identification. Plants for sale; all raised at Dunskey. Tearoom with warming soups and tea. Please refer to website in extreme weather conditions.

Directions: One mile from Portpatrick on B738 off A77.

Disabled Access:
Partial

Opening Times:
Sat & Sun 14 - 15 February
10:00am - 4:00pm
Sat & Sun 21 - 22 February
10:00am - 4:00pm
All dates open for the Snowdrop Festival.

Admission:
£4.00, under sixteen £0.50, families £12.00

Charities:
Donation to SG Beneficiaries

9 GLENWHAN GARDENS

Dunragit, by Stranraer DG9 8PH
Mr and Mrs W Knott T: 07787 990702
E: www.glenwhangardens.co.uk

Glenwhan Garden has been described as one of the most beautiful gardens in Scotland, situated at 300 feet, overlooking Luce Bay and the Mull of Galloway, with clear views to the Isle of Man. Thirty-five years ago there was wild moorland, but with dedication and vision, you can now see glorious collections of plants from around the world. There is colour in all seasons and the winding paths, well placed seats, and varied sculptures, focusing around small lakes, add to the tranquil atmosphere. There is a seventeen acre moorland wildflower walk, the chance to see red squirrels and a well marked Tree Trail.

Other Details: Thriving plant nursery and tearoom with delicious home produce. Parties catered for with notice. Although disabled access is partial, access is available in most parts.

Directions: Seven miles east of Stranraer, one mile off A75 at Dunragit (follow brown VisitScotland signs).

Disabled Access:
Partial

Opening Times:
1 April - 31 October
10:00am - 5:00pm

Admission:
£5.00, season ticket £15.00, family ticket £12.00 (up to three children)

Charities:
Donation to SG Beneficiaries

10 LOCHNAW CASTLE
Lochnaw, By Leswalt, Stranraer DG9 0RW
Mr and Mrs Geoffrey Anderson

The garden is very much a work in progress and presently there is not a great deal of formal garden. We are in the process of designing and restoring what was the Victorian flower garden and a new garden has been created in what was the Victorian wing of the house which was demolished in the 50s. There is an extensive double walled garden housing the largest satellite of the National Apple Collection which was previously at Brogdale and also a large selection of red, white and pink currants and gooseberries.

Other Details: Access to the walled garden can be on foot through the woodland or by car for those who cannot manage the walk. It is also possible to walk around the loch but not in a complete circle as the northern end is near the road. If wet suitable footwear is recommended.

Directions: Turn left at the church in Leswalt and follow Glen Road until Drumlockart Caravan Park (which is on the right). Entrance to the Castle is just after, on the left. Great care should be taken when driving on this road.

Disabled Access:
None

Opening Times:
Sunday 16 August
2:00pm - 5:00pm

Admission:
£4.00, children free

Charities:
Macmillan Nurses receives 20%, Help for Heroes receives 20%, the net remaining to SG Beneficiaries

11 LOGAN BOTANIC GARDEN
Port Logan, by Stranraer DG9 9ND
A Regional Garden of the Royal Botanic Garden Edinburgh
www.rbge.org.uk

At the south western tip of Scotland lies Logan which is unrivalled as the country's most exotic garden. With a mild climate washed by the Gulf Stream, a remarkable collection of bizarre and beautiful plants, especially from the southern hemisphere, flourish out of doors. Enjoy the colourful walled garden with its magnificent tree ferns, palms and borders along with the contrasting woodland garden with its unworldly gunnera bog. Visit the Logan Conservatory, new in 2014 and housing a special collection of tender South African plants.

Other Details: National Plant Collection®: Gunnera/Leptospermum/Griselinia. Champion Trees: Polylepis/Eucalyptus. Home baking, botanic shop, Discovery Centre, audio tours available and Logan Exhibition studio.

Directions: Ten miles south of Stranraer on A716 then two and a half miles from Ardwell village.

Disabled Access:
Full

Opening Times:
Suns 1, 8, 15, 22 Feb 11:00am - 4:00pm for Snowdrop Festival
Sun 24 May 10:00am-5:00pm
15 March - 31 October
10:00am - 5:00pm

Admission:
£6.00, conc £5.00, under 16 free (incl small donation to Garden, for prices without donation check rbge.org.uk)

Charities:
RBGE receives 40%, the net remaining to SG Beneficiaries

12 LOGAN HOUSE GARDENS
Port Logan, By Stranraer DG9 9ND
Mr and Mrs Andrew Roberts

The Queen Anne house is surrounded by sweeping lawns and a truly spectacular woodland garden. Rare and exotic plants together with champion trees and fine species of rhododendrons provide an excellent habitat for an interesting variety of wildlife.

Other Details: Champion Trees: seven UK and eleven Scottish Champions. Teas and plant stall on 17 May opening only.

Directions: On A716 thirteen miles south of Stranraer, two and a half miles from Ardwell village.

Disabled Access:
Partial

Opening Times:
Sunday 17 May
2:00pm - 5:00pm
1 March - 30 September
10:00am - 5:00pm

Admission:
£4.00, children under 16 free

Charities:
Port Logan Hall receives 40%, the net remaining to SG Beneficiaries

THE HOMESTEAD WITH DAMNAGLAUR HOUSE
Damnaglaur, Drummore, Stranraer DG9 9QN
Carol Rennison T: 01776 840323
E: rennison267@btinternet.com

A developing garden around a modern bungalow, completed in 2007. The garden has mixed planting in raised beds and borders with a large lawned area with uninterrupted views towards the sea and the Galloway Hills. Garden features are highlighted by the use of natural driftwood, shells and other treasures found on the nearby beaches.

Directions: 100 yards north of Junction of B7041/B7065.

Disabled Access:
Partial

Opening Times:
Sunday 21 June
1:00pm - 5:00pm

Admission:
£4.00 (includes both gardens)

Charities:
Kirkmaiden Parish Church receives 40%, the net remaining to SG Beneficiaries

WHITEHILLS HOUSE
Minnigaff, Newton Stewart DG8 6SC
Dr and Mrs Davie

This garden extends to ten acres with landscaping all round the house, much of the garden is woodland with a large collection of rhododendrons.

Directions: From centre of Newton Stewart turn right over Cree Bridge and then turn first left after 50 metres. Follow the road through the village of Minnigaff for ½ mile. Turn left at sign for RSPB, continue past Monnigaff Church on right then continue on main road as it turns left for 300 metres. Whitehills is first on left at black wrought iron gates.

Disabled Access:
Partial

Opening Times:
Saturday 6 June
11:00am - 4:00pm

Admission:
£4.00

Charities:
Help the Aged, Parkinsons UK and Marie Curie Cancer Care receive 40%, the net remaining to SG Beneficiaries

WOODFALL GARDENS
Glasserton DG8 8LY
Ross and Liz Muir
E: woodfallgardens@btinternet.com www.woodfall-gardens.co.uk

This lovely three acre 18th century triple walled garden has been thoughtfully restored to provide year round interest. Many mature trees and shrubs including some less common species; herbaceous borders and shrub roses surround the foundations of original greenhouses; grass borders; a knot garden; extensive beds of fruit and vegetables; a herb garden; a woodland walk. This unusual garden is well worth a visit.

Other Details: Teas and home baking on 21 June only.

Directions: Two miles south-west of Whithorn at junction of A746 and A747 (directly behind Glasserton Church).

Disabled Access:
Partial

Opening Times:
Sunday 21 June
10:30am - 4:30pm
Sunday 12 July
10:30am - 4:30pm
Also by arrangement on request

Admission:
£4.00, children free (must be accomp. by a responsible adult)

Charities:
Glasserton Parish Church and Macmillan Cancer Support each receive 20%, the net remaining to SG Beneficiaries

INDEX OF GARDENS

INDEX OF ADVERTISERS

WOULD YOU LIKE TO OPEN YOUR GARDEN FOR CHARITY?

If you would like information on how to open your garden for charity please write to us at the address below, call 0131 226 3714 or email info@scotlandsgardens.org

We welcome gardens large and small and also groups of gardens.

To: Scotland's Gardens, 42a North Castle Street, Edinburgh EH2 3BN

Please send me more information about opening my garden for charity.

Name _____

Address _____

_____

Postcode _____ Tel _____

Email _____

OUR GUIDEBOOK FOR 2016

ORDER NOW
and your copy will be posted
to you on publication in December 2015.

Send order to:

Scotland's Gardens, 42a North Castle Street, Edinburgh EH2 3BN

Please send me ___ copy / copies of **Our Guide for 2016**,

price £8.99, to include postage and packing, as soon as it is available.

I enclose a cheque / postal order made payable to Scotland's Gardens.

Name   _____

Address   _____

  _____

Postcode   _____

Copies of Our Guide for 2016 may also be purchased on our website:
www.scotlandsgardens.org